The United Nations in Latin America

Routledge Studies in Latin American Politics

The United Nations in Latin America

Aiding Development

Francis Adams

Routledge
Taylor & Francis Group

NEW YORK AND LONDON

First published 2010
by Routledge
711 Third Avenue, New York, NY 10017

Simultaneously published in the UK
by Routledge
2 Park Square, Milton Park, Abingdon, Oxfordshire OX14 4RN

First issued in paperback 2014

Routledge is an imprint of the Taylor and Francis Group, an informa business

© 2010 Taylor & Francis

Typeset in Sabon by
RefineCatch Limited, Bungay, Suffolk

Library of Congress Cataloging in Publication Data
Adams, Francis.
　The United Nations in Latin America : aiding development / by Francis
Adams.
　　p. cm.— (Routledge studies in Latin American politics v.2)
　Includes bibliographical references and index.
　1. Latin America—Economic policy.　2. Economic development—Latin
America.　3. Economic assistance—Latin America.　4. Sustainable
development—Latin America.　5. United Nations Development
Programme.　6. United Nations Development Group.　7. Latin
America—Foreign relations.　8. Latin America—Politics and
government.　I. Title.
HC125.A297 2009
338.98—dc22　　　　　　　　　　　　　　　　　　2009026866

ISBN 978-0-415-80613-8 (hbk)
ISBN 978-1-138-87476-3 (pbk)
ISBN 978-0-203-86191-2 (ebk)

Contents

vi Contents

List of Acronyms

AIDS	Acquired Immunodeficiency Syndrome
AMR	Annual Ministerial Reviews
BRT	Bus Rapid Transport
CABEI	Central American Bank for Economic Integration
CCA	Common Country Assessment
CCAD	Central American Commission on Environment and Development
CEB	Chief Executives Board for Coordination
CEDAW	Convention on the Elimination of All Forms of Discrimination Against Women
CEP	Caribbean Environmental Program
CFC	chlorofluorocarbons
CFS	Committee on World Food Security
CMR	child mortality rate
CONGO	Conference on Nongovernmental Organizations in Consultative Relationship with the United Nations
CSD	Commission on Sustainable Development
CSO	civil society organization
CSW	Commission on the Status of Women
DCF	Development Cooperation Forum
DELC	Division of Environmental Law and Conventions
DEPI	Division of Environmental Policy Implementation
DESA	Department of Economic and Social Affairs
DEWA	Division of Early Warning and Assessment
ECESA	Executive Committee of Economic and Social Affairs
ECOSOC	Economic and Social Council
EPTA	Expanded Program of Technical Assistance
EPZ	export processing zone
ERD	Emergency Response Division
FAO	Food and Agriculture Organization
FOCADES	Central American Environment and Development Fund
GAVI	Global Alliance for Vaccines and Immunization
GDI	Gender-Related Development Index

GDP	Gross Domestic Product
GEF	Global Environmental Facility
GEM	Gender Empowerment Measure
GEMS	Global Environmental Monitoring System
GEO	Global Environmental Outlook
GNP	Gross National Product
GRID	Global Resource Information Database
HDI	Human Development Index
HDR	Human Development Report
HIPC	Heavily-Indebted Poor Countries
HIV	Human Immunodeficiency Virus
AIDS	Acquired Immunodeficiency Syndrome
HPI	Human Poverty Index
ICJ	International Court of Justice
ICPD	International Conference on Population and Development
IDB	Inter-American Development Bank
IDP	internally displaced person
IFAD	International Fund for Agricultural Development
IFI	international financial institution
IIHR	Inter-American Institute of Human Rights
ILAC	Latin American and Caribbean Initiative for Sustainable Development
ILO	International Labour Organization
IMF	International Monetary Fund
IMR	infant mortality rate
INSTRAW	International Research and Training Institute for the Advancement of Women
IPC	International Poverty Center
ISI	import substitution industrialization
MBC	Meso-American Biological Corridor
MDG	Millennium Development Goals
MERCOSUR	Common Market of the South
MYFF	Multi-Year Funding Framework
NAFTA	North American Free Trade Accord
NAM	Non-Aligned Movement
NCSA	National Capacity Needs Self-Assessment
NGO	nongovernmental organization
OCHA	Office for the Coordination of Humanitarian Affairs
ODA	official development assistance
ORT	oral rehydration therapy
PAHO	Pan American Health Organization
PARLATINO	Latin American Parliament
PEI	Poverty-Environment Initiative
PRRO	Protracted Relief and Recovery Operations
PRSP	Poverty Reduction Strategy Paper

RBLAC	Regional Bureau for Latin America and the Caribbean
RCF	Regional Cooperation Framework
ROLAC	Regional Office for Latin America and the Caribbean
SAP	structural adjustment program
STD	sexually transmitted disease
SUNFED	Special United Nations Fund for Economic Development
SU/TCDC	Special Unit for Technical Cooperation Among Developing Countries
UN	United Nations
UNCDF	United Nations Capital Development Fund
UNCED	United Nations Conference on the Environment and Development
UNCLOS	United Nations Convention on the Law of the Sea
UNCTAD	United Nations Conference on Trade and Development
UNDAF	United Nations Development Assistance Framework
UNDG	United Nations Development Group
UNDP	United Nations Development Programme
UNECA	United Nations Economic Commission for Africa
UNECE	United Nations Economic Commission for Europe
UNECLAC	United Nations Economic Commission for Latin America and the Caribbean
UNEP	United Nations Environmental Programme
UNESCAP	United Nations Economic and Social Commission for Asia and the Pacific
UNESCO	United Nations Education, Scientific and Cultural Organization
UNESCWA	United Nations Economic and Social Commission for Western Asia
UNFPA	United Nations Population Fund
UN-HABITAT	United Nations Human Settlements Programme
UNHCHR	United Nations High Commissioner on Human Rights
UNHCR	United Nations High Commissioner for Refugees
UNICEF	United Nations Children's Fund
UNIDO	United Nations Industrial Development Organization
UNIFEM	United Nations Development Fund for Women
UNITAR	United Nations Institute for Training and Research
UNRISD	United Nations Research Institute for Social Development
UNSF	United Nations Special Fund
UNV	United Nations Volunteers
WCED	World Commission on Environment and Development
WCMC	World Conservation Monitoring Center
WFP	World Food Programme
WFS	World Food Summit
WHO	World Health Organization
WSSD	World Summit on Sustainable Development

Acknowledgments

I would like to acknowledge the assistance and encouragement I received during the course of this project. I am especially grateful to Benjamin Holtzman, Editor of Routledge Research, who was exceedingly helpful throughout the entire preparation of this manuscript. Elaine Dawson assisted with formatting and word processing during the latter stages of this project. I also received research assistance from Andrew Townsend and continued support from my colleagues in the Department of Political Science and Geography and the Graduate Program in International Studies here at Old Dominion University. The book is dedicated to my partner Maria Esther and our two sons Jayden and Adryan. Although I could not have completed this project without the support of these individuals, its shortcomings are solely my responsibility.

Francis Adams
May 2009

1 Introduction

Economic conditions in Latin America have changed dramatically in recent years. The gleaming glass skyscrapers, upscale shopping centers, and luxurious subdivisions attest to a fairly remarkable expansion of income and wealth. More people are living with greater affluence now than at any other time in the history of the continent.

Unfortunately, most Latin Americans have not benefitted from this economic transformation. Urban areas continue to be plagued by immense slums and shanty towns, often placed precariously on hillsides or along river basins, and rural communities lack such basic necessities as clean water, adequate nutrition, primary health care, and decent education. Conditions can be especially difficult for women who earn less and have fewer resources than men. Economic growth is also threatening natural environments in the region.

Distributing the benefits of economic growth more equitably without compromising natural ecosystems is the central challenge for Latin American nations today. Meeting this challenge will depend on the energy, commitment, and resources of people throughout the region. Genuine progress is only possible if it emanates from within these societies. Clearly governments bear considerable responsibility for stimulating growth, promoting equity, and protecting natural environments. Nongovernmental groups can also play a role in achieving these objectives. Ultimately, success requires forging effective partnerships between the state and civil society.

At the same time, Latin American nations do not have the resources needed to fully meet basic human needs while preserving natural environments and external assistance remains imperative. The United Nations (UN) has long sought to aid Latin American development. UN agencies have worked to improve basic nutrition, preventative health care, and primary education. The UN has also sponsored initiatives to promote gender equity and preserve natural environments.

This book reviews the UN's development assistance to Latin America during the early years of the twenty-first century. Focus is placed on the five subsidiary agencies that are most directly engaged in meeting the needs of the poor, improving the lives of women, and protecting natural environments: the United Nations Development Programme (UNDP), World Food Programme (WFP), United Nations Children's Fund (UNICEF), United Nations Population Fund (UNFPA), and United Nations Environmental Programme (UNEP). Together these agencies have made important, though rarely recognized, contributions to the sustainable development of Latin America.

DEFINING DEVELOPMENT

Before turning to the work of the United Nations in Latin America, it is important to consider how the idea of *development* has evolved over time. Initially, development was equated almost exclusively with economic growth.[1] When a nation's economy was expanding from one year to the next it was considered developing. Economic growth, it was argued, would increase employment and raise real incomes. The process of development thus required spurring growth, typically through public investments in infrastructure or industry.

Equating development with economic growth was challenged on a number of accounts. While such growth may be *necessary* for development, critics charged, it is by no means *sufficient* and should be considered just one component of the development process.[2] In fact, economic growth alone may not lead to improvements in the basic living conditions of poor communities. A nation could have an expanding economy while living conditions actually deteriorate. This has occurred in Latin America in the past, especially in those nations marked by the greatest inequalities of income and wealth. Economic growth rates alone do not indicate how the benefits of growth are distributed.

The idea of development was thus expanded to include changes in the physical quality of life of poor communities. Development, it was argued, should constitute real improvements in living conditions for the poor. Those nations increasingly able to meet the basic human needs of their citizens, such as clean water, sound nutrition, primary health care, basic education, and decent housing, were considered developing.[3] Composite indices were devised that went beyond economic growth to include such measures as caloric intake, infant and child mortality, life expectancy, average years of schooling, and adult literacy.[4]

This new emphasis on basic needs was also challenged. Simply providing nutrition, health care, and education, while certainly important, should not be equated with development. Rather, it was argued, development should be associated with "empowerment."[5] The poor should be able to obtain the knowledge, skills, and resources needed to provide for themselves and their families on a long-term basis. Emphasis thus shifted to capacity development, self-reliance, and the ability of all people to achieve their full potential.[6]

The idea of "empowerment" also engendered some criticism. It was frequently argued that environmental considerations must be included in any definition of development. If economic and social progress contributes to air and water pollution, soil erosion, the depletion of scarce resources, and the destruction of natural habitats, then a nation should not be considered developing. Rather, meeting human needs must be balanced with the protection and preservation of natural environments. "Sustainability," which signifies meeting present needs without jeopardizing the needs of future generations, should be recognized as a central component of the development process.[7]

Today the idea of "development" is sufficiently broad to encompass these various elements. It is typically associated with a growing economy that empowers poor communities so they can meet their own needs on a long-term basis while simultaneously preserving and protecting natural environments. It is this idea of "development" that is utilized throughout this book.

WORK OF THE UNITED NATIONS

Latin American nations currently face enormous economic, social, and environmental challenges. Although meeting these challenges will largely depend on the efforts of local governments and community groups, the United Nations can play a complementary and supportive role in this process. The organization's subsidiary agencies have worked to meet basic human needs, promote gender equity, and protect natural environments throughout the region.

Meeting the basic needs of poor communities has long been prioritized. UN agencies have distributed clean water and food to vulnerable populations and helped meet the nutritional needs of displaced populations at times of social crisis or natural disaster. These agencies have also worked to improve basic health care, sponsoring immunization campaigns to combat infectious diseases and programs to train and equip public health workers. The UN has also worked to strengthen education systems, allocating resources for school construction, basic supplies, teacher training, instructional materials, and curricular reform. The United Nations Development Programme has been at the forefront of these efforts while the World Food Programme, United Nations Population Fund, and United Nations Children's Fund have played complementary roles.

The UN has also worked to promote gender equity. Particular focus has been placed on ensuring women have access to adequate health and reproductive care. UN agencies have also enhanced training and employment opportunities for women. Working with local governments and community groups, the UN has supported policy and legal measures to more effectively protect and advance the rights of women. The UNFPA, UNDP, and WFP have supported these initiatives.

Lastly, the UN has worked to preserve and protect natural environments. This includes programs to combat air and water pollution, reduce soil erosion, enhance forest management, and protect biodiversity. Public policy reform and the promotion of regional cooperation on environmental issues have also been prioritized. Here UNEP has played a lead role while other agencies, most notably UNDP, have also sponsored environmental initiatives.

RATIONALE FOR THIS BOOK

Attention to the economic, social, and environmental work of the United Nations counters the common tendency to focus almost exclusively on the organization's political and security agenda. There is, of course, an expansive literature on the work of the United Nations Security Council and its related agencies, especially with respect to mediating conflicts, controlling the proliferation of weapons, and dispatching peacekeeping troops to troubled areas around the world. Less attention has been accorded the economic, social, and environmental work of the UN.[8] This is true despite remarkably large resource allocations in these areas. Economic, social, and environmental work constitutes the largest part of overall UN operations, consuming roughly 70 percent of all human and financial resources each year.[9]

This book also challenges some of the more common assumptions in the study of international affairs. Scholars typically adopt the fundamental assumptions of *realism*. Nation-states are considered the central actors in world politics, operating within the context of an anarchical yet highly competitive world system, and decision makers are thought to be rational utility maximizers, adopting foreign policies that advance their unique and unitary national interests vis-à-vis all other states. Realists tend to minimize the importance of global institutions, assuming such institutions simply reflect the interests of their most powerful member states. They are created, maintained, and manipulated by these states and only supported as long as they do not diminish the power of these states. The UN is thought to reflect the particular interests of the world's dominant powers and have little impact on how these states define and pursue these interests.

This book counters the *realist* view of global affairs. The analysis that follows demonstrates the role global institutions play in determining international outcomes. Although nation-states remain preeminent actors on the world stage, international institutions, most notably the UN, have greatly expanded their capabilities and are increasingly in a position to condition the behavior of member states.

The importance of international institutions is clearly evident with respect to the provision of collective goods; the creation of universal norms, rules, and regimes; the enforcement of international law; and the resolution of economic, social, and environmental crises. This reflects an era of deepening interdependence in which state sovereignty is giving way to global governance. It also underscores the need to adopt a more *nuanced* view of the UN which differentiates among its component parts. While the Security Council may reflect the interests of its most powerful member states, other bodies within the UN exhibit an increasing degree of decision-making autonomy and capacity to influence global outcomes. This is evident with respect to the economic, social, and environmental agencies reviewed in this book.

PARAMETERS AND QUALIFICATIONS

This book surveys United Nations efforts to promote sustainable development in Latin America. A broad definition of the region is employed that includes Mexico, the nations of Central and South America, and the Caribbean islands. However, the book does not offer detailed case studies of specific projects in individual countries. Such an approach is well beyond the scope of a single volume. Rather, emphasis is placed on the general character of the UN's development work in Latin America during the early years of the twenty-first century.

It is also important to acknowledge that this study does not include all of the areas in which the UN is engaged. Rather, I am focusing on the three areas outlined earlier that are critical to the contemporary idea of development: provision of basic human needs, enhancement of gender equity, and protection of natural environments. Development certainly involves improving living conditions of poor communities and ensuring access to adequate nutrition, health care, and education. Moreover, it is increasingly recognized that development necessitates special attention to the needs of women. Gender equity is an essential prerequisite for broader social progress. Lastly, development must be sustainable, balancing human needs with environmental preservation. These three challenges are central to the comprehensive definition of development outlined earlier and encompass much of the work of the UN in Latin America.

At the same time, other challenges that Latin American nations face are not emphasized in this study. Efforts to stimulate economic growth or improve basic infrastructure, although obviously important, tend to be associated with the work of the World Bank, International Monetary Fund (IMF), and Inter-American Development Bank (IDB). The UN has not been heavily involved in these areas. Also, this analysis does not examine short-term relief efforts. Although certainly critical at times of social crisis or natural disaster, emergency assistance and care for refugees are largely separate from initiatives to promote the long-term development of the region.

Lastly, this study does not focus on political reform. This is not meant to deny the importance of such reform to the development process. Although it was traditionally assumed that economic and social progress *preceded* political reform, it is now widely recognized that development depends, to a considerable extent, on the quality of governance within each nation. Broad-based economic and social progress, which enhances living conditions of poor communities, requires inclusive and effective political systems. Governments should carefully manage scarce resources, create opportunities for investment, elevate productivity, and meet the needs of disadvantaged groups. The UN has played a central role in the promotion of political reform in Latin America. In fact, improving governance is now considered essential for fostering sustainable human development.[10] However, the UN's work in this area has been extensively examined elsewhere and there is little need to revisit the same territory in this volume.[11]

It is also important to reiterate that I am not including all UN institutions that are aiding development in Latin America. Rather I have limited my analysis to the five subsidiary agencies identified earlier: the United Nations Development Programme, World Food Programme, United Nations Children's Fund, United Nations Population Fund, and United Nations Environmental Programme. Together, these five agencies encompass much of the direct work of the UN in Latin America. The book does not examine the various specialized agencies that are affiliated with the UN, such as the World Health Organization (WHO), Food and Agriculture Organization (FAO), United Nations Educational, Scientific and Cultural Organization (UNESCO), International Fund for Agricultural Development (IFAD), or United Nations Industrial Development Organization (UNIDO). With their own charters, secretariats, memberships, and funding sources, these agencies are largely independent of formal UN control.[12] This study also excludes the various functional and regional commissions and the research and training institutes of the UN.

BOOK OUTLINE

This book begins with a general overview of the development work of the United Nations before turning to specific initiatives in Latin America. The second chapter outlines the different UN institutions that sponsor economic, social, and environmental programs in the developing world. The chapter also reviews the basic purpose, history, structure, and activities of the five subsidiary agencies emphasized in this book. I conclude with a brief chronology of how the development agenda of the UN evolved over time.

Subsequent chapters turn to the contemporary reality of Latin America and the corresponding assistance of the UN. Chapter 3 describes living conditions in the region, with focus placed on access to basic nutrition, health care, and education. Both, the recent progress achieved in meeting these needs and the continued challenges that Latin American nations face, are reviewed. The latter half of this chapter identifies the major causes of poverty in the region, highlighting social and political factors along with the impact of the global economy. Chapter 4 outlines UN efforts to meet basic human needs, especially with respect to nutrition, primary health care, and public education.

The next two chapters turn to the lives of Latin American women. Chapter 5 focuses on the continued problem of gender inequality in the region. Emphasis is placed on women's access to health and reproductive care, and gender differences in income and employment. Again, both the recent progress achieved in improving the lives of women and the continued challenges they face are considered. The second part of the chapter identifies the various factors that account for gender inequality. Chapter 6 reviews UN efforts to promote gender equity and improve the lives of women. Emphasis is placed on improving access to health and reproductive care, enhancing training and employment opportunities, and reforming public policies.

The next two chapters focus on natural environments. Chapter 7 outlines the central environmental challenges in Latin America, including threats to air and water, the overuse of land, and the destruction of tropical rainforests. The chapter concludes with an analysis of the domestic and international forces that contribute to environmental deterioration in the region. Chapter 8 examines UN efforts to preserve natural resources and ecosystems. Focus is placed on specific environmental projects as well as broader efforts to promote environmentally responsible policy and legal reforms. Regional cooperation on common environmental threats is also considered.

The concluding chapter offers a series of recommendations for aiding Latin American development. This includes specific proposals for meeting basic human needs, promoting gender equity, and protecting natural environments. The chapter also identifies various institutional reforms which would strengthen the developmental capacity of the UN and ways of forging effective partnerships between the UN, local governments, and nongovernmental organizations (NGO).

The UN has always been controversial, attracting both high praise and virulent criticism. This book is not intended to replicate the positions of its most devoted supporters or fiercest critics. Rather, my central objective is to identify and describe the economic, social, and environmental work of the UN in Latin America during the early years of the twenty-first century. Such work constitutes a clear manifestation of the emergent era of global governance.

2 The United Nations and Development

The United Nations has long maintained an institutional commitment to economic and social progress in the developing world. One of the fundamental purposes of the UN is "to employ international machinery for the promotion of the economic and social advancement of all peoples."[1] In fact, promoting cooperation on economic and social matters is considered just as important as fostering international peace and security. The UN has consistently stressed a direct connection between its economic and security objectives. Because poverty and inequality frequently engender armed conflict between and within nations, enhancing peace and security depends, to a considerable extent, on meeting the needs of the world's poor.[2]

This chapter reviews the economic, social, and environmental work of the UN in the developing world. The first section considers the various institutional components of the UN that are engaged in aiding development. This includes three of the organization's principal bodies and a wide range of functional and regional commissions, research and training institutes, specialized agencies, and subsidiary programs. I then turn to the five agencies emphasized in this volume: the United Nations Development Programme, World Food Programme, United Nations Children's Fund, United Nations Population Fund, and United Nations Environmental Programme. The central purpose, history, organizational structure, funding sources, and activities of each agency are outlined. The last section reviews how the development agenda of the UN evolved over time.

UNITED NATIONS MACHINERY

The United Nations has an exceptionally large and continually expanding number of organs, commissions, institutes, agencies, funds, and programs that are directly engaged in development. As noted in the preceding chapter, the economic, social, and environmental work of the UN consumes a substantial proportion of the organization's resources each year. Roughly 70 percent of all financial and human resources are devoted to development.

Three of the six principal organs of the UN—the Secretariat, General

Assembly, and Economic and Social Council (ECOSOC)—share development responsibilities. The other three organs—the Security Council, International Court of Justice (ICJ), and Trusteeship Council—are generally not engaged in development. The Security Council responds to global security threats through mediation, instituting sanctions, dispatching peacekeeping troops, or authorizing the collective use of force. The ICJ adjudicates disputes between member states and issues advisory opinions regarding international law. The Trusteeship Council was established to administer various *trust territories* that the UN inherited at its founding. Since these territories have now attained either self-governance or formal political independence, the council has suspended operations. Because the Security Council, ICJ, and Trusteeship Council have little direct role in development they are not examined in this volume. The Secretariat, General Assembly, and ECOSOC, on the other hand, play important roles in promoting economic, social, and environmental progress in the developing world.

SECRETARIAT

The Secretariat is the principal administrative arm of the United Nations. It is headed by the Secretary-General, who is considered the organization's chief administrative officer.[3] The Secretariat, which has a staff of 15,000 from 170 different countries, is primarily responsible for aiding the other principal organs.[4] It is organized into various departments, divisions, offices, and programs. The Department of Economic and Social Affairs (DESA), which was established in 1997, has the most extensive development responsibilities.[5] DESA has specialized divisions on sustainable development, the advancement of women, social policy, population, development policy, and financing development. These divisions undertake policy analysis, generate economic and social data, facilitate cooperation among member states, and extend technical assistance to member governments.[6]

GENERAL ASSEMBLY

The General Assembly plays a central role in the developmental mission of the United Nations. The assembly, which includes all member states and holds regular sessions from September to December each year, is the chief deliberative, policy making, and representative body of the United Nations. Although its resolutions are not legally binding, they do reflect the will of the global community. Moreover, conventions and treaties adopted by the General Assembly become part of international law upon ratification by a threshold number of member states. The assembly also approves the UN budget and apportions expenditures.

The General Assembly is responsible for overseeing the development work of the UN. Most of its substantive work during the regular session is conducted through six committees that are composed of representatives from all member states.[7] The Economic and Financial Committee focuses on issues related to economic growth and development, including financing for development, human settlements, and international debt. The Social, Humanitarian, and Cultural Committee examines issues related to human rights, the advancement of women, the protection of children, the needs of indigenous communities, and the treatment of refugees. These committees also supervise the economic and social activities of various subsidiary funds and programs.

ECONOMIC AND SOCIAL COUNCIL

The Economic and Social Council has the most direct role in development.[8] The council may initiate studies with respect to economic and social matters, make policy recommendations to the General Assembly or to member states, and prepare draft conventions.[9] ECOSOC is also involved in planning international conferences on economic, social, and environmental issues and coordinating follow-up to these conferences. Although ECOSOC meets in a four-week formal session each July, alternating between New York and Geneva, the work of its various committees continues throughout the year.[10] The council can also convene ad hoc meetings in response to humanitarian emergencies.

Coordination is among the central responsibilities of ECOSOC. The council is charged with coordinating the work of the subsidiary funds and programs as well as various functional and regional commissions.[11] ECOSOC is also expected to coordinate the work of the specialized agencies, though in practice these agencies are largely autonomous and the council is limited to offering nonbinding recommendations. ECOSOC also negotiates consultative arrangements between the UN and nongovernmental organizations.

FUNCTIONAL AND REGIONAL COMMISSIONS

As noted earlier, the Economic and Social Council oversees various functional and regional commissions. The functional commissions most relevant for this study include the Commission on Sustainable Development (CSD), which monitors international efforts to promote development; Commission on Population and Development, which studies global demographic trends; Commission for Social Development, which offers policy advice on social issues; and Commission on the Status of Women (CSW), which works to advance the economic, social, and political rights of women. The regional commissions focus on the specific challenges of different geographic areas of the world.[12] Much of their work involves collecting data, undertaking macroeconomic studies, and formulating policy recommendations.[13] They typically focus on such issues as economic growth, foreign trade, regional integration, population trends, agricultural production, and environmental threats. The regional commissions also assist member governments prepare development plans and projects.

RESEARCH AND TRAINING INSTITUTES

ECOSOC is also responsible for supervising various research and training institutes. The institutes most directly engaged in development are the United Nations Research Institute for Social Development (UNRISD), United Nations Institute for Training and Research (UNITAR), and United Nations International Research and Training Institute for the Advancement of Women (INSTRAW). UNRISD conducts research on some of the central challenges facing developing countries, including urban and rural poverty, infrastructure weaknesses, and environmental deterioration. The institute professes a *holistic* approach to development that prioritizes equity, empowerment, and sustainability. UNITAR offers training programs in the field of economic and social development. Its primary mission is to strengthen national capacities to implement comprehensive development programs and meet international commitments. INSTRAW conducts research on gender issues in the developing world and sponsors training programs for women.

SPECIALIZED AGENCIES

Many of the specialized agencies are also engaged in development work. These agencies have been brought into formal relationships with the United Nations through negotiated agreements.[14] Although these agreements encourage reciprocal representation at meetings, information exchange, and coordination of activities, each agency operates largely independent of UN control and policy direction derives solely from its own governing bodies. These agencies also have their own charters, mandates, memberships, organizational structures, budgets, and funding sources.

The Economic and Social Council is expected to coordinate the activities of the specialized agencies. However, its role is largely limited to initiating consultations and drafting nonbinding recommendations. In fact, these agencies, some of which actually predate the UN itself, have resisted central coordination. This is especially true of the World Bank and the International Monetary Fund (IMF), the largest and most influential of the specialized agencies. Other agencies engaged in development work include the International Labor Organization (ILO), Food and Agriculture Organization (FAO), United Nations Educational, Scientific and Cultural Organization (UNESCO), World Health Organization (WHO), United Nations Industrial

Development Organization (UNIDO), and International Fund for Agricultural Development (IFAD).

SUBSIDIARY FUNDS AND PROGRAMS

The subsidiary funds and programs are directly engaged in development work. These agencies were created by the United Nations and are supervised by the General Assembly, either directly or through the Economic and Social Council. Most of their resources derive from the voluntary contributions of member states. Five of the largest funds and programs—the United Nations Development Programme, World Food Programme, United Nations Children's Fund, United Nations Population Fund, and United Nations Environmental Programme—constitute the central focus of this volume and are described in some detail below. Other subsidiary agencies include the United Nations Conference on Trade and Development (UNCTAD), United Nations High Commissioner for Refugees (UNHCR), United Nations High Commissioner on Human Rights (UNHCHR), and United Nations Human Settlements Programme (UN-HABITAT).

UNITED NATIONS DEVELOPMENT PROGRAMME

The United Nations Development Programme has the broadest mandate of the various subsidiary agencies included in this volume. It plays a significant role in the poverty alleviation efforts of the UN and supports initiatives to promote gender equity and environmental preservation.[15] As the world's largest source of multilateral grant assistance, UNDP is sometimes considered the development agency of the South.

UNDP, which was established in 1965 through the merger of the Expanded Programme of Technical Assistance (EPTA) and the United Nations Special Fund (UNSF), sponsors programs and projects throughout the developing world. Its central objective is to build national capacity for poverty reduction and sustainable development. Of UNDP's 6,500 staff members, 85 percent work in the developing world and the vast majority are locally recruited from host countries.

UNDP is governed by a 36-member Executive Council made up of representatives from both donor and recipient countries. The council is elected by ECOSOC and is responsible for overall policy formation. The Administrator of UNDP is appointed by the Secretary-General and confirmed by the General Assembly. UNDP, which is headquartered in New York City, has regional bureaus for Africa, the Arab States, Asia and the Pacific, Europe and the Commonwealth of Independent States, and Latin America and the Caribbean. Each bureau coordinates all sponsored programs in that region and promotes cooperation among neighboring states.

UNDP maintains 136 country offices worldwide, the largest number of any development assistance agency, which support programs in 166 countries. Each country office is led by a Resident Coordinator who is considered the chief representative of the UN in that country and is responsible for supervising all development activities.[16] As UNDP operations have become increasingly decentralized, more responsibility for program development, monitoring, and evaluation has been transferred to the country offices.[17]

UNDP receives most of its funds through the voluntary contributions of UN member governments or affiliated agencies. This currently totals about US$1 billion per year. Resources are allocated on the basis of each country's population and per capita income.[18] While most assistance is in the form of grants, recipient countries are expected to contribute local facilities, equipment, and supplies. Country contributions often constitute half of total project costs. Projects supported by UNDP typically receive collaborative funding from other multilateral institutions, such as the World Bank and the regional development banks, or from private sources.

UNDP projects are generally consistent with each country's development objectives. Program officials consult with government officials on project design and implementation is typically carried out by local governments or nongovernmental organizations. UNDP currently supports more than 6000 projects around the world with the majority of these projects designed to meet basic nutritional, health care, and educational needs.

In recent years, UNDP has worked to improve the lives of women. Emphasis is placed on ensuring access to land, credit, training, and technology. This is done, at least in part, through the United Nations Development Fund for Women (UNIFEM) which is administered by UNDP. UNIFEM provides direct financial and technical support for projects that contribute to the equitable and sustainable development of women. The fund also supports the participation of women in development planning and practice.

UNDP emphasizes gender mainstreaming in all social and economic programs. Gender mainstreaming is defined as a

> process of assessing the implications for women and men of any planned action, including legislation, policies or programs, in all areas and at all levels. It is a strategy for making women's as well as men's concerns and experiences an integral dimension of the design, implementation, monitoring and evaluation of policies and programs in all political, economic and societal spheres so that women and men benefit equally and inequality is not perpetuated. The ultimate goal is to achieve gender equality.[19]

The UNDP's Policy and Program Manual calls for all projects to be examined from the standpoint of women's role in development.[20] A Division for Women in Development was established to ensure women's needs and capabilities are systematically considered in all sponsored activities. One administrator in each country office is responsible for ensuring project proposals are responsive to the needs of women. A Gender Programme Team promotes gender equality across issues areas, regional bureaus, and interagency networks, a Gender Equality and Diversity Unit ensures gender parity in the management of work plans and budget submissions, and a Gender Steering and Implementation Committee ensures a gender perspective is included in all programs and projects.[21]

UNDP has also become increasingly engaged in the sustainable management of natural resources. It is one of the implementing agencies, along with UNEP and the World Bank, of the Global Environmental Facility (GEF). GEF allocates US$2 billion per year to help developing countries meet international environmental obligations. Emphasis is placed on six focal areas: biological diversity, climate change, international waters, ozone layer depletion, land degradation, and the management of hazardous wastes. Within GEF, UNDP is responsible for capacity building, pre-investment activities, technical assistance, and management of a small grant program.[22]

UNDP is also a major source of technical assistance to governments in the developing world. Focus is placed on ensuring access to the scientific knowledge and advanced technologies needed for social and economic progress. UNDP administers a Special Unit for Technical Cooperation among Developing Countries (SU/TCDC) and cosponsors, along with the Brazilian government, the International Poverty Center (IPC). The center conducts research on poverty and inequality and provides technical support for the preparation of poverty reduction strategies.[23] UNDP even plays a role in relief and recovery operations. The Resident Coordinator is responsible for mobilizing international assistance in countries recovering from natural disasters or other emergencies and the Emergency Response Division (ERD) aids countries in post-conflict reconstruction and the safe return of refugees.[24]

In recent years UNDP has become heavily engaged in policy dialog with governments in the developing world. Programme staff assist public officials in the formulation of national development strategies. This is done, at least in part, through the preparation of Poverty Reduction Strategy Papers (PRSP). These papers, which derive from a series of consultations between UNDP representatives, local government officials, and civil society groups, are formal statements of a country's development strategy.

UNDP also administers the United Nations Capital Development Fund (UNCDF) and the United Nations Volunteers (UNV). UNCDF generally supports infrastructural projects, including improvements in water and irrigation systems, and the construction of feeder roads, schools, and hospitals. The fund also promotes greater access to credit for poor communities, especially in rural areas. UNV oversees thousands of volunteers throughout the developing world who assist community-based initiatives in development, humanitarian relief, and rehabilitation.

Lastly, UNDP regularly publishes the *Human Development Report* (HDR). This report, which is prepared by an independent team of consultants from the public and private sector, provides basic data on nutrition, health, and education in the developing world. The HDR also advocates a broader approach to development that goes beyond economic growth to emphasize equity, empowerment, and sustainability.[25] Its Human Development Index (HDI) offers a broad measure of national development by including such indicators as life expectancy, educational attainment, purchasing power, and per capita income.[26]

WORLD FOOD PROGRAMME

The World Food Programme is the largest provider of international food assistance. Its central purpose is to extend food aid to countries whose populations suffer from acute or chronic hunger. WFP offers humanitarian relief to meet the short-term needs of people displaced by civil conflict or natural disaster and works to promote long-term nutritional security.[27]

WFP was established by the General Assembly and the Food and Agriculture Organization (FAO) in 1961 and began operations in 1963. It is based in Rome and has a staff of 10,000. The Executive Director of WFP is appointed jointly by the UN Secretary-General and the Director-General of FAO for a fixed five-year term. WFP has a 36-member Executive Council, with 18 members elected by the Economic and Social Council and 18 members elected by FAO for renewable three-year terms. The Executive Council coordinates food aid policies, reviews and approves projects, and sets the overall budget. WFP has regional bureaus for Latin America and the Caribbean (Managua), West Africa (Dakar), East and Southern Africa (Kampala), Central Africa (Yaounde), Asia (Bangkok), the Middle East, Central Asia and the Mediterranean (Cairo), and Eastern Europe (Rome). Its annual budget, currently about US$2 billion, is largely obtained from the voluntary contributions of UN member states. Additional support is provided by multilateral institutions, corporations, foundations, and non-governmental organizations.

WFP plays a central role in the provision of emergency food relief at times of natural disaster. Its Food-for-Life programs aid refugees and internally displaced persons (IDP) and its Protracted Relief and Recovery Operations (PRRO) provide post-crisis rehabilitation to achieve food security. Both initiatives offer temporary support to poor families to help rebuild communities, homes, schools, clinics, and basic infrastructure. In countries most vulnerable to natural disasters, WFP helps develop emergency response systems.

WFP is also the world's largest organizer of school feeding programs. These programs are designed to improve the nutrition of children and increase enrollment rates. When nutritious food is provided, parents have an additional incentive to enroll and maintain their children in school. WFP also has a Food-for-Growth program that targets vulnerable groups such as pregnant and nursing women, newborn children, and the elderly.

WFP also supports Food-for-Work programs that provide food assistance in exchange for work on development projects. Projects can include building clinics and schools, terracing hillsides, replanting forests, repairing irrigation canals, or implementing soil and water conservation projects. Because food assistance is typically procured within each country or region, local farmers are also direct beneficiaries.

UNITED NATIONS CHILDREN'S FUND

The United Nations Children's Fund works to ensure the survival, protection, and development of children. The fund plays a key role in the provision of basic needs for children and youth, including safe water, nutrition, primary health care, and basic education. Priority is accorded victims of extreme poverty, natural disaster, or warfare.

UNICEF, which was originally called the United Nations International Children's Emergency Fund, was established in 1946 to provide food, medicine, and clothing to children suffering in the aftermath of the Second World War, especially in Europe.[28] In 1953 the General Assembly extended UNICEF's mandate indefinitely and it became a permanent subsidiary agency. The fund's central purpose also shifted to improving the lives of children in the developing world.

UNICEF, which is based in New York City, has a 36-member Executive Board. Member nations are elected to the board by ECOSOC for three year terms. The Executive Board sets overall policy for the fund, in addition to approving specific programs and budgets. UNICEF has eight regional offices that are responsible for providing direction and technical assistance to 126 country offices. Most of the fund's 8000 staff members work in the country offices. UNICEF's annual budget, which is currently US$1.2 billion, is largely derived from the voluntary contributions of member states. The fund also receives support from foundations, businesses, and nongovernmental organizations.[29]

UNICEF activities are carried out in cooperation with host governments and are typically based on a "Situation Report" that analyzes the current and projected needs of each country. Considerable resources are devoted to the provision of basic health care. Emphasis is placed on ensuring children are vaccinated against six of the most common childhood diseases: diphtheria, measles, polio, tetanus, tuberculosis, and whooping cough. UNICEF is a co-founder of the Global Alliance for Vaccines and Immunization (GAVI) that strives to improve access to vaccines and strengthen immunization systems.

UNICEF works to ensure immunization coverage in a number of ways. It forecasts vaccine needs, collaborates with governments and donors to secure funding, helps purchase and transport vaccines, and encourages parents to have their children immunized. The fund also trains health workers on the proper use of vaccines and the importance of maintaining accurate immunization records. Priority is accorded to those countries with low immunization rates and districts in those countries where children are least protected. UNICEF also coordinates with governments and nongovernmental organizations to conduct national immunization campaigns that reach tens of thousands of children.[30]

UNICEF works to decrease child death from dehydration. The fund supports oral rehydration therapy (ORT) that allows water to stay in the digestive tract long enough to be absorbed.[31] UNICEF is also working to combat malaria, especially through the provision of insecticide-treated mosquito nets to children and pregnant women, and HIV/AIDS, by preventing parent-to-child transmission of HIV and caring for children orphaned or made vulnerable by the disease.

Childhood nutrition is also a priority. UNICEF supports training programs to teach parents the best ways to identify and prevent malnutrition and sponsors education campaigns to promote breastfeeding. UNICEF is also working to combat vitamin A deficiency. Because children suffering from vitamin A deficiency have weak immune systems, they are at greater risk of dying from measles or diarrhea. The fund's Vitamin A Global Initiative works with local governments to provide children with semi-annual vitamin A supplements. UNICEF also fortifies food, such as sugar or flour, with vitamin A and provides vitamin A to pregnant women.

Strengthening education systems in the developing world has also been a central component of UNICEF's mission. The fund works to ensure all children have access to quality education. It supports schools that use participatory teaching methods, maintain safe environments for children, and have strong links to local communities. The fund also supports pre-school, special education, and outreach services for orphans and other vulnerable children.

Lastly, UNICEF provides technical assistance to member governments. Such assistance helps governments design, administer, and evaluate projects that deliver essential services to children. UNICEF frequently engages in policy advocacy on behalf of children's rights. The fund was instrumental in drafting the 1989 *Convention on the Rights of the Child* and actively lobbies governments to ensure children have access to adequate nutrition, health care, and education.

UNITED NATIONS POPULATION FUND

The United Nations Population Fund is the world's largest source of family planning and reproductive health services. More than one-fourth of all international population assistance is channeled through UNFPA. Its family planning and reproductive health programs have been credited with preventing unintended pregnancies, slowing the spread of sexually transmitted diseases (STD), reducing maternal mortality, and improving the health of newborns.[32]

UNFPA was established by the General Assembly as a Trust Fund in 1967 and began operations in 1969. It was originally called the United Nations Fund for Population Activities. Although the fund's name was altered in 1987, it retains its original acronym. UNFPA's initial purpose was to analyze global population trends and assist governments obtain basic demographic data. Its mission later expanded to aiding countries in the formulation of family planning strategies and assisting pregnant and nursing women. UNFPA was originally administered by the United Nations Development Programme but became an independent subsidiary agency in 1972. The fund, which reports to the General Assembly through ECOSOC, is based in New York City and has a staff of 1000. A joint UNDP/UNFPA Executive Board, composed of 36 member countries, supervises all sponsored programs and projects.[33] The fund has regional bureaus for the Arab States and Europe, the Pacific, Latin America and the Caribbean, and sub-Saharan Africa.

The annual budget of UNFPA is about US$500 million, with most resources derived from the voluntary contributions of UN member states. A total of 172 countries currently contribute to the fund. UNFPA also receives donations from other intergovernmental organizations, foundations, corporations, and nongovernmental organizations. Since becoming operational in 1969, the fund has provided over six billion dollars of population assistance to developing countries.

The mandate of UNFPA, as established by ECOSOC in 1973 and reaffirmed in 1993, is to respond to population and family planning needs, promote awareness on how best to deal with population problems, assist individual countries with population pressures, and help stabilize population growth. Family planning is a central component of UNFPA's mission. The fund works to ensure access to safe and affordable contraceptive methods and other reproductive health commodities. UNFPA also seeks to ensure safe childbirths. This includes the provision of prenatal care for pregnant women, expanded access to skilled attendants at birth, and emergency obstetric care. The fund also supports postpartum care for mothers and infants.

Improving sexual health is also an important part of UNFPA activities. The fund works to prevent the spread of STDs, especially HIV/AIDS. Its programs are designed to ensure young people have accurate information, nonjudgmental counseling, and comprehensive services to prevent sexually transmitted infections.

Lastly, UNFPA aids developing countries in the collection and analysis of demographic information. The annual *State of the World Population* report contains demographic indicators for each country and region of the world along with general information on population trends. UNFPA officials work with local governments to ensure population issues are included in national planning processes and to build capacity in family planning and reproductive health. The fund provides assistance in the organization and evaluation of family planning programs and promotes legal and policy reforms that improve the lives of women.

UNITED NATIONS ENVIRONMENTAL PROGRAMME

The United Nations Environmental Programme was established to oversee the ever-expanding environmental agenda of the United Nations. Its central objective is to promote international cooperation on environmental issues and problems. Priority is placed on ensuring the sustainable management of natural resources; preserving air, water, land, forests, and biodiversity; developing renewable sources of energy; and mitigating climate change. Particular attention is accorded developing countries where resources available to protect and preserve natural environments are limited.[34]

UNEP was first proposed at the 1972 United Nations Conference on the Human Environment in Stockholm. At that time it was generally acknowledged that existing programs were not adequate to meet global environmental challenges. UNEP was formally established by the General Assembly later that same year. Although the program does not have a separate charter, General Assembly Resolution 2997 describes its basic purpose and the structure and functions of its Governing Council and Secretariat.[35]

UNEP, which is based in Nairobi and has a staff of 900, reports to the General Assembly through ECOSOC. Its work is overseen by an Executive Director who is nominated by the Secretary-General and elected by the General Assembly. UNEP also has a 58-member Governing Council that sets broad policy guidelines.[36] Council members, who are typically the environmental ministers of their respective countries, are elected to four-year terms by the General Assembly.[37] UNEP has regional offices for Africa, Asia and the Pacific, Europe, Latin America and the Caribbean, North America, and West Asia. These offices play a lead role in devising collective responses to regional environmental threats. UNEP also has divisions that focus on early warning and assessment, policy development and law, and multilateral environmental agreements. Because the annual budget of UNEP is relatively small (about US$100 million per year), it does not play a large role in funding environmental projects.[38] Rather, UNEP works to ensure environmental concerns are incorporated into the policies and programs of other UN agencies.[39] UNEP is also responsible for environmental policy coordination and information exchange within the UN.

UNEP's priorities, as defined by the fifth special session of its Governing Council, are environmental monitoring, coordination of environmental conventions, and development of environment policy instruments. Monitoring global environmental conditions is a major responsibility. The environmental data that UNEP collects is published in a number of publications, most notably its *Global Environmental Outlook* (GEO) report. UNEP maintains the Global Environmental Monitoring System (GEMS) that coordinates a network of 150 stations worldwide, providing information on climate, ocean and atmospheric conditions, natural resources, and transboundary pollution. The program also maintains the Global Resource Information Database (GRID), the World Conservation Monitoring Center

(WCMC), the Millennium Ecosystem Assessment Project, the Risøe Centre on Energy, Climate and Sustainable Development, and the Collaborating Centre on Water and Environment. The Division of Early Warning and Assessment (DEWA) monitors the state of the world environment, assesses global and regional environmental trends, and identifies emerging environmental threats.

UNEP also works to promote international environmental norms and standards. Much of this work is undertaken by its Division of Environmental Law and Conventions (DELC). This division initiated negotiations on most of the major environmental treaties and protocols that have been adopted over the past three decades. UNEP is also responsible for implementing various environmental conventions, including those on biodiversity, desertification, climate change, migratory species, endangered species, ozone protection, hazardous wastes, organic pollutants, and regional seas.[40]

In the developing world, UNEP helps integrate environmental concerns into the economic planning processes. Much of this work is carried out by its Division of Environmental Policy Implementation (DEPI). This division works to strengthen government institutions responsible for the management of the environment. Programme officials also assist governments in the formulation of environmental regulations and adoption of legislation that complies with international treaty obligations. UNEP offers training programs for government officials on the application of international environmental laws and treaties. The agency even sponsors a small number of initiatives to educate the general public on the appropriate use of natural resources.

Although UNEP is not a major source of financing for environmental projects, it does administer a select number of demonstration projects. Successful projects are later expanded by member states and other UN agencies. UNEP is one of the implementing agencies, along with the United Nations Development Programme and the World Bank, of the Global Environmental Facility. As noted earlier, GEF assists developing countries meet international environmental obligations. UNEP's responsibilities within GEF include providing scientific and technical support for projects and guidance on national environmental assessments.[41]

DEVELOPMENT AGENDA OF THE UNITED NATIONS

The United Nations has played a lead role in setting the global developmental agenda.[42] This is reflected in various funding initiatives, global conferences, and policy declarations during the past five decades. The development work of the UN is consistent with its founding documents. One of the central purposes of the UN, as stated in its charter, is "[t]o achieve international co-operation in solving international problems of an economic, social, cultural or humanitarian character."[43] Chapter 9 of the charter, which is exclusively devoted to international economic and social concerns, calls for promoting "higher standards of living, full employment, and conditions of economic and social progress and development" and devising "solutions of international economic, social, health and related problems."[44] The developmental mission of the UN is also informed by the 1948 *Universal Declaration of Human Rights* (see Appendix 1). Article 25 of the declaration states that "[e]veryone has the right to a standard of living adequate for the health and well-being of himself and of his family, including food, clothing, housing and medical care and necessary social services."[45] The subsequent article stresses the right to basic education.[46]

Because the *Universal Declaration of Human Rights* is not a legally binding document within the framework of international law, a separate *International Covenant of Economic, Social and Cultural Rights* was prepared (see Appendix 2). The covenant, which was adopted by the General Assembly in 1966 and entered into force in 1976, focuses on the provision of basic human needs, such as nutrition, health care, education, and shelter. It recognizes the right of all people "to be free from hunger," and to enjoy "the highest attainable standard of physical and mental health."[47] State parties to the covenant are expected to "take steps, individually and through international assistance and co-operation, especially economic and technical, to the maximum of its available resources, with a view to achieving progressively the full realization of the rights recognized in the present Covenant."[48] The covenant is thus phrased in aspirational terms, with governments expected to fulfill these rights to the maximum extent possible. ECOSOC supervises implementation of the covenant. State parties are required to submit reports to its Committee on Economic, Social and Cultural Rights on the progress they have achieved in fulfilling the covenant.[49] The committee also issues legislative and policy recommendations to assist governments meet their obligations.

EARLY INSTITUTIONS

The early years of the United Nations coincided with the independence of many new nations in the developing world. The UN was under increased pressure from the representatives of these nations, especially from Africa and Asia, to redirect resources toward economic and social development. A number of institutions were established to achieve this objective. As early as December 1948, the General Assembly called for international experts to advise governments on economic development.[50] The following year, the Expanded Programme of Technical Assistance for the Economic Development of Underdeveloped Countries (EPTA) was established. EPTA was designed to transfer knowledge, skills, and technology to the local managers of economic and social projects in the developing world.[51] The program was financed largely through voluntary contributions and its annual operating fund never surpassed US$20 million.

Leaders from the developing world soon lobbied for additional resources. They proposed establishing a Special United Nations Fund for Economic Development (SUNFED) that would provide grants and long-term, low-interest loans to finance the construction of hospitals, schools, and industrial plants. SUNFED was expected to support development projects that were unable to attract private investment capital. Despite a vigorous campaign by developing countries, this fund never came into existence. Western leaders were generally opposed to the proposal, arguing that such a fund would largely duplicate work already being carried out by the World Bank. Rather, a United Nations Special Fund (UNSF) was established in 1959 with a more limited purpose. While UNSF undertook feasibility studies and provided some pre-investment grants for development projects, its central objective was to stimulate new capital investments either by recipient governments or the private sector. EPTA and UNSF were merged in 1965 to become the United Nations Development Programme.

DEVELOPMENT DECADES

As noted earlier, decolonization heightened pressures on the United Nations to allocate greater resources for economic and social development. The newly independent countries of Africa and Asia, along with a number of Latin American countries, called for increased attention to the needs of their societies. In 1961, many of these nations formed the Non-Aligned Movement (NAM). Originally designed to consolidate the political independence of member states, NAM's focus soon shifted to global economic issues. Many of these same countries established the Group of 77 in 1964 to strengthen their position within the General Assembly.[52] The United Nations Conference on Trade and Development (UNCTAD), also established in 1964, became an additional vehicle for advancing the interests of developing countries within the United Nations.

In response to the increased activism of African, Asian, and Latin American countries, the General Assembly designated the 1960s the "decade of development." The central objective of this decade was to accelerate progress toward sustainable economic growth and social progress.[53] A 1962 General Assembly resolution entitled *Permanent Sovereignty over Natural Resources* stated:

> It is desirable to promote international co-operation for the economic development of developing countries and that economic and financial agreements between the developed and developing countries must be based on the principles of equality and the right of peoples and nations to self-determination.[54]

The UN called on the industrialized nations to support progress in the developing world by pledging economic assistance equal to 1 percent of their Gross National Product (GNP). Toward the end of this decade the UN commissioned an internal report to assess its development work. The report, formally entitled *Study of the Capacity of the United Nations Development System*, recommended that economic assistance be managed by UNDP and ECOSOC become more of a policy center.[55]

While a second Development Decade was declared for the 1970s, the agenda advanced during this decade went well beyond increasing economic assistance. Leaders from the developing world advocated fundamental reforms to the global economy. A special session of the General Assembly convened in 1974 adopted a *Declaration and Program of Action for the Establishment of a New International Economic Order*. The declaration called for: 1) ensuring the economic sovereignty of developing countries, 2) according developing countries greater purchasing power for their primary product and raw material exports, 3) offering developing countries preferential access to the markets of industrialized countries, 4) ensuring that developing countries control the level and nature of foreign direct investment, 5) transferring new technologies to developing countries, 6) rescheduling or cancelling most international debts, and 7) expanding the decision-making power of developing countries in global financial institutions. Although these proposals were advanced with considerable resolve, they were resisted by most industrialized nations and few reforms were ever adopted.

The UN commissioned a second report in 1975 to consider how it could better meet the needs of developing countries.[56] The report expressed concern about the proliferation of institutions engaged in development and proposed establishing a single United Nations Development Agency. It also recommended replacing UNCTAD with an international trade organization. Although neither recommendation was adopted, the UN continued to play a role in setting the global development agenda by sponsoring conferences and preparing conventions that focused on the needs of developing countries.

CONFERENCES AND CONVENTIONS

During the latter part of the twentieth century the United Nations sponsored a number of international conferences that focused on various aspects of development. Each conference typically concluded with an ambitious action plan. During the 1970s alone the UN sponsored the 1972 Conference on the Human Environment, 1974 World Food Conference, 1974 World Population Conference, 1976 Conference on Human Settlements, and 1979 World Conference on Agrarian Reform and Rural Development.

The 1980s, which was declared the third Development Decade, began with the publication of a report by the Independent Commission on International Development Issues. This ad hoc commission, set up by the UN and World Bank and chaired by former West German Chancellor Willy Brandt, was charged with examining global inequality. Its final report recommended comprehensive international trade, aid, and monetary reforms.[57] Two subsequent reports followed soon thereafter. The 1983 *Report of the World Commission on Environment and Development* emphasized the link between economic development and environmental issues and the 1985 *Bertrand Report* again called on the UN to radically restructure its development machinery.[58] The latter report recommended replacing ECOSOC with an Economic Security Council limited to 23 member states and establishing a single development agency responsible for agriculture, health, education, and industry.

In 1986 the General Assembly adopted a *Declaration on the Right to Development* (see Appendix 3), which stated that development is an "inalienable human right by virtue of which every human person and all peoples are entitled to participate in, contribute to, and enjoy economic, social, cultural and political development."[59] The declaration established specific recommendations for both member countries and the international community. According to Article 2:

> [S]tates have the right and the duty to formulate appropriate national development policies that aim at the constant improvement of the well-being of the entire population and of all individuals, on the basis of their active, free and meaningful participation in development and in the fair distribution of the benefits resulting therefrom.[60]

Article 4 stated that "international co-operation is essential in providing these countries with appropriate means and facilities to foster their comprehensive development."[61]

While the 1990s was declared the fourth Development Decade, the agenda was not nearly as ambitious as that of previous decades. Instead of advocating fundamental reform of the global economy, which was deemed unlikely, the UN stressed more practical measures to reduce poverty, enhance the capacity of the poor, and protect natural environments. The 1992 UN Conference on Environment and Development in Rio de Janeiro emphasized the link between the environment and development, the 1993 World Conference on Human Rights identified poverty alleviation as a basic human right, the 1994 International Conference on Population and Development (ICPD) linked basic human needs with sustainable development, and the 1995 World Summit for Social Development focused on reducing unemployment, combating poverty, and promoting sustainable development. The final declaration from the last conference stated that "economic development, social development, and environmental protection are interdependent and mutually reinforcing components of sustainable development"[62] and pledged to make poverty reduction, full employment, and social integration the central objectives of development. A Commission for Social Development was established to monitor progress in fulfilling these goals.

Secretary-General Boutros Boutros-Ghali added momentum to UN development efforts through two policy documents. *An Agenda for Peace* (1992) drew a direct connection between development and the prevention of warfare. Because conflict stems from such social problems as population growth, inequality, and debt, he argued, social and economic progress is essential for achieving international security. The second document, *An Agenda for Development* (1994), identified development as the most significant challenge of the time and highlighted the UN's role in promoting economic and social progress. The document advocated a holistic approach to development that included economic, social, cultural, political, and environmental considerations. Boutros-Ghali also stressed the importance of grassroots participation in the development process.

MILLENNIUM DEVELOPMENT GOALS

An Agenda for Development offered a broad statement of how the United Nations viewed the development process, a perspective that grew out of the lessons learned from the experiences of the 1970s and 1980s. At the same time, the document offered only a general statement of UN aspirations. Translating these aspirations into concrete goals and practical programs was a more difficult task. In an attempt to meet this challenge, a Millennium Summit was convened in September 2000 at the UN headquarters in New York under the leadership of Secretary-General Kofi Annan.[63] The summit concluded with the adoption of the *United Nations Millennium Declaration* (see Appendix 4) and Millennium Development Goals (MDGs) (see Appendix 5) that established eight fundamental goals (along with 18 specific targets and 48 indicators) for the new century.[64] The target date for achieving these goals is 2015.[65]

The MDGs include: 1) eradicating extreme poverty and hunger, 2) achieving universal primary education, 3) promoting gender equality and the empowerment of women, 4) reducing child mortality, 5) improving maternal health, 6) combating HIV/AIDS, malaria and other diseases, 7) ensuring environmental sustainability, and 8) developing a global partnership for development. These goals are designed to serve as a common policy framework for the entire UN system. Member governments are also encouraged to include these goals in their national development policies and to submit annual reports on the progress achieved in meeting specific targets. The UNDP was assigned primary responsibility for overseeing the progress of each nation.[66]

Although leaders from the developing world embraced the MDGs, most nations did not have the resources needed to meet each specific target. In an attempt to enhance the resources available to developing countries, the UN sponsored a follow-up conference in March 2002. The International Conference on Financing for Development, which took place in Monterrey

Mexico, focused on mobilizing the resources needed to achieve the MDGs. The conference adopted the *Monterrey Consensus* that advocated increased foreign economic assistance, along with promoting private investment and international trade, and lessening the burden of international debt. ECOSOC was assigned primary responsibility for monitoring progress in each of these areas. The Secretariat also established a Financing for Development Office within the Department of Economic and Social Affairs to ensure commitments reached at the conference were fulfilled.

A World Summit on Sustainable Development (WSSD) was held in Johannesburg in 2002 to mark the tenth anniversary of the UN Conference on Environment and Development. The summit concluded with the *Johannesburg Declaration*, a broad statement of commitment to sustainable development, and a "plan of implementation" which included quantifiable goals and targets with specific deadlines. In September 2005 the UN organized another World Summit to evaluate progress achieved toward realizing the MDGs during the preceding five years. The summit, which marked the opening of the 60th session of the General Assembly, reaffirmed that "sustainable development in its economic, social and environmental aspects constitutes a key element of the overarching framework of United Nations activities."[67] Member states also called for a continued commitment to official development assistance (ODA).

CONCLUSION

The United Nations has played a notable role in setting the global development agenda. This chapter reviewed the different UN institutions that are engaged in the promotion of economic, social, and environmental progress in the developing world. This includes three principal organs—the Secretariat, General Assembly, and Economic and Social Council—along with a number of functional and regional commissions, research and training institutes, and specialized agencies. Particular attention was accorded the five subsidiary agencies that are most directly involved in development: the United Nations Development Programme, World Food Programme, United Nations Children's Fund, United Nations Population Fund, and United Nations Environmental Programme. The chapter also considered the UN's broader role in promoting development, with focus placed on its early institutions, the activities associated with consecutive Development Decades, and the sponsorship of various conferences and conventions, culminating with the adoption of the *Millennium Declaration* and MDGs.

The UN's efforts to promote economic, social, and environmental progress in the developing world have attracted both praise and criticism.[68] Critics charge that the UN is far too bureaucratic and cumbersome to have much of an impact. Its vast collection of councils, commissions, agencies, and programs often have overlapping mandates and missions.[69] Vested interests and a continued defense of the status quo make it difficult to dissolve institutions that are no longer needed. The UN is also faulted for poor collaboration and coordination among its various agencies.

Critics also point to a lack of transparency and accountability on budgetary matters. Poor financial supervision, it is argued, results in contracts being awarded and money disbursed with little regard for standard accounting procedures.[70] Since departments and agencies are rarely audited, they have little incentive to improve financial practices. Spending priorities are also questioned. Critics point to development projects that never achieved their stated purpose or reached intended beneficiaries.

The UN is also faulted for having a large proportion of its resources allocated for salaries and overhead. Many UN officials, who are appointed to satisfy demands for geographic diversity, are considered poorly qualified for their positions. Member governments exert considerable influence over personnel and administrative decisions.[71] When incompetence is evident, officials are typically transferred to another department rather than being dismissed.[72]

Proponents of the UN offer an alternative perspective. The UN has a fairly impressive record of accomplishments, it is argued, in the promotion of sustainable development. This record is rarely recognized, however, because institutional weaknesses and failed projects receive much greater attention than every day achievements. Moreover, the limitations of the UN are largely due to the intransigence of member governments. With few independent sources of financing, the UN is dependent on the contributions of member states. Yet many states are in arrears in their regular dues and reluctant to fully fund the subsidiary agencies. Member countries continually expand the mandate of the UN without a comparable expansion of resources.[73]

Proponents also stress the unique advantages of the UN. After many years of working in the developing world, the organization has accumulated considerable managerial and technical expertise. The UN's reputation for neutrality allows it to operate in individual countries with less suspicion than other multilateral or bilateral assistance programs. It is thus in a better position to develop relationships based on trust and goodwill with both local governments and societal groups.

While proponents and critics of the UN advance opposite extremes, the reality is considerably more complex. Any assessment of the development work of the UN necessitates review of the activities of specific agencies. The chapters that follow survey the work of five subsidiary agencies in Latin America during the early years of the twenty-first century with focus placed on meeting basic human needs, improving the lives of women, and preserving natural environments. My central objective is to identify and describe the economic, social, and environmental work of the UN in the region.

3   Poverty in the Americas

Poverty reduction is the foremost objective of development. If nothing else, development signifies improving living conditions for the poor and ensuring access to basic nutrition, health care, and education. International assistance is typically structured to meet the basic needs of poor communities in the developing world.

This and the following chapter consider the problem of poverty in Latin America. Approximately 200 million people live in poverty throughout the region.[1] Tens of millions of people are unable to obtain clean water or sufficient nutrition. The poor are also excluded from quality and affordable health care. Clinics and hospitals are largely inaccessible to poor communities, especially in rural areas. The region is also marked by major weaknesses in public education systems. This is reflected in low enrollments, irregular attendance, late matriculation, and high dropout rates.

This chapter first reviews social conditions in Latin America, with focus placed on access to nutrition, primary health care, and basic education. I then turn to the principal causes of poverty in the region. Social factors, especially profound inequalities in the distribution of income and wealth, clearly contribute to the problem, but governments have also been unable or unwilling to significantly improve socioeconomic conditions. External factors, most notably international trade, foreign debt, and economic adjustment, also contribute to poverty in the region.

NUTRITION

The nutritional status of Latin Americans has slowly improved over time. More people have access to clean water and quality foodstuffs now than in the past. Unlike other regions of the developing world, severe problems of hunger or famine are relatively rare. At the same time, serious nutritional deficiencies remain. Roughly 120 million Latin Americans lack access to safe drinking water.[2] This includes about 7 percent of the urban population and 35 percent of the rural population. The poor quality of water systems is a major cause of gastrointestinal diseases and a primary contributor to child mortality.

Food insecurity also affects large numbers of people in Latin American.[3] There are 60 million chronically malnourished people in the region, representing 11 percent of the total population. 100 million people are unable to meet their minimal caloric requirements on a daily basis. In some of the poorest countries—Bolivia, El Salvador, Guatemala, Haiti, Honduras, and Nicaragua—nearly half of the population is malnourished. Malnutrition reduces resistance to malaria, measles, pneumonia, tuberculosis, and a number of other illnesses.

Malnutrition is *especially* debilitating for children. At present, about 10 percent of all Latin American children are severely underweight for their age.[4] When children are poorly nourished, their health, cognitive skills, and learning capacity are all compromised. Moreover, because malnutrition undermines immune systems, children are more vulnerable to infectious diseases. A high percentage of children have vitamin A deficiency, which is a major cause of blindness and a contributing factor to childhood deaths from diarrhea, malaria, and measles, as well as iron deficiency anemia, which lowers resistance to infections and limits physical and cognitive development.

HEALTH

Latin America has registered some improvements in public health in recent years.[5] Increases in both community health services and the number of trained health workers have expanded access to primary health care. Enhanced medical care and childhood vaccinations have contributed to steady improvements in health indicators. While the infant mortality rate (IMR) was 126 in 1950, it stands at 22 today.[6] Similarly, the child mortality rate (CMR) has fallen from 81 in 1970 to 33 today.[7] Average life expectancy has increased from 53 to 73 during the past five decades.[8]

Despite these gains, health systems remain highly segmented. While middle and upper income families have access to quality private care, the poor are dependent on public clinics and hospitals plagued by unsanitary conditions, poorly trained personnel, outdated equipment, and shortages of basic medicines.[9] Per capita spending on health care in Latin America (US$438) is below the world average (US$640) and well behind that of high income countries (US$2514). The limited availability of health insurance means most costs are absorbed directly by individuals and families.

Access to health care also varies between urban and rural areas. Because most hospitals and medical facilities are located in national or provincial capitals, they are largely inaccessible to the rural poor. Major urban hospitals and clinics received about two-thirds of public sector expenditures while serving just one-fifth of the overall population. Even in urban areas, quality medical services primarily benefit middle and upper income families as emphasis is placed on expensive treatments to cure illness rather than preventative care.

Despite improvements in vaccination coverage, many children do not receive routine immunization against such common childhood diseases as cholera, diphtheria, hepatitis, measles, meningitis, tetanus, typhoid, tuberculosis, and whooping cough. Moreover, even in those countries where vaccination coverage is fairly strong, drug resistant forms of some diseases have emerged in recent years. Infections of the digestive system, especially diarrhea, are a major cause of child mortality.

HIV/AIDS has emerged as a major threat to the health and well-being of people in Latin America.[10] The region currently has 2.5 million people who are HIV-positive. The virus is especially prevalent in Brazil, where 20,000 new HIV/AIDS cases are reported each year, and the Caribbean nations of Barbados, the Dominican Republic, Guyana, Haiti, Jamaica, Suriname, and Trinidad. The Caribbean has the second highest incidence of HIV/AIDS in the world after sub-Saharan Africa and AIDS has become the leading cause of death for both men and women aged 15–24. The disease is also spreading rapidly in the Central American nations of Belize, Honduras, and Panama. Transmission of HIV is primarily through sexual contact and the sharing of needles among intravenous drug users, though the epidemic has recently spread beyond high risk populations to the more general public. It is largely concentrated in poor communities where access to health care and sexual education is limited.[11] Women also face the risk of transmitting the infection to their babies during pregnancy, delivery, or breastfeeding.

The HIV/AIDS pandemic often places entire families at risk. When wage earners become ill, household assets are depleted. The impact on children can be especially harmful. Children who live in households with HIV-positive family members often drop out of school because their parents can no longer afford school fees. Moreover, an increasing number of children must care for themselves when their parents or guardians become ill.

EDUCATION

Latin America has also registered some advances in education. Most countries have increased public spending on education, both in terms of expenditures per student and expenditures as a percentage of gross domestic product (GDP). This has contributed to an increase in the number of teachers and better quality instructional materials. The region is close to achieving universal access to primary education.[12] Literacy rates in the region have doubled since the 1930s to 86 percent and the average years of schooling have also doubled since 1960 to seven years.[13]

At the same time, there remain serious weaknesses in education systems throughout Latin America.[14] Public education is characterized by low enrollment, late matriculation, irregular attendance, high dropout rates, and poor student performance. A quarter of all children do not complete primary school and nearly 40 percent do not complete secondary school. Dropout rates are especially high in poor communities where children are often needed to augment family income. Approximately 36 million adults are illiterate.[15]

Although enrollment rates have increased in recent years, the quality of education remains deficient. Despite increased public spending, the total amount allocated for education is limited.[16] Low salaries make it difficult to attract qualified teachers and those teachers who are employed are often poorly trained and motivated. Teaching methods tend to focus on rote memorization rather than participatory learning, critical thinking, or problem solving. Schools are typically overcrowded and poorly equipped. Latin American students perform worse in international assessments than their peers in other regions of the world.[17]

Public education systems in rural areas are especially deficient. Rural schools are invariably characterized by a lack of trained teachers and inadequate facilities. In Bolivia, only 7 percent of children in rural areas complete primary school within the standard eight years and over half of rural primary schools offer only three of eight grades. In Guatemala, although 60 percent of the school age population lives in rural areas, only 25 percent of the nation's schools are located outside of cities. While 50 percent of students who enter primary school in urban areas go on to complete primary school, the comparable figure is just 20 percent in rural areas.[18]

SOCIAL CAUSES

Clearly a major reason for poverty is simply the poor distribution of income and wealth. Inequalities are more pronounced in Latin America than in any other region of the world.[19] At present, the richest 10 percent of the population receives 40 percent of total income, while the poorest 20 percent of the population receives just 3 percent of income. In countries with the greatest inequality, such as Bolivia, Brazil, El Salvador, Guatemala, and Nicaragua, the wealthiest 20 percent of the population earns nearly 30 times that of the poorest 20 percent. In Haiti, 4 percent of the population controls two-thirds of the nation's wealth.

Inequality has its roots in the early formation of these nations. A landed oligarchy emerged during the colonial period and retained control over the best lands after independence. *Latifundias* have been passed down from one generation to the next and continue to constitute an important source of power and wealth. A similar concentration of ownership is evident in the industrial and manufacturing sectors. The region is marked by rigid class structures and restricted social mobility. The landed and industrial elite are followed by a small middle class and a large underclass. Many of the poorest people are relegated to the informal economy, without regular wages, social benefits, or job security.[20]

There is also a strong correlation between the class structure and ethnicity.[21] A distinct ethnic hierarchy is evident in most Latin American countries. People of European origin, the descendants of those who immigrated to the region during the colonial period or the early years of independence, generally have the greatest income and wealth. The wealth accumulated by these families is passed down over time.

Indigenous peoples, on the other hand, have long endured poverty, exclusion, and discrimination.[22] Much of their land and resources were appropriated during the colonial period and they have continued to be marginalized in the period since independence.[23] This is especially evident in the areas with the largest indigenous populations, such as the Andes and Middle America.[24] Living conditions for indigenous peoples are considerably below national averages in almost all respects. While the majority of the indigenous live in rural areas, they are often landless. Those who do own land typically have plots that are too small to be economically viable. Low incomes generally result in poor nutrition, health care, and education which, in turn, undermine the prospects for succeeding generations.

People of African descent have also been marginalized and exploited.[25] The Afro-Latino population is highest in the Caribbean and the Atlantic coast of Central and South America, especially Brazil, Colombia, French Guiana, Guyana, Panama, Suriname, and Venezuela. Most Afro-Latinos trace their ancestry to people brought to the continent during the colonial era slave trade. Income and living standards of people of African descent are far below national averages. This is reflected in a number of social indicators, including infant and child survival rates, life expectancies, and adult literacy.

Poverty can also be linked to population growth. This is true despite the fact that fertility rates have declined dramatically throughout Latin America, from 5.6 children per woman in 1970 to 2.5 children per woman today. Some countries are already approaching an overall fertility rate equivalent to population replacement (about 2.1 children per woman) and passing into the last stage of demographic transition.[26] Improvements in educational and economic opportunities have enhanced the status of women and altered traditional gender roles. This has led women to postpone marriage and childbirth until later in their reproductive years. Women also have greater access to contraception and family planning programs.

Population growth does *not* seem to be outstripping natural resources.[27] As a whole, Latin America is not overpopulated. In fact, population density in the region is only half the global average. The dependency ratio in the region is also declining, since there are fewer dependents (people under age 15 or over 65) over time for each working age person (age 15–65).[28] Latin America is also endowed with tremendous natural resources. With just

9 percent of the world's people, the region has 31 percent of the world's freshwater, 23 percent of arable land, almost half of all tropical forests, and an extraordinary diversity of plant and animal life. Latin America also has considerable mineral wealth, including bauxite, chromium, copper, diamonds, gold, iron ore, lead, lithium, manganese, nickel, silver, tin, and zinc. The region has large petroleum and natural gas reserves, especially in Mexico and Venezuela, but also in Argentina, Bolivia, Brazil, and Ecuador.

At the same time, population growth does contribute to poverty. Latin America's population has increased *fourfold* since 1940 to its present level of 580 million people. Although population growth rates have declined in recent years, they still average about 1.6 percent.[29] This is due, at least in part, to the phenomenon of "population momentum." Because of previously high fertility levels, 40 percent of the people are under 15 years of age.[30] As a result, each year a large number of young women enter their reproductive years. Although these women typically have fewer children than their mothers and grandmothers, the overall population continues to increase. The region's population is expected to reach 628 million by 2015.[31] Because population growth is typically more rapid that economic growth, it is difficult to meet increased demands for basic services or absorb all of the new entrants into the job market.

It can also be argued that economic progress has been slowed by the emigration of professionals to North America and Europe. Often the best educated individuals leave their home country in search of better paying positions abroad.[32] This is especially true of health care professionals, but is also evident with respect to teachers, engineers, and scientists. This constitutes a double loss for these societies, since resources were expended to train these individuals and the skills that they now have are often the very skills most needed at home.

At the same time, Latin American countries benefit from emigration in some respects. It typically acts as a safety valve, since, as noted earlier, local economies cannot absorb all of the new entrants into the job market each year. Emigrants also send money earned abroad to family members back in their home countries. Such remittances have become a major source of income for many families, especially in Mexico and Central America.[33] Remittances to Latin America have grown exponentially in recent years and now total US$60 billion per year.[34] For some countries in the region, remittances are equal to 10 percent of gross domestic product and 30 percent of export earnings.[35] They thus constitute a crucial source of foreign exchange which helps countries balance their external accounts.

POLITICAL CAUSES

Poverty can also be linked to the poor quality of governance in Latin America.[36] In general, governments have *not* played a positive role in promoting social and economic progress. In fact, they have often constituted a major obstacle to such progress.[37] Governments can be faulted for poor economic policy making, with the adoption of import substitution industrialization (ISI) during the 1950s and 1960s being a prominent example.[38] The central objective of this strategy was to replace imports with domestically produced goods. This, it was thought, would help diversify local economies away from a heavy dependence on a few primary product and raw material exports. The development of some lead industries would then expand other sectors of the economy. To spur this process, Latin American governments invested heavily in the development of a manufacturing sector. Firms were often created and owned by the state.[39] Governments also provided the private sector with tax breaks, subsidized financing, and preferential access to foreign exchange. To limit foreign competition, protectionist trade policies, including steep tariffs, numerical quotas, license fees, and domestic content requirements were enacted. Restrictions were also imposed on foreign investment. Such investment was typically limited to certain sectors of the economy and required some level of local content, local equity ownership, and capital reinvestment.

ISI policies did diversify Latin American economies, especially in Mexico and some of the larger South American countries such as Argentina, Brazil, Chile, and Venezuela. From 1950 to the mid-1970s, annual growth in the manufacturing sector averaged 7 percent. This helped expand employment, raise living standards, and broaden the middle class. However, the strategy ultimately produced debilitating budget deficits. Governments spent well beyond their means to promote domestic industrialization. Moreover, with a protected market and few incentives to modernize, state-owned firms were highly inefficient. Latin American nations were unable to deepen the industrialization process or realize greater economies of scale because their home markets were relatively small and domestic firms were not competitive in external markets.[40]

Import substitution industrialization also produced severe balance of payments problems. Foreign reserves rapidly deteriorated because these nations were selling fewer products abroad and receiving less foreign investment. However, they remained dependent on critical imports, such as energy, capital goods, and advanced technology. This led to large foreign exchange deficits and heavy borrowing from abroad. The sizable external debts that many nations are grappling with today are a legacy of these past policies.

Budget deficits and external debts have limited government spending on basic nutrition, health care, and education. Inattention to agriculture also led to the decline of rural economies.[41] In some of the poorest countries— Bolivia, Guatemala, Honduras, Nicaragua, Paraguay and Peru—at least 50 percent of the population lives in rural areas. As noted earlier, malnutrition, poor health, and illiteracy are all the more severe in the countryside. In Brazil, for example, there are major differences between the largely rural

North and West of the country and the more urban South-East. This is also true for Peru and Ecuador where the urbanized coastal areas are better off than the Andean sierra or tropical lowlands.

Governments in Latin America do not have an especially strong record of allocating public resources to promote the general well-being. A relatively small elite dominates most governments in the region, effectively excluding the poor and working class from meaningful participation in political affairs. Political systems rely heavily on patronage, with the private interests of a few outweighing the public welfare of many.[42] Public sector corruption, which includes kickbacks on state contracts, influence peddling, the solicitation of bribes to circumvent regulations or obtain government licenses, the direct embezzlement of government revenue, and the appointment of family members or close associates to government offices, is relatively extensive.[43]

Public sector corruption is certainly not unique to Latin America. Many of the conditions that produce corrupt behavior, however, are especially prevalent in the region. The misuse of public office for private gain is more likely when upward mobility is restricted, the salaries of civil servants are low, and resources are scarce. Corruption is also likely when institutional transparency is limited, public officials have considerable discretion over the allocation of resources, and poor oversight makes the disclosure of illegal acts unlikely.

Public sector corruption undermines social and economic progress by lowering the quality of public services, reducing tax revenues, and distorting incentives. Since corruption tends to benefit privileged groups at the expense of the poor and dispossessed, it intensifies existing inequalities. The diversion of public monies limits the availability of resources to adequately fund social programs. Because corruption raises both the costs and uncertainties for transnational corporations, it discourages foreign investment.

EXTERNAL CAUSES

There are also a number of international factors that have contributed to poverty in Latin America.[44] It is frequently argued that the poor progress of countries in the region is due, at least in part, to their historical insertion into the global economy. The underdevelopment of the region can be traced to the pattern of specialization imposed during colonial rule and continued throughout the postcolonial period.

Clearly trade relations have often worked against the interests of Latin American nations. Despite public sector support for industrialization, the most important exports from the region remain primary products and agricultural goods. This is reflected in the heavy dependence of Argentina on beef and grain exports, Bolivia on tin, Brazil and Colombia on coffee, Chile on copper, Cuba and the Dominican Republic on sugar, and many of the Central America nations on bananas, coffee, and cotton. The value of these

primary products has consistently declined relative to the value of manufactured products and capital goods. These nations are thus required to
increase their exports from one year to the next simply to earn the foreign
exchange needed to purchase the same volume of manufactured and capital
goods from abroad.

External debt also constitutes a major obstacle to economic and social
progress. The combine debt of Latin American countries today—US$750
billion—is equivalent to 35 percent of the region's gross national income.
Annual debt servicing equals 8 percent of GNP and absorbs nearly one-third
of total foreign exchange earnings. Resources that could be allocated for
productive or social investments are used to make interest payments on
foreign debts. The costs incurred in servicing external debts are often greater
than public spending on health care and education combined.

As noted earlier, the debt crisis has its origins in the import substitution
industrialization policies of the past. Governments borrowed heavily from
abroad to offset foreign exchange shortages. External finance was abundant
and real interest rates were relatively low at the time. Toward the end of the
1970s, creditor nations encountered severe inflationary pressures and
responded with tight monetary policies that drove up interest rates. Because
many of the loans were extended under floating rate agreements, Latin
American nations suddenly faced much greater debt service obligations. The
global recession of the early 1980s only compounded problems for these
nations as markets for traditional exports collapsed and commodity prices
plummeted. The combination of reduced export earnings and higher debt
payments led to chronic foreign exchange shortages. New commercial lending also declined as commercial banks lost confidence in the ability of these
nations to repay past loans.

Latin American countries then turned to international financial institutions (IFI), most notably the World Bank, International Monetary Fund
(IMF), and Inter-American Development Bank (IDB), for assistance. Support
from these institutions was contingent on the adoption of structural adjustment programs (SAP) designed to restore equilibrium to each nation's
internal and external accounts. Moreover, other sources of credit, including
the Paris Club, many bilateral programs, and most commercial banks, made
further loans contingent on reaching an agreement with the World Bank
and IMF.

The economic reforms required under structural adjustment reflected a
strong bias in favor of market-based allocation of resources between and
within nations. They included reducing government services and subsidies in
such areas as nutrition, health care, education, housing, and transportation.[45] The accords also called for lessening regulatory constraints on the
private sector and adopting measures to protect private property, reward
risk taking, promote competitive markets, and enforce commercial transac-
tions. IFI also advocated privatization of state-owned enterprises. In subsequent years, Latin American nations undertook one of the most extensive

privatization processes in the developing world. State ownership of companies in telecommunications, electricity, fuel, water and other basic services was transferred to the private sector. IFI also worked with Latin American governments to identify and reduce barriers to foreign trade and investment. This included placing greater emphasis on expanding exports and establishing export processing zones (EPZ) to attract foreign capital.

Structural adjustment produced some positive results: reducing public sector spending helped balance government budgets, deregulation stimulated private sector growth, privatization allowed governments to rid themselves of inefficient public enterprises, greater exports increased foreign exchange reserves, and new foreign investment expanded employment opportunities.

At the same time, neoliberal market reforms frequently intensified inequalities in the region.[46] Poor and working class people were often the most adversely affected by these reforms. Low income communities were obviously hurt by the loss of publicly funded nutrition, health care, education, and housing programs. Private sector investments were typically concentrated in those sectors—such as transportation, mining, and industry—that produced the highest returns rather than met basic human needs. Deregulation also undermined the economic position of poor communities. The removal of price controls on basic necessities was hardest for those with fixed or low incomes.

The benefits of privatization were also unevenly distributed. While private investors gained from the purchase of public corporations, often at substantial discounts, divestiture led to a significant loss of public sector employment. Workers lost positions as the managers of newly privatized companies streamlined their workforces. Those who retained public sector employment often saw their wages cut.

Trade liberalization was also problematic in a number of respects. As noted earlier, because trade relations take place in a highly monopolized world market, largely dominated by the industrialized states, Latin American exports are often undervalued relative to their manufactured imports. Reliance on a small number of export products increased the vulnerability of these nations to market fluctuations. Moreover, free trade tended to increase domestic inequalities. Larger landowners benefitted from expanding markets for their products, but peasant farmers were frequently displaced as production of cash crops for export replaced the production of staples to meet local needs. Small-scale artisans also saw their market position decline due to the influx of mass-produced consumer goods.[47]

Foreign investment also intensified inequality. Such investment tended to benefit a fairly narrow elite with direct ties to transnational firms. Local businesspeople, for example, gained from joint venture arrangements or supply contracts, and professionals often improved their salaries by working for foreign corporations. The poor and working class, however, rarely benefitted from such investment. While some new manufacturing jobs were created, these jobs were generally characterized by low wages, poor health and safety conditions, long hours, and forced overtime. Working conditions frequently deteriorated as governments competed with one another to attract foreign investors.[48]

CONCLUSION

This chapter considered the problem of poverty in Latin America. Despite some improvements in recent years, the overall standard of living remains low. Approximately 200 million people live in poverty. Tens of millions of people lack access to clean water, adequate nutrition, and quality health care while public education systems are plagued by teacher shortages, decaying facilities, and outdated instructional materials.

Basic human needs are interrelated, as weaknesses in one area produce negative outcomes in other areas. Poor nutrition typically undermines basic health as the malnourished are more vulnerable to illness and disease. This can be especially debilitating for children since poor nutrition during the early years can produce lifelong health problems. Malnutrition also undermines the ability of children to do well in school. When a child lacks proper nutrition their cognitive development is impaired and they are unable to concentrate on their studies. The same is true with respect to health. When children are ill they either perform poorly in school or miss school altogether. When parents are poorly educated they are generally less capable of meeting the nutrition and health needs of their children.

A number of factors contribute to poverty. Clearly a major cause is simply the poor distribution of income and wealth. Inequalities are more pronounced in Latin America than in any other region of the world. Economic inequalities closely correspond with ethnicity as minority groups, especially the indigenous and Afro-Latinos, are among the poorest segments of the population. Population increases are also part of the problem. Although population growth rates have declined considerably in recent years, they continue to average about 1.6 percent annually in the region. This strains each nation's economy and natural resources. The emigration of professionals to high income countries in North America and Europe is also thought to impede economic progress.

Latin American governments have not been especially effective in promoting economic and social progress. In fact, the economic strategies pursued have often drained public sector resources and expanded budget deficits. Governments have rarely made sufficient investments in basic human needs or capacity development. In fact, endemic corruption has led to the diversion of public monies from social investments. Corruption has also hampered economic growth by distorting incentives, reducing tax revenues, and lowering the quality of public services.

Lastly, external forces have undermined development. Clearly trade relations have often worked against the interests of Latin American nations.

While the major exports of the region remain primary products and agricultural goods, the value of these exports has consistently declined relative to the value of manufactured products. External debt has also constituted a major obstacle to advancement. Annual debt service and interest payments alone are about 8 percent of gross national product and absorb nearly one-third of total foreign exchange earnings. Resources that could be used for productive investments or meeting basic needs are diverted into debt service payments. Externally-mandated structural adjustment reforms further intensified inequalities in the region.

While poor living standards are an obvious symptom of underdevelopment, they also restrict economic and social progress. Malnutrition, illness, and poor education all limit capacity development, labor productivity, and the efficient use of national resources. Meeting the basic needs of all is essential for Latin American development. The next chapter turns to the economic and social initiatives of the United Nations in the region.

4　Meeting Basic Human Needs

The preceding chapter surveyed economic and social conditions in Latin America. Despite some progress in recent years, a large segment of the population continues to live in poverty. Tens of millions of people lack access to clean water and adequate nutrition. The region's poor are also unable to obtain quality and affordable health care. Public schools are plagued by teacher shortages, decaying facilities, and outdated instructional materials.

Meeting basic human needs is essential for the overall development of Latin America. A healthy, well-educated population is the foundation for labor productivity, technological innovation, economic growth, and the sustainable use of natural resources. While achieving this objective will largely depend on the efforts of local governments and societal groups, most countries do not have the resources necessary to fully meet basic needs and external assistance remains critically important.

This chapter surveys United Nations' efforts to meet basic human needs. I begin with the organization's general work in this area before turning to specific initiatives in Latin America during the early years of the twenty-first century. Particular attention is accorded the United Nations Development Programme which has the most expansive mandate of the various subsidiary agencies. As noted in chapter 2, the UNDP Resident Representative coordinates poverty reduction efforts in each country. UNDP has a Regional Bureau for Latin America and the Caribbean (RBLAC). Each year this bureau establishes a Regional Cooperation Framework (RCF) that identifies the central challenges in the region and priority areas for work. The United Nations Children's Fund, World Food Programme, and United Nations Population Fund have also supported poverty reduction initiatives in Latin America.

GENERAL WORK OF THE UNITED NATIONS

Nutrition has long been prioritized by the United Nations. The *Universal Declaration of Human Rights* states that "[e]veryone has the right to a standard of living adequate for the health and well-being of himself and of his family, including food"[1] (see Appendix 1). The *International Covenant on Economic, Social and Cultural Rights* identifies freedom from hunger as a universal right and calls on state parties

> [t]o improve methods of production, conservation and distribution of food by making full use of technical and scientific knowledge, by disseminating knowledge of the principles of nutrition and by developing or reforming agrarian systems in such a way as to achieve the most efficient development and utilization of natural resources[2] (see Appendix 2).

The UN also sponsored a number of conferences that focused on global nutrition, beginning with the 1974 World Food Conference. The conference's *Universal Declaration on the Eradication of Hunger and Malnutrition* asserted that "every man, woman, and child has the inalienable right to be free from hunger and malnutrition in order to develop their physical and mental faculties."[3] The conference concluded with an agreement to improve food production, storage facilities, land use, and water quality in the developing world. Member nations agreed to establish an International Fund for Agricultural Development (IFAD) to finance agricultural projects in the developing world and to increase the access of poor farmers to markets, technology, land, and other productive resources. The UN also established a World Food Council as a ministerial forum on food and agricultural issues.[4] The 1979 World Conference on Agrarian Reform and Rural Development emphasized the importance of land reform and peasant rights.

In 1992, the Food and Agriculture Organization (FAO) and the World Health Organization (WHO) jointly sponsored an International Conference on Nutrition where governments pledged to substantially reduce chronic hunger, malnutrition, and micronutrient deficiencies. The 1995 World Summit for Social Development adopted a plan to meet global nutritional needs and the World Food Summit (WFS), which was convened the following year, called for "an ongoing effort to eradicate hunger in all countries, with an immediate view to reducing the number of undernourished people to half their present level no later than 2015."[5] A Committee on World Food Security (CFS) was established to monitor implementation of the plan.

Nutrition is also an important component of the Millennium Development Goals (see Appendix 5). Nations committed to reducing by half the proportion of people without access to safe drinking water or adequate nutrition. The 2002 World Summit on Sustainable Development (WSSD) established timetables for enhancing global food security and the 2005 World Summit affirmed that agricultural and rural development are integral to national development efforts.

The UN has also been committed to promoting global health care. The *Universal Declaration of Human Rights* states that everyone has the right to medical care[6] (see Appendix 1) and the *International Covenant on Economic, Social and Cultural Rights* affirms the right to "the highest attainable standard of physical and mental health"[7] (see Appendix 2). A number of conferences have focused on global health issues. The 1974 World Population Conference called for a comprehensive strategy to improve the management of existing health services and to widen their coverage to reach rural, remote, and underprivileged groups. The 1978 International Conference on Primary Health Care resolved that health is "a fundamental human right and that the attainment of the highest possible level of health is a most important worldwide social goal."[8] Governments were called upon to "formulate national policies, strategies and plans of action to launch and sustain primary health care as part of a comprehensive national health system."[9]

In 1981 WHO adopted a *Global Strategy for Health for All* that called for advances in primary health care, disease prevention, diagnosis, therapy, and health promotion. The 1994 International Conference on Population and Development (ICPD) in Cairo linked health care with sustainable development and called for universal access to reproductive health services. The 1995 World Summit for Social Development advocated strengthening both school-based and community-based health education programs for children, adolescents, and adults and for all countries to ensure universal, non-discriminatory access to health services. A follow-up to the Cairo conference, the ICPD + 5, assessed progress toward implementing the ICPD *Program of Action* and identified strategies for moving forward.[10]

The Millennium Development Goals also prioritized health care (see Appendix 5). The goals include reducing infant and child mortality by two-thirds, improving maternal health, and reversing the spread of HIV/AIDS, malaria, and other major diseases. The 2002 WSSD called for strengthening the capacity of health systems to deliver basic services in an efficient, accessible, and affordable manner and for integrating health concerns into strategies for poverty reduction and sustainable development. The 2005 World Summit launched a Partnership for Maternal, Newborn and Child Health that was predicated on the belief that reproductive health is essential for achieving international development goals.[11]

The UN has also worked to improve education systems in the developing world. The *Universal Declaration of Human Rights* states that "[e]veryone has the right to education" and that

> [e]ducation shall be free, at least in the elementary and fundamental stages. Elementary education shall be compulsory. Technical and professional education shall be made generally available and higher education shall be equally accessible to all on the basis of merit.[12] (See Appendix 1)

The *International Covenant on Economic, Social and Cultural Rights* recognizes the universal right to education (see Appendix 2).[13] State parties to the covenant are expected to provide primary education free to all, and make secondary education generally available and accessible by every appropriate means.

A number of conferences highlighted the importance of universal education. The 1990 World Conference on Education for All resolved that every child, youth, and adult should be able to benefit from educational opportunities.[14] Emphasis was placed not only on access to basic education, but also on the quality of education and actual learning outcomes.[15] The 1994 International Conference on Population and Development (ICPD) adopted a *Programme of Action* that called for universal primary education. The 1995 World Summit for Social Development proposed strengthening national strategies for eradicating illiteracy and universalizing basic education. The 2000 World Education Forum adopted a *Framework for Action* that included the following goals: 1) expand and improve comprehensive early childhood education, especially for the most vulnerable and disadvantaged children, 2) increase primary school enrollment to at least 90 percent, 3) eliminate gender disparities in primary and secondary education, 4) ensure children achieve recognized and measurable learning outcomes, especially in numeracy, literacy, and essential life skills, and 5) achieve a 50 percent improvement in adult literacy.[16]

The Millennium Development Goals also highlight the importance of education (see Appendix 5). One of the central goals is to achieve universal primary education by 2015. The 2002 WSSD called for ensuring all children are able to complete primary education and the 2005 World Summit emphasized "the critical role of both formal and informal education in the achievement of poverty eradication and other development goals."[17]

WORK IN LATIN AMERICA

The general commitment to basic nutrition, health care, and education outlined above is reflected in the work of the United Nations in Latin America. UN agencies provide food assistance to those vulnerable to nutritional shortages, especially expectant and nursing mothers. School feeding programs ensure poor children have at least one nutritious meal a day and Food-for-Work programs allocate food in exchange for work on community improvement projects. The provision of basic health care and prevention of infectious diseases are also central components of the UN's work in the region. Efforts to strengthen education systems include school construction, updating instructional materials, and training teachers. The UN also works to enhance public sector capacity to meet the basic needs of poor communities.

NUTRITION

The United Nations places special emphasis on meeting the nutritional needs of expectant and nursing mothers. In Guatemala and Nicaragua, the World Food Programme provided a cereal fortified with iron and vitamins to expectant and nursing mothers. Additional food aid (rice, beans, soybeans, and oil) was offered to pregnant women in exchange for undergoing regular medical checkups.[18] In Cuba, where iron deficiency is common, expectant and nursing mothers were provided with a supplement enriched with micronutrients. These supplements lowered anemia rates and helped improve the health of newborn babies.[19] In Bolivia, food aid was dispersed to pregnant and nursing women in combination with nutritional training and in Haiti, pregnant and nursing women received a monthly ration of rice, beans, oil and iodized salt in addition to iron and folic acid supplements.

WFP has also sought to meet the nutritional needs of children. Its early childhood program informs young mothers of the benefits of breastfeeding.[20] Breast milk includes all the vitamins, minerals, and enzymes needed for a baby's growth and the antibodies needed to lessen risks of contracting infectious diseases. The frequency and severity of upper respiratory infections, ear infections, and even chronic conditions such as asthma and allergies are significantly reduced when infants are breastfed. Babies are also less likely to develop diabetes, meningitis, pneumonia, and some forms of childhood cancer later in life. Breastfeeding is also beneficial for new mothers since it replenishes iron lost during pregnancy and childbirth, helps reduce the uterus to its normal size, and may even reduces the risk of serious illnesses such as breast cancer, cardiovascular disease, diabetes, hypertension, osteoporosis, and ovarian cancer.

WFP also fortifies foods with micronutrients, such as vitamin A and iron for distribution to children from six months to two years of age. In the Peruvian Sierra, *Inka Mix*, which includes barley, maize flour, peas, soy protein, vegetable oil and other local ingredients, was developed to meet the specific nutritional requirements of children. Similar food fortification programs in Cuba, Guatemala, and Haiti over the past five years helped reduce anemia and malnutrition among children.[21]

Improving the nutrition of older children has also been a component of WFP's work in Latin America. WFP is the largest organizer of school feeding programs in the region. These programs, which typically provide an enriched cereal-based drink and fortified biscuits, contribute toward the intake of calories, protein, and micronutrients, including Iodine and vitamin A. By relieving short-term hunger, school feeding programs improve the learning capacity of children. They also raise attendance rates by increasing the incentive for parents to send their children to school.

WFP sponsored school feeding programs in virtually all Latin American countries. In Colombia, the program focused on children who had been displaced by civil conflict.[22] In Bolivia, primary schools in the most food-insecure municipalities were targeted.[23] Indigenous children in the Peruvian highlands were given an enriched dairy drink and a fortified biscuit while Nicaraguan children received a corn-soya based drink that was fortified with micronutrients and produced locally with equipment donated by WFP.[24] In Ecuador, WFP provided kitchen and service equipment for elementary school feeding programs in 19 rural provinces. Two meals a day were delivered to primary schools in Guatemala, with parents largely responsible for the preparation and transport of these meals.[25]

WFP also supported Food-for-Work programs in which participants received food aid in exchange for their work on community improvement projects. These programs have multiple benefits. The poor are better able to meet their nutritional needs while simultaneously making improvements to their local communities. Participants also gain the skills necessary to compete more effectively in the formal economy.

Most Food-for-Work activities involve the construction of physical infrastructure. In El Salvador, dams and drainage systems were installed in flood prone areas and water containment structures and deep wells were built in drought-affected areas.[26] In Peru, 250 pre-school and primary education facilities were renovated. Food-for-Work programs in Nicaragua and Guatemala contributed to the construction of dykes and bridges, the maintenance of roads, and improvements in water and sanitation facilities.[27] In Honduras, focus was placed on the rehabilitation of agricultural lands and infrastructure damaged by natural disasters.[28] Food-for-Work programs in Colombia targeted people displaced by civil conflict.[29] Similar programs were extended to Colombian refugees in Ecuador.

WFP also offered training programs in food preparation and family health. In Colombia, Ecuador, El Salvador, and Nicaragua, the staff of both health institutions and education centers were trained in nutrition, hygiene, and sanitation. Training activities in Guatemala and Honduras focused on preservation of potable water, food preparation, and nutritional health for expectant and nursing mothers.[30] WFP also offered training in hygiene, nutrition, and food preparation for indigenous communities in Bolivia and Peru. In Cuba, WFP monitored the health status of expectant and nursing women and provided nutritional education.[31] In Haiti, school cooks were trained in nutrition, meal preparation, and hygiene.[32]

WFP also worked to increase food cultivation. This included campaigns to develop sustainable farming methods in Colombia, improve soil and livestock management in Peru, and enhance the access of peasant farmers to basic implements in mountainous areas of Haiti. When possible, food assistance was procured locally as a further means of aiding domestic farmers.[33]

The UN also worked to strengthen public sector capacity to meet the nutritional needs of poor communities. In Guatemala and Nicaragua, WFP assistance with vulnerability analysis permitted a more geographically focused approach to food distribution in the drought corridor and selected areas prone to flooding. Similarly, in El Salvador and Honduras, WFP helped improve public sector mechanisms for monitoring nutritional needs in areas vulnerable to seasonal food insecurity and natural disasters. Programme support allowed both governments to establish food security surveillance systems. WFP also worked with the Ministry of Health of Honduras in the same year to prepare a national plan to eradicate malnutrition in children under five.[34] In Colombia, the government's technical capacity to identify and meet the nutritional needs of internally displaced persons (IDP) was improved.[35] WFP supported the decentralization of public sector food distribution mechanisms in Peru and enhanced the distribution of foodstuffs in those regions of Bolivia with the highest child malnutrition rates.[36]

HEALTH CARE

The United Nations also worked to improve health care in Latin America, with special attention placed on the needs of children.[37] UNICEF played a lead role in vaccinating children against common childhood diseases and newer viruses such as Hepatitis B. Vaccination campaigns were frequently coupled with the provision of vitamin and iron supplements.[38] UNICEF's Early Childhood Program in Cuba dramatically increased immunization levels of children under five. The fund also worked jointly with the governments of the Dominican Republic and Haiti to implement a cross-border immunization campaign. Both countries are free from measles and polio, at least in part, because of this campaign.[39] In Ecuador, UNICEF ensured 95 percent coverage for basic immunizations and in Peru, children in indigenous communities were given the Hepatitis B vaccine.

UNICEF also sponsored other initiatives to protect children from illnesses. In a number of countries the fund aided provincial governments purchase medicines and health supplies.[40] UNICEF regularly distributed oral rehydration packets that helped prevent dehydration and diarrhea. The fund also distributed high dose vitamin A capsules. As noted in the preceding chapter, vitamin A deficiency is a major cause of blindness and a contributing factor to childhood deaths from diarrhea, malaria, and measles.

The UN also worked to combat sexually transmitted diseases (STDs). This includes both preventing the spread of these diseases and caring for those already infected. Considerable focus was placed on HIV/AIDS.[41] As noted in the previous chapter, the spread of HIV/AIDS is among the greatest public health threats in the region. Much of this work was carried out by UNDP. In Ecuador, programme staff worked with the municipal governments of Quito and Guayaquil to develop a consistent set of policies for controlling the spread of HIV/AIDS. This led to establishing testing and counseling centers in both cities.[42] UNDP also supported national HIV/AIDS prevention campaigns that targeted poor communities in Peru and Uruguay. In Trinidad and Tobago, programme staff helped formulate a national strategic plan for HIV/AIDS and worked to mainstream HIV/AIDS initiatives into sectoral planning. Technical assistance was also provided for establishing the AIDS Coordinating Committee that is responsible for managing a national response to the pandemic.[43]

Reducing the transmission of HIV/AIDS has been a priority. Most Latin Americans do not know their HIV status and many are not sure how to protect themselves from the virus. UNICEF worked with young people to overcome the social stigma that has limited HIV/AIDS prevention and treatment. In the Caribbean, the fund helped develop a regional Health and Family Life Education curriculum to deliver information about HIV/AIDS to young people. The curriculum was adopted by public school systems in Antigua, Barbados, Grenada, and St. Lucia. In Haiti and Honduras, workshops provided information about sexuality and HIV/AIDS. UNICEF offered training in safe and responsible behavior to adolescents in Brazil and Cuba, especially among those groups known to be at the greatest risk.

UNFPA also worked to stem the spread of HIV/AIDS. In Haiti, UNFPA worked with various government agencies to prepare a national strategic plan to combat HIV/AIDS.[44] In the Dominican Republic, a national logistics system for HIV/AIDS education was developed.[45] UNFPA helped draft El Salvador's national plan on STDs, including HIV/AIDS and, in Panama, provided assistance for voluntary counseling and testing among pregnant women.[46] UNFPA also enhanced the managerial and technical capacities of civil society organizations (CSO) working with HIV/AIDS victims. UNFPA supported a joint initiative by the Brazilian and Jamaican governments to expand HIV counseling and testing. In Ecuador, Guatemala, and Venezuela, AIDS education was integrated into school curricula.[47] UNFPA provided culturally sensitive education in sexual health to adolescents in Belize, Costa Rica, and the Dominican Republic.[48] In Haiti prevention activities focused on commercial sex workers. UNFPA funded a center for sex workers in Port au Prince that provided them information on how best to protect themselves from HIV/AIDS and other STDs.[49]

UNFPA also worked with police and military units to control the spread of HIV/AIDS. In Bolivia and Paraguay, education programs on sexual and reproductive health were developed for the armed forces. The militaries of both countries now provide reproductive health services, including contraceptives and information on preventing HIV/AIDS and other STDs. Similarly, sexual and reproductive health services were expanded in the armed forces of Colombia.[50]

The UN also worked to reduce mother-to-child transmission of HIV. In Bolivia, UNICEF trained 400 doctors on how best to prevent such transmission. In Brazil, Ecuador, Guatemala, and Haiti, free counseling and testing was provided to pregnant women, followed by anti-retroviral therapy for those who tested positive for HIV. The number of HIV tests conducted on pregnant women has nearly doubled in these countries since 2000.

The training of health workers in HIV/AIDS prevention has also been prioritized. In the Dominican Republic and Haiti, UNFPA sponsored training programs for reproductive health service providers, community health workers, and peer educators.[51] Technical assistance was also provided for health training in Colombia.[52] WFP also supported HIV/AIDS prevention. In Guatemala, Nicaragua, and Paraguay, the programme strengthened community participation in prevention activities through the training of local health volunteers.

Improving care for people living with AIDS was also a central component of these efforts. This included providing counseling services and access to anti-retroviral pharmaceuticals. WFP provided nutritional support for HIV-positive individuals throughout Latin America.[53] In Honduras, UNFPA supported a 24-hour nursing service for HIV/AIDS patients.[54] UNICEF organized care for HIV-positive parents with small children in Brazil and Jamaica. The UN also sought to protect the rights of people living with AIDS. A UNFPA project helped identify weaknesses in the existing laws in Central America and the Caribbean, the two sub-regions with the highest AIDS rates in Latin America. The project also strengthened laws governing discrimination in the workplace and increased the legal rights of HIV-positive individuals.[55]

EDUCATION

The United Nations also worked to strengthen public education systems in Latin America. UNICEF has played a lead role in these efforts. The fund contributed to the renovation of existing schools and the construction of new schools. In Bolivia, UNICEF supported the Indigenous Girls' Education Project that built boarding schools for more than 2000 girls. As part of the "School Going to the Child" campaign in Colombia, the fund helped build schools in conflict areas that gave thousands of displaced children a chance to resume their education. In Haiti, 55 new schools were built and water and sanitation facilities were improved in 75 other schools.

UNICEF also worked to ensure schools had sufficient textbooks and other instructional materials. The fund's "Educate Your Child" program provided school libraries in Cuba with books for children and adolescents. In Brazil, UNICEF supported the *EducAmazônia Project* that improved the quality of basic education for children attending rural schools in the Amazonian state of Para. Schools in this region, which are often located along tributaries in the rainforest, are among the most isolated in Brazil. In Ecuador, the "Textbooks for All" program provided free textbooks to more than 400,000 children in seven provinces.

Teacher training was also a component of this work. In Brazil, UNICEF helped launch a comprehensive training program for elementary, high school, and vocational education teachers, with emphasis placed on the use of new information and communication technologies. Fund staff also worked with the Ministry of Education of Brazil to develop educational standards. UNICEF also promoted curriculum reform in the region. In Guyana, instructional methodologies were revised to improve the transition from pre-primary to primary school and from primary to secondary school.

Improving schools, updating instructional materials, and training teachers are all designed to achieve universal primary and secondary education. The UN also supported other initiatives to increase enrollments. In Bolivia, UNICEF supported the "Integrated Early Childhood Development" program that expanded preschool education and adopted new alternative education initiatives. A nationwide program in Argentina was supported to strengthen school attendance in those provinces with the highest dropout rates. New transportation systems were developed in rural parts of Bolivia and Brazil to ensure children are able to attend school. UNICEF also supported *Chile Crece Contigo* (Chile Grows with You) which increased the number of preschools in poor communities. Chile's Ministry of Education also partnered with UNICEF to aid children who had dropped out of school. Family involvement in schools was strongly encouraged, with parent-teacher councils established in nearly every school district of the country. UNICEF worked with the Ministry of Education of Guatemala to increase education funding and create scholarships for poor children while a "Back-to-School" initiative in Haiti encouraged thousands of adolescents to resume their education.[56]

School enrollment can be especially challenging in communities with large indigenous populations since these communities are often located in remote parts of the country, have higher poverty levels, and speak local languages. UNICEF supported a range of educational initiatives to reach indigenous children. In Bolivia, where 32 indigenous cultures constitute over half of the population, the fund worked with the Ministry of Education to improve bilingual and multicultural education programs. Similarly, local bilingual and intercultural education initiatives were supported at the preschool level in Venezuela. In Brazil, UNICEF developed teaching materials to reflect local customs and cultures.

PUBLIC POLICY REFORM

While the United Nations directly supported a range of nutrition, health care, and education initiatives in Latin America, maintaining these programs once international assistance ends was also emphasized. UN agencies worked to ensure governments have the capacity, resources, and technology needed to meet basic needs on a long-term basis. These efforts typically began with a diagnosis of current living conditions. UNDP carried out household surveys to measure poverty levels in Barbados, Bolivia, the Dominican Republic, Guatemala, Nicaragua, Panama, and Suriname.[57] In Honduras, a system for gathering quantitative and qualitative data on socioeconomic conditions was established. Local municipal authorities were then trained in the use of this data.[58] Similarly, in Trinidad and Tobago, UNDP helped map areas of systemic poverty and establish a comprehensive social database.[59] In Guyana, Nicaragua, Paraguay, and Venezuela, the capacity of local governments to measure, monitor, and analyze poverty indicators was strengthened.[60] UNDP aided Haiti's Institute of Statistics and Information Science to draw up a profile of socioeconomic living conditions.[61] The World Food Programme also helped monitor the nutritional status of families, with most of this work focusing on the Central American drought corridor. The information gathered from community interviews, focus group discussions, and household surveys allowed local governments to better structure public sector nutritional programs.

Possibly the most extensive research and data collection was undertaken by the United Nations Population Fund. In Guatemala, the fund worked with the National Statistical Institute to gather the data necessary to formulate and evaluate social policies.[62] Similarly, in the Dominican Republic, UNFPA expanded the availability of reliable information related to population dynamics and socioeconomic conditions. The fund also aided the National Statistics Office in the analysis, processing, and dissemination of census results.[63] UNFPA helped train government officials in Bolivia to use demographic data in planning and policy formulation.[64] In Brazil, standardized methodologies and tools among state planning organs were instituted. This included analysis of issues related to adolescents, reproductive health, population, and migration. UNFPA also supported the use of sociodemographic data in the formulation and evaluation of public policies and programs.[65]

UN agencies also worked to improve public sector capacities to meet basic human needs. Here UNDP was most directly involved. Programme staff offered policy advice on socioeconomic issues and supported governments in planning and managing development programs. UNDP officials also advised governments throughout the region on how to integrate specific poverty reduction targets into national economic policies. As noted in Chapter 2, Poverty Reduction Strategy Papers (PRSP) are based on a participatory process of consultations between state and civil society actors.

UNDP helped strengthen government capabilities in most South American countries. Following Argentina's 2001 economic collapse, UNDP worked with local authorities to establish a program that provided a monthly stipend to 2 million of the most impoverished households and basic medicines to nearly 15 million people.[66] In Peru, an emergency jobs program was established that provided short-term employment for over 125,000 urban dwellers. In Uruguay, public sector services for children, women, and families living in poverty were improved.[67] Focus was placed on harmonizing government social services and reforming health and education systems. UNDP helped formulate and implement a national poverty reduction strategy in Paraguay and contributed to the design and implementation of initiatives to improve access of the poor to services, employment, and productive resources in Bolivia.[68]

UNDP also worked to enhance public sector capacities in Central America and the Caribbean. In Costa Rica, government institutions were modernized to ensure social investments were equitably distributed.[69] UNDP helped strengthen the capacity of regional, municipal, and local institutions in Nicaragua to incorporate a sustainable human development perspective into their plans and programs. Emphasis was placed on increasing the technical capacity of regional bodies to participate in national development.[70] In El Salvador, UNDP supported the formulation of national poverty reduction programs and improved instruments for assessing results. The programme also worked with the Social Investment Fund for Local Development to strengthen municipal and community development initiatives.[71] In Cuba, municipal capacities for managing social services and long-term development planning were strengthened.[72] UNDP helped develop a strategic framework for poverty reduction in Haiti that incorporated macroeconomic modeling, public expenditure analysis, and aid coordination.[73]

CONCLUSION

This chapter surveyed United Nations efforts to meet basic human needs in Latin America during the early years of the twenty-first century. Particular focus was placed on improving basic nutrition. The UN distributed food to expectant and nursing mothers, provided school meals, and allocated food assistance in exchange for work on community improvement projects. The UN also worked to expand access to healthcare and prevent the spread of contagious diseases. UN efforts to strengthen education systems included constructing schools, updating instructional materials, and training teachers. The UN also supported public policy reform to enhance the long-term capacity of governments to meet the basic needs of poor communities.

UN programs have clearly improved the nutrition, health, and education of children and adults throughout Latin America. At the same time, the sustainability of these programs has sometimes been limited. It is often difficult to maintain these initiatives once UN assistance ends. This is due, at least in part, to the inability or unwillingness of local governments to fully fund these programs. It is also evident in those cases where civil society participation in the design, implementation, and evaluation of these programs is negligible.

Meeting basic human needs is essential for the overall development of Latin America. How children are nurtured has a major impact on their ability to learn and develop. Well-nourished, healthy children are more likely to attend school and are better able to concentrate on their studies. Healthy children also mean reduced household and societal spending on medical care. Healthy, well-educated adults are more productive in the labor force and lose fewer days of work. Education also expands the capacity of people to enter the work force, make better use of technology, and adapt to change. As economic opportunities become available to more people, inequalities in the distribution of income and wealth typically decline, along with overall levels of poverty.

5 Women in the Americas

Enhancing gender equity is essential for development. Social and economic progress depends, to a considerable extent, on improving the lives of women.[1] Higher incomes and greater control over productive assets allow women to more effectively provide for themselves and their families, and women's work in both formal and informal economies contributes to broader social progress. International institutions increasingly recognize these basic realities and are structuring development assistance to better meet the needs of women.

This chapter and the chapter that follows focus on women in Latin America, a region long characterized by patriarchy and gender inequality. Women have less access to basic services than men and when they enter the labor market are typically relegated to lower status positions, working longer hours, under more difficult conditions, for less pay. Women also have less control over land, capital, credit, and technology.[2]

This chapter first reviews gender relations in Latin America, with focus placed on women's access to health and reproductive care as well as their comparative position in the labor market. I then examine those factors that contribute to patriarchy in the region. This includes cultural attitudes that have been passed down from one generation to the next and public policies that systematically favored men over women. The influence of international financial institutions (IFI) is also considered.

HEALTH AND REPRODUCTIVE CARE

Health systems in Latin America are more responsive to women's needs today than in the past. Women now enjoy greater access to family planning services, prenatal care, assisted childbirth, and postpartum care than previous generations. At the same time, the coverage and quality of health care remains inadequate, especially for poor women.[3] Inadequate screening for breast and cervical cancer results in these cancers often going undetected until their later stages. Cervical cancer is the most common form of cancer death for women in the region. In fact, Latin America has the highest cervical cancer mortality rates in the world. There are also substantial disparities in non-communicable or chronic diseases between men and women. The rate of cardiovascular disease, for example, is higher in women aged 15–44 and again above 60 than for men in the same age groups. Women are also more likely to develop diabetes and musculoskeletal diseases than men.

Latin American women are also more vulnerable than men to STDs. Because women are more likely to have asymptomatic infections, and diagnosis is delayed, they typically develop more serious long-term complications. Moreover, because sexual education programs are limited, adolescent girls and women are often not fully informed of the best means of protection from these diseases. HIV/AIDS, in particular, has emerged as a serious threat.[4] The percentage of women who are HIV-positive has increased dramatically in recent years.[5] Women now constitute 30 percent of adults in Central and South America and close to 50 percent of adults in the Caribbean who have contracted this virus.

There are also shortcomings with respect to family planning and reproductive care.[6] Many women do not have access to safe and reliable contraception. The limited availability of birth control accounts for relatively high numbers of unintended pregnancies. Women wishing to terminate a pregnancy have few safe options as most nations have adopted stringent laws prohibiting abortion.[7] However, the region's abortion rate is actually among the *highest* in the world, higher than in the United States or Western Europe where first trimester abortions are legal in most cases. About five million abortions are performed each year in Latin America, roughly equivalent to 25 percent of all pregnancies. Because the majority of these abortions are performed under clandestine, dangerous, and unsanitary conditions, 40 percent of women who have abortions suffer complications. Roughly 4000 women die from clandestine abortions each year and hundreds of thousands of women are injured. The percent of maternal deaths caused by unsafe abortions is higher in Latin America than any other region of the world. Nearly one-fifth of maternal deaths are due to abortion-related complications.

Pregnancy also poses a risk for women. Poor women often lack access to quality prenatal care. This compromises their health and increases the potential for complications during childbirth. On average, 20 percent of expectant mothers begin their pregnancy with low weight or experience insufficient weight increases during their pregnancy. This typically results in low birth weights for their babies. Moreover, 35 percent of expectant mothers suffer from iron deficiency anemia which increases the risk of premature delivery and low birth weight, as well as maternal and fetal mortality.

Childbirth can also be precarious. Poor women and women living in remote areas typically lack access to basic and emergency medical treatment during childbirth.[8] This can be especially dangerous when women experience obstructed labor, hemorrhage, eclampsia, infection, toxemia, or hypertensive disorder. Maternal mortality rates are relatively high, with about 22,000 deaths each year.[9] Maternal mortality rates are especially high for women between 15–19 who are twice as likely as women in their twenties and thirties to die during childbirth.

INCOME AND EMPLOYMENT

There have also been some positive changes with respect to the relative position of Latin American women in the labor market. Educational improvements have closed the gap between males and females at the primary, secondary, and even post-secondary level. In fact, women now average *more* years of schooling than men.[10] This has allowed women to enter the workforce in most all economic sectors, including those fields historically dominated by men.[11] At present, women constitute one-third of the overall labor force and 40 percent of the working population in urban areas. The income differentials between men and women have also declined. Latin American governments have adopted legislation to promote more equitable workplaces, including equal pay provisions, protections for pregnant women, and maternity benefits. Property rights that have historically favored men have been altered to treat women more equally under the law.[12]

Despite these advances, poverty rates continue to be higher for women than men.[13] Seventy percent of the poor are women and female-headed households have much higher poverty rates than other families.[14] Women also constitute a disproportionately higher percentage of the unemployed and underemployed. A total of 20 percent of women seeking work are unemployed, compared with 10 percent of men. Those women who have jobs are generally paid at a rate lower than their male counterparts. Women receive about 25 percent less income than men, even when performing the same or similar tasks and controlling for the number of hours worked.[15] Although women have largely gained formal equality of property rights, sizable gaps in the actual ownership of land and other productive assets remain.

Labor laws and employment practices sometimes reinforce gender inequality. In most countries, women are prohibited from certain types of employment.[16] Moreover, companies are reluctant to employ women full-time and resort to strategies such as subcontracting, part-time employment, and paying for piecework done at home. When women do obtain full-time employment, they are generally clustered into lower-status jobs, working longer hours for less pay.

Women constitute a large percentage of the workforce in the various export processing zones (EPZ) that have been established in the region. Nearly 80 percent of all employees in the *maquiladoras* (assembly plants) of Northern Mexico, the Caribbean, and Central America are women. This is especially true in the labor-intensive factories producing textiles or electronics. In these factories, women are typically paid less than the minimum wage, are more likely to be laid off during economic downturns, and are less likely to have health insurance or retirement pensions. Because occupational health and safety standards are poorly enforced, working conditions are frequently hazardous.[17]

Women are also more likely than men to be employed in the informal sector.[18] This includes street vendors, market sellers, and those working in home-based microenterprises. Working conditions in the informal sector are generally not covered by national labor legislation and there are few legal protections. Latin America has also seen the feminization of agriculture as men increasingly migrate from rural areas to larger towns and cities. Women currently constitute about 65 percent of all agricultural workers in the region.[19]

A large number of women work as domestic servants for middle and upper income families. Almost 20 percent of the females in the labor force are domestic servants. Once again, income and employment protections are minimal. Most countries have separate regulations governing domestic servants. While employment in the formal economy is generally limited to between 40 and 48 hours a week, the work day for domestic servants can be extended to 12 hours, and the work week can be as much as 72 hours. These women have few legal protections with respect to wages, rest periods, and personal safety.[20]

HISTORICAL CAUSES

Patriarchy and gender discrimination can be found throughout Latin American history. In pre-colonial societies men assumed positions of power and privilege while women were relegated to home and child care. These roles were reinforced during the period of Spanish and Portuguese colonization. Under the colonial order men were granted positions of authority in the government and economy while women were largely confined to the private arena of family and child care.[21]

Male dominance of the political arena continued throughout the post-colonial period. Governments maintained gender inequalities by privileging men in public programs.[22] Gender was rarely considered in design of these programs and expenditures on women's nutrition, health, and education were minimal. Governments also enacted laws that favored men over women. This included limits on women's participation in certain occupations and legal barriers to owning land and other properties. Although some legal protections for women have been adopted in recent years, they are often poorly communicated and enforced.[23]

Catholicism, which was introduced during the colonial period, reinforced strict gender roles. The Spanish and Portuguese established a close relationship between the state and the church. Catholicism was an important foundation for these nations and a source of legitimacy for the political elite. In return, governments extended special privileges to the church, including control over religious education in public schools.

The very structure of the Catholic Church, with leadership exclusively in the hands of men, tends to legitimize the notion that men are naturally in positions of authority. Church teachings, which emphasize women's role as wife and mother, also validate patriarchy. The *Virgin Mary* is used to glorify motherhood, female suffering, and self-denial. The church has also played a significant role in shaping family law in Latin America. Church opposition to sex education, contraception, abortion, and divorce has greatly influenced legislation throughout the region.[24]

Conservative evangelical protestant churches, which have expanded rapidly in recent years, also reinforce strict gender roles. This is especially evident with respect to Pentecostal and other charismatic churches.[25] Pentecostals currently represent 13 percent of all Latin Americans (roughly 75 million people) and 73 percent of all Protestants in the region. These churches are especially common in poor communities.[26] By emphasizing personal experiences with the *Holy Spirit*, such as speaking in tongues, diving healing, and prophesying, Pentecostalism constitutes an important source of hope and comfort for the poor. These churches generally sanction traditional gender roles, with women occupying a subordinate place in the family. A husband's authority is deemed preeminent and women are expected to be deferential. Again, a devoted mother who nurtures and serves her husband and children is the ideal.[27]

These historical forces have produced gender roles that are sometimes characterized as *Machismo* and *Marianismo*. *Machismo*, which derives from the Spanish word for male, reflects the idea that men are expected to be aggressive, competitive, courageous, strong, and virile. Men should dominate their household and family. Any hint of gentleness and moderation is considered feminine and not respected. *Marianismo*, on the other hand, which derives from the notion that women should emulate the *Virgin Mary*, encourages women to be subservient, docile, passive, gentle, obedient, humble, pious, and self-sacrificing. These culturally constructed gender roles, which are internalized and passed down from both mothers and fathers to daughters and sons, limit the power and independence of women.

At the same time, it is important to avoid oversimplifying the reality of gender relations in Latin America. Gender roles are exceedingly complex and not fully captured by the aforementioned dichotomies.[28] Over time women have gained greater power over their lives and their relations with men and feminist movements have emerged throughout the region to challenge traditional gender roles.[29] Gender expectations also vary considerably by country, region, income, and ethnicity.

EXTERNAL CAUSES

External influences have also contributed to gender inequality in Latin America. International development banks, such as the World Bank and Inter-American Development Bank (IDB), traditionally supported projects in which men were the primary beneficiaries. Only recently has gender mainstreaming been adopted by these institutions.[30] Many of the policies of these institutions are also inimical to the interests of women. Structural adjustment reforms, for example, often undermine the economic position of women. As noted in chapter 3, these reforms involve reducing public sector spending, removing restrictions on the private sector, selling off government-owned industries, and integrating domestic economies into global markets.

Structural adjustment often works *against* the interests of women.[31] Cutbacks in public sector nutrition, health care, education, and child care programs typically have more adverse impacts on women because they are more dependent on these programs. Deregulation has encouraged more insecure, non-union, poorly paid work in sectors where female employment is most prevalent. It has also depressed wages and increased prices for consumer goods and services. Government layoffs due to privatization have disproportionately affected women who are often the last hired and first fired. Trade and investment liberalization have created jobs in export processing zones that draw heavily on female workers, but, as noted earlier, are characterized by low pay, long hours, and difficult working conditions. Trade liberalization has led to the displacement of female-dominated subsistence agriculture by male dominated export-oriented farming. The influx of mass-produced imports has contributed to the destruction of small handicrafts, prepared by women's collectives, as an industry. Overall, these reforms tend to place the burden of adjustment more on women than men and thus intensify gender inequalities in the region.

CONCLUSION

This chapter reviewed economic and social conditions of women in Latin America. Although some progress has been achieved in recent years, women continue to face significant obstacles in their daily lives. Many women are unable to obtain adequate health and reproductive care, especially gynecological, prenatal, and obstetric services. In the workplace, women tend to be concentrated in positions with low pay, few benefits, and little security. Women have less control than men over land and other productive assets.

The difficulties women face are interrelated. When women suffer from poor nutrition or health, they are not able to effectively compete in the labor market. Unable to advance in the formal economy, women are relegated to the low wage, less stable informal economy. As women fall further into poverty, they have even less access to decent health care and education for themselves and their families. The *feminization of poverty* is thus reproduced from one generation to the next.

A number of factors contribute to patriarchy in Latin America. Gender roles established in pre-colonial and colonial periods and passed down over time generally favor men over women. Men have historically used their political and economic power to ensure dominance over women. Governments have reinforced gender inequality, either by directly imposing legal limitations on women or by simply not enforcing laws designed to protect and advance the interests of women. Governments have also been reluctant to channel resources into programs where women are the primary beneficiaries. Catholic and conservative protestant churches have reinforced patriarchy by legitimizing and sanctioning strict gender roles. Lastly, international development banks traditionally supported projects in which men were the primary beneficiaries and advanced policies that were detrimental to women.

Gender inequality clearly limits overall economic and social progress in Latin America. When women are malnourished, the physical well-being of their children is compromised. Because women who suffer from ill health or illiteracy are less capable of providing for their children, these children are at a greater risk of developing illnesses or dropping out of school. When women's talents are restricted, both national productivity and economic growth are limited. More effectively meeting the needs of women is clearly necessary for the overall advance of Latin America. United Nations' efforts to enhance health and reproductive care and expand employment opportunities for women are described in the following chapter.

6 Promoting Gender Equity

The preceding chapter surveyed the contemporary reality of women in Latin America. Despite some progress, women continue to face greater hardships in their daily lives, and more obstacles to advancement, than men. Many women are unable to obtain quality and affordable health and reproductive care. When women enter the labor market they are typically relegated to lower paid, less secure positions. Women have less control over land and productive assets than men and are more likely to live in poverty.

Improving the lives of women is essential for the overall development of Latin America. Women are the primary care givers for their families and, when afforded the opportunity, make significant contributions to broader economic and social progress. While closing the gender gap will largely depend on the work of local governments and community groups, domestic resources are limited and international institutions can support this process of social change.

This chapter examines United Nations efforts to improve the lives of women. The first section reviews how work in this area evolved over time. While gender issues have long been recognized by the UN, they have only recently been placed near the top of the organization's priorities. The remainder of the chapter focuses on specific initiatives in Latin America since 2000. The United Nations Population Fund has played a lead role in working to meet the needs of women followed by the United Nations Development Programme and World Food Programme.

GENERAL WORK OF THE UNITED NATIONS

Attention to gender issues can be traced to the early institutions and documents of the United Nations.[1] In 1946 the Economic and Social Council established a Commission on the Status of Women (CSW).[2] The commission, which is comprised of 45 member countries, monitors the economic, social, and political conditions of women worldwide and makes recommendations for reducing global gender disparities.[3] CSW has been at the center of the UN's gender-related work, sponsoring global conferences, drafting international accords, and establishing universal standards for the advancement of women.

CSW ensured that gender issues were addressed in the early activities of the UN. The *Universal Declaration of Human Rights* stressed the need to advance human rights and fundamental freedoms, without distinction of any kind, including sex (see Appendix 1)[4] The 1952 *Convention on the Political Rights of Women* called on member states to ensure women have the same rights as men to vote, compete in elections, and hold public office. When the first Development Decade was declared in 1961, a special effort was made to channel funds to women's groups. The *International Covenant on Civil and Political Rights* and the *International Covenant on Economic, Social and Cultural Rights* affirmed the equal rights of men and women and prohibited discrimination on any grounds, including sex (see Appendix 2). The General Assembly's *Declaration on the Elimination of Discrimination against Women*, adopted in 1967, called for all appropriate measures "to abolish existing laws, customs, regulations and practices which are discriminatory against women, and to establish adequate legal protection for equal rights of men and women."[5]

The second Development Decade, which began in 1970, continued to stress gender issues and the need to involve women in the development process. The year 1975 was designated International Women's Year and the period 1975–85 the UN Decade for Women. The General Assembly established guidelines for member governments that included distributing nutritional and health services more equitably, strengthening education and training programs for women, integrating women into the labor force, and involving women in the preparation of development plans.

The UN also sponsored the First World Conference on Women in 1975.[6] This conference, which took place in Mexico City, initiated the process of bringing women together to collectively address gender issues. It concluded with a *Declaration on the Equality of Women and their Contribution to Development and Peace.* The declaration enumerated the economic, social, and political rights of women and offered recommendations on a wide range of subjects, including health and reproductive care, family planning, literacy, education, technical and vocational training, access to credit, and employment.[7] The Mexico City conference created the impetus for the International Research and Training Institute for the Advancement of Women (INSTRAW). Established by ECOSOC in 1976 and based in the Dominican Republic, INSTRAW conducts research on economic, social, and political obstacles to the advancement of women and sponsors training seminars for government officials and civic leaders on topics related to gender equality.[8] The Mexico City conference also recommended establishing a fund to improve economic and social conditions for women in developing countries. Within a year, the General Assembly established the Voluntary Fund for the United Nations Decade for Women. Renamed the United Nations Development Fund for Women (UNIFEM) in 1985 when it became an autonomous body of the UN in association with UNDP, the fund provides technical and financial support for projects where women are the primary beneficiaries and promotes female participation in development programs.[9]

In 1979 the General Assembly adopted the *Convention on the Elimination of All Forms of Discrimination against Women* (CEDAW) which codified many of the principles contained in the earlier *Declaration on the Elimination of Discrimination against Women.*[10] CEDAW was the first legally binding international instrument to advance the rights of women. The convention defines discrimination against women as:

> Any distinction, exclusion or restriction made on the basis of sex which has the effect or purpose of impairing or nullifying the recognition, enjoyment or exercise by women, irrespective of their marital status, on the basis of equality of men and women, of human rights and fundamental freedoms in the political, economic, social, cultural, civil or any other field.[11]

Those states that ratify the convention are legally obligated to repeal all laws that favor men over women and enact new provisions that protect women from gender discrimination. The convention covers a range of areas, including access to health and reproductive care, equality of educational and employment opportunities, and the right to participate in public life. The UN also established a Committee on the Elimination of Discrimination against Women to monitor implementation of CEDAW.[12] Governments must report to this committee every four years on their efforts to meet the provisions of the convention. The committee then responds with a series of recommendations for adjusting domestic policies and laws to better conform to international standards.[13]

The UN sponsored a Second World Conference on Women in 1980.[14] The conference, which took place in Copenhagen, reviewed and evaluated the progress achieved during the first half of the Decade for Women. Emphasis was placed on women's health, education, and employment. It concluded with a declaration that outlined existing obstacles to the advancement of women and recommended a range of policy and legal reforms.

The third UN Development Decade began in 1980. The General Assembly declaration that initiated this decade stressed the importance of women's participation in the development process, both as beneficiaries and agents. It called for eliminating the structural imbalances that perpetuate gender inequality and for fundamental social and economic changes to enhance professional opportunities for women. The Third World Conference on Women, which took place in Nairobi in 1985, adopted a *Plan of Action* that reaffirmed concern regarding the status of women and provided a framework for eliminating gender-based discrimination.[15] The integration of women in the development process was again stressed. Women's participation in decision making was recognized not only as a legitimate right but also as a social and political necessity that should be incorporated into all institutions of society.[16]

Soon after the conclusion of this conference the UN introduced new initiatives to ensure it was faithful to the same principles required of member states. The 1986 *Declaration on the Right to Development* stated that "[e]ffective measures should be undertaken to ensure that women have an active role in the development process" (see Appendix 3).[17] In 1987 the UNDP established a Division of Women in Development within its Bureau for Program and Policy Evaluation. The central objective of this division was to mainstream gender issues into all UNDP policies and programs.[18] Similarly, the Secretariat established a Division for the Advancement of Women (DAW) in 1988 to monitor implementation of resolutions on gender equity and support national efforts to advance the rights of women.[19]

The 1992 United Nations Conference on Environment and Development (UNCED) emphasized the importance of gender equity and the vital role of women in environmental management and sustainable development. UNCED's program of action *Agenda 21* which included a chapter on women, called on governments to eliminate legal, cultural, social, and other barriers to women's participation in public life.[20] It also recommended enabling women to play an enhanced role in sustainable development through better health care, improved educational opportunities, greater access to credit, and enhanced property rights.

These goals were reiterated in subsequent conferences during the remainder of the decade. The 1994 International Conference on Population and Development (ICPD) focused on women's health and education. Its *Programme of Action* committed governments to expand resources for reproductive health services and enhance opportunities for girls to complete both primary and secondary education.[21] The importance of gender equality was also highlighted at the 1995 World Summit for Social Development. As stressed in the final declaration:

> Social and economic development cannot be secured in a sustainable way without the full participation of women and that equality and equity between women and men is a priority for the international community and as such must be at the centre of economic and social development.[22]

The UN sponsored a Fourth World Conference on Women later that same year. The conference, which took place in Beijing, adopted a *Declaration and Platform of Action* that included a number of recommendations with respect to health care, education, and employment. It also called for women's equal access to economic resources, including land, credit, technology, and vocational training.[23]

The UN also pressed for gender equity in the early years of the twenty-first century. The 23rd Special Session of the General Assembly in June 2000, which was entitled "Women 2000: Gender Equality, Development and Peace in the Twenty-first Century," assessed the progress achieved in women's rights since the Beijing conference. Governments were encouraged to eliminate legislative gaps that leave women without effective legal protections against gender-based discrimination. In September of the same year, the *United Nations Millennium Declaration* highlighted the importance of gender equality for sustainable development (see Appendix 4). It called on states "[t]o promote gender equality and the empowerment of women as effective ways to combat poverty, hunger and disease and to stimulate development that is truly sustainable."[24] Promoting gender equality and the empowerment of women was also one of the eight MDGs (see Appendix 5).

The 2002 World Summit on Sustainable Development (WSSD) highlighted the importance of women's access to decision making at all levels, mainstreaming gender perspectives into the policy-making process, eliminating all forms of discrimination against women, and improving the health and well-being of women through equal access to health care, education, credit, and land. The 2005 World Summit reaffirmed that "gender equality and the promotion and protection of the full enjoyment of all human rights and fundamental freedoms for all are essential to advance development."[25] The final declaration called for ensuring access to reproductive health care, eliminating gender inequalities in education, promoting access to labor markets, guaranteeing the right to own and inherit property, and ensuring access to productive assets.

WORK IN LATIN AMERICA

The consistent emphasis on gender equity outlined above is also reflected in the work of the UN in Latin America. Particular attention is placed on ensuring access to health and reproductive care. UN agencies offer education on human sexuality, provide family planning services, and work to ensure safe childbirth. The UN also supports literacy and vocational training programs to improve the economic position of women, as well as initiatives to reduce gender gaps in access to productive resources. Strengthening public sector capacity to meet the needs of women is also prioritized. This includes improving assessment capacity, mainstreaming gender considerations into public policy, strengthening programs in which women are the primary beneficiaries, and promoting gender-sensitive legal reform.

HEALTH AND REPRODUCTIVE CARE

Improving women's access to health and reproductive care is a central component of the work of the United Nations in Latin America. The United

Nations Population Fund plays a lead role in these efforts. The fund has worked to prevent unintended pregnancies, especially among adolescent girls. Infants born to adolescent mothers are more likely to be premature and have low birth weights. Because young mothers are generally less able to provide the type of compensatory care needed, infant and child mortality rates are generally higher.

UNFPA worked to ensure adolescent girls received information on human sexuality. The fund supported the introduction of family life education in public school curricula, including subjects like reproductive health and physiology, family planning, and responsible parenthood. In Peru, UNFPA developed instructional methodologies to improve the quality of sexual and reproductive health components in formal and non-formal education and organized sex education training for primary and secondary teachers.[26] UNFPA worked with the Department of Education of Bolivia to strengthen sex education programs. Materials were developed to encourage safe sex behavior and prevent unintended pregnancies.[27] UNFPA made a similar contribution in Colombia. Working with the ministries of Health and Education, the fund expanded sex education for adolescents in rural and remote areas.[28] In Brazil, UNFPA helped develop instructional tools for sexual and reproductive health in schools. The fund also instituted a system for measuring the impact of sexual and reproductive health educational activities on the knowledge, attitudes, and practices of adolescents.[29] In Cuba, UNFPA helped expand educational activities on sexual and reproductive health in various types of schools, including teacher training institutes.[30] UNFPA worked with the Ministries of Education of Ecuador, El Salvador, Guatemala, and Nicaragua to integrate sexuality education into curriculum at all levels of basic education. Teachers were trained on how best to address adolescent sexual and reproductive health issues. Similarly, the fund promoted a school curriculum in Mexico that focused on the importance of making informed and responsible decisions on reproductive health issues. Adolescents were involved in developing this curriculum.[31] In Panama, UNFPA worked with parents, community leaders, and teachers to develop sexuality education programs and in Paraguay, the fund incorporated information on reproductive health into school curricula.[32]

UNFPA also developed programs to reach adolescents outside of formal education systems. In Ecuador and Venezuela the fund supported non-formal sexuality education activities in regions where school attendance and completion rates are low.[33] UNFPA also helped integrate sexuality education into alternative education programs in Bolivia.[34] Public sector health clinics in Tegucigalpa were used to offer sex education to Honduran adolescents with peer counselors employed to overcome social and cultural barriers.[35]

UNFPA was directly involved in the provision of contraceptives and other voluntary family planning services. The fund strengthened the national system for ensuring the availability of contraceptives in Bolivia and helped expand the range of contraceptive methods covered by health plans in Colombia.[36] Technical assistance to Brazil's Ministry of Health improved access to a range of contraceptive methods at the state and local levels.[37] UNFPA worked with the Honduran Family Planning Association to improve the supply management system for contraceptives.[38] In Nicaragua and Peru, technical support was extended to guarantee the supply of reproductive health commodities, especially in rural areas. The fund estimated contraceptive needs, facilitated procurement, and organized distribution efforts.[39] UNFPA supported Costa Rica's Social Security Fund in evaluating reproductive health services and improving the quality of those services, especially family planning counseling in hospitals, clinics, and health centers.[40]

UNFPA also worked to improve prenatal care. The training of reproductive health providers was a central part of this effort. In Cuba and Nicaragua, training programs strengthened prenatal health services.[41] Prenatal training was provided in those regions of Bolivia, Brazil, and Peru with the highest number of indigenous populations. UNFPA instituted a national training program in prenatal care in Ecuador and enhanced the maternal health surveillance system in Colombia.[42] Emphasis was placed on those regions of each country with the highest rates of maternal mortality.

UNFPA also supported programs to ensure women have the assistance of a skilled attendant during childbirth and access to emergency obstetric services. In Nicaragua, UNFPA worked with the Ministry of Health to strengthen obstetric care units in ten hospitals and health centers and in Panama the first emergency obstetric care unit was established in the Comarca Ngobe Buglé region to serve indigenous communities.[43] The fund worked with the Ministry of Health of the Dominican Republic to strengthen health services networks that specialize in delivery and postpartum care.[44] In Ecuador and Guatemala, a program was supported to better identify and respond to obstetric emergencies. Participants in the program included community leaders, traditional birth attendants, and voluntary health workers.[45] The fund also helped train managerial and technical health sector personnel in emergency obstetric care in El Salvador and Peru.[46]

Ensuring service providers are respectful of women from diverse social and cultural backgrounds was also emphasized.[47] In the Peruvian departments of Apurimac, Cajamarca, and Cusco, UNFPA adapted its reproductive health services to better conform to indigenous beliefs and practices. A similar project was supported in Ecuador that combined traditional prenatal and childbirth practices with modern medicine.[48] In Bolivia, UNFPA worked with indigenous groups to develop strategies for the delivery of reproductive health information and services.[49] Additional initiatives were undertaken with Aymarás women in Chile and Mbya women in Paraguay.[50]

TRAINING AND EMPLOYMENT

The United Nations also worked to enhance training and employment opportunities for women. Considerable emphasis was placed on improving female literacy rates. The World Food Programme often conditioned food aid on participation in literacy classes. In Honduras, women received annual food assistance as an incentive for attending literacy classes. In the Ayacucho region of Peru, WFP provided training to illiterate and semiliterate women in nutrition, hygiene, and income generating activities. Functional literacy courses were also offered to Haitian women who had not been able to complete their education. WFP supported bilingual literacy classes for Guatemalan women.

The UN also supported vocational training for women. In Jamaica, pregnant teens who received training through UNFPA were more likely to continue their education and eventually enter the labor force. The fund also sponsored vocational training for homeless women in Haiti. A UNFPA program in Nicaragua encouraged women to participate in decision making within organizations and businesses such as schools, mills, dairies, and poultry operations. The fund also helped strengthen women's leadership roles in Guatemalan community organizations by training local women in bookkeeping and accounting.

WFP was also committed to reducing gender gaps in access to productive resources and leadership skills. Food aid was typically distributed directly to the household's senior female. Women also participated in the planning, management, and implementation of food assistance activities. In Bolivia women played a central role in establishing kitchens, orchards, and greenhouses. In El Salvador, at least 70 percent of participants in the management of WFP resources were women. Women assumed leadership roles on food distribution committees in Honduras.[51] An initiative in Guatemala emphasized the creation and control of assets by women, providing training and alternative income generation options, and strengthening their roles in communal organizations.[52] WFP also supported Generosidad, a gender equity project in Mexico that focused on improving income opportunities for women. Technical assistance and training was extended to Peruvian women to establish agro-industrial enterprises.[53] In Brazil, UNDP supported the government's efforts to strengthen the legal rights of women. Because women can now receive civil documents at no cost, they have greater access to credit, technology, and income generating opportunities.

PUBLIC POLICY REFORM

The UN also sought to strengthen the capacity of Latin American governments to meet the needs of women. These efforts typically began with an assessment of socioeconomic conditions in the region. UNDP utilized its Gender-Related Development Index (GDI) to measure differences between men and women with respect to life expectancy, educational attainment, and income and its Gender Empowerment Measure (GEM) to assess the extent to which women are represented in positions of economic and political influence.[54]

UNDP commissioned a series of country reports to analyze progress toward achieving the gender components of the Millennium Development Goals. Between 2003 and 2008 country reports were completed for Argentina, Bolivia, Brazil, Colombia, Ecuador, Guatemala, Nicaragua, Paraguay, Peru, and Venezuela. UNDP worked with Mexico's Institute for Social Development to establish a gender-responsive poverty monitoring system. In Chile, research on the status of women was used to inform public sector budgets and institute educational reforms.

UNFPA also helped assess conditions for women in Latin America. The fund worked with the Venezuelan government to track changes in population structure, distribution, and size. In Brazil, Cuba, and Paraguay, training programs helped government officials monitor changes in gender inequality more effectively. UNFPA also promoted the use of sociodemographic data in the formulation and evaluation of public policies. In Guatemala, national capacity to produce census and survey data that incorporated gender perspectives was strengthened. UNFPA also supported the Secretariat for Planning and Programming in policy-oriented research on population issues.[55] This allowed for better integration of population and gender concerns into the preparation of development programs. Similarly, UNFPA aided Bolivia's Ministry of Planning to use population data in development planning and monitoring public services at the municipal and community levels.[56] In Costa Rica, the fund strengthened institutional capacities to generate, collect, and analyze information on population, reproductive health, and poverty reduction.[57] UNFPA also provided technical assistance to incorporate gender-related data in the design and evaluation of public policies. In Ecuador, public sector capacity to include population data in the policy-making process was strengthened. UNFPA worked with national and local institutions to ensure population data was utilized in the design of health and education policies.[58] Similarly, UNFPA increased the capacity of the National Institute of Statistics of Honduras to collect, analyze, and disseminate demographic information and helped establish a national system of sociodemographic data, disaggregated by gender, in the Dominican Republic.[59]

UNFPA also worked with the Latin American and Caribbean Women's Health Network to monitor the health of women. The fund developed a database that provides gender-sensitive information to governments. Among Caribbean nations, UNFPA improved public sector capacity to utilize sociodemographic data in the formulation, implementation, and evaluation of development policies. Support was provided to examine population factors in existing policies within the framework of each country's poverty reduction efforts.[60]

Mainstreaming gender issues was also emphasized. UNDP worked with governments to ensure public sector budgets, policies, and programs benefitted men and women equally and to design initiatives that contribute to the advancement of women.[61] In Chile, gender-sensitive budgeting was introduced at both national and local levels. Gender issues were also included across sectoral lines in the design of public policies.[62] Similarly, UNDP helped establish program targets, disaggregated by gender, into national policy planning frameworks in Brazil.[63] Gender considerations were also included in the development of training methodologies.

The United Nations Development Fund for Women (UNIFEM), which is administered by UNDP, also worked to include gender considerations in the preparation of public sector budgets. In Bolivia, leaders of women's organizations were trained to more effectively participate in public policy making. Municipal budgetary guidelines now require that resources be allocated to programs that promote gender equality. Similarly, in Ecuador and Peru, UNIFEM helped make budget policies more responsive to the principles of gender equality. This work was recently expanded beyond the Andean region. In Costa Rica, UNIFEM improved the capacity of national and local institutions to develop policies and programs addressing gender inequities, focusing on reproductive rights and women's economic autonomy.[64] In Guatemala, the fund helped strengthen the participation of indigenous women in local and provincial policy-making processes.

UNFPA also promoted gender mainstreaming in Latin America. In the Dominican Republic, the inclusion of gender concerns in government development plans was enhanced through the establishment of an interinstitutional group on population and development.[65] UNFPA also worked with the Ministry of Women's Affairs to create Gender Equity and Development Offices in all government ministries. In Nicaragua, gender issues were mainstreamed into the Emergency Fund for Social Investment, the leading anti-poverty program. In Colombia and Paraguay, UNFPA ensured population and gender factors were included in poverty reduction and development strategies.[66] The fund aided preparation of gender-sensitive projects in Panama that linked population to poverty reduction.[67]

UN agencies also strengthened public sector programs that directly assisted women. Particular focus was placed on improving health and reproductive care. UNFPA assisted Guatemala's Ministry of Health in the design and implementation of a national policy on reproductive health.[68] Similarly, the fund provided technical assistance to the Nicaraguan government for the development of national reproductive health policy.[69] UNFPA worked with Ecuador's Ministry of Health to develop national health care norms and protocols. Focus was placed on family planning, prenatal care, and strengthening reproductive health service delivery networks.[70] In El Salvador, national capacity to deliver reproductive health services was enhanced. National policies and norms were revised to improve the quality of reproductive health care.[71] UNFPA worked with Venezuela's Ministry of Health and Social Development to establish standards for the provision of family planning services.[72] Similarly, UNFPA aided the Ministry of Environment and Population of Colombia to improve reproductive health in regions characterized by significant social inequality, political violence, and high numbers of displaced persons.[73] In Peru, technical assistance was extended for the development of family planning programs and a national policy on adolescent reproductive health.[74] UNFPA aided the Ministry of Health of Honduras update reproductive health norms and establish more effective monitoring and evaluation systems.[75] The fund strengthened national capacity in the Dominican Republic to provide sexual and reproductive health services, including prenatal and postpartum care.[76]

The UN also supported public institutions that advance the rights of women. In Peru, UNFPA supported creation of the Ministry for the Promotion of Women and Human Development. The fund also helped draft legislation to create a new Secretariat for Women in the Dominican Republic. In Brazil, UNIFEM provided technical support to the Ministry of Agrarian Development to ensure at least 30 percent of resources allocated for agrarian reform were channeled to women. New measures were also adopted to increase female access to land, training, and technical assistance. Technical assistance was also extended to El Salvador's Ministry of Education to incorporate gender issues into public school curriculums.

Lastly, the UN promoted legal reforms to better protect the rights of women. This work typically began with an examination of existing laws from a gender perspective. In Brazil, national and international experts were recruited to evaluate legal frameworks designed to guarantee reproductive rights.[77] Similarly, in the five Andean countries, UNFPA examined national legislation affecting women's economic, social, and cultural rights. UNFPA worked with Haiti's Ministry of Women's Affairs to amend legal statutes that discriminated against women and helped revise Peruvian laws that restricted access of adolescent girls to reproductive health services.[78] In Honduras and Panama, UNFPA helped formulate laws in the areas of population, sexual and reproductive health, and gender equality.[79] The fund strengthened the capacity of Bolivia's judicial system to adjudicate on sexual and reproductive health issues.[80] UNFPA also worked to ensure women are aware of their legal rights. In Ecuador, the Free Maternity Law guarantees access to family planning, care for pregnant women, and health care for children up to five years of age. The fund helped inform women of their rights under the law and educated medical staff on the law's implication for reproductive health care.

CONCLUSION

This chapter surveyed recent United Nations efforts to promote gender equity in Latin America. Particular attention was placed on improving women's access to health and reproductive care. The UN was extensively engaged in efforts to expand education on human sexuality, provide family planning services, and ensure safe childbirth. The UN also worked to improve the position of women in the formal economy. This included providing support for literacy and vocational training programs, as well as initiatives to reduce gender gaps in access to productive resources. UN efforts to strengthen public sector capacity included mainstreaming gender considerations into public policy, expanding social programs that benefit women, and promoting legal and regulatory reform.

UN agencies have clearly helped advance gender equity in Latin America. However, the overall contribution has sometimes been compromised by poor coordination among different agencies. This has led to the duplication of activities or the misallocation of resources. Enhanced coordination would allow for greater joint programming, information sharing, and pooling of resources. The impact of UN programs has also been limited by local governments that rarely prioritize gender issues. With little support from public sector actors, the UN has not been able to scale up its activities in the region. Part of the problem is simply the cultural environment in which the UN is operating. Given the long-standing nature of patriarchy in the region, and the continued strength of strict gender roles, real change in the lives of women will continue to be incremental.

Improving the lives of women is essential for Latin American development. As women obtain wider access to education and employment they gain greater control over their lives. As income levels increase, women typically choose to have fewer children, which lessens pressures on local economies and natural environments. Moreover, the children they do have are typically better off. Women are more likely than men to use their income to improve their children's nutrition and health. As women's educational and income levels increase, they also place greater emphasis on their children's education. When women enter the labor force in greater numbers and more varied positions they make significant contributions to the economic and social progress of their nations.

7 Ecology of the Americas

Preserving and protecting natural environments is an integral part of the development process. Social and economic progress is not sustainable if it causes the rapid depletion of natural resources or destruction of local habitats. Economic growth and environmental preservation constitute complementary parts of the same process of change, and development assistance is increasingly structured to meet these twin objectives.

This chapter and the following chapter turn to environmental issues in Latin America. The degradation of natural resources and ecosystems has increased over the past three decades, often at alarming rates.[1] Emissions from factories and vehicles have produced some of the worst urban air pollution in the world, while the dumping of agricultural, mining, and industrial wastes has damaged lakes, rivers, streams, coastal waterways, and coral reefs. The increased use of chemical fertilizers, pesticides, and herbicides has reduced the long-term productivity of agricultural land. Latin America has the *highest* rate of deforestation in the world.

This chapter first reviews the major environmental challenges in Latin America, with focus placed on current threats to the region's air, water, land, and forests. I then turn to those factors most responsible for environmental decline. Social factors, such as poverty, population growth, and urbanization, are clearly part of the problem, but governments have been slow to enact environmental laws or effectively manage natural resources. In fact, the development model pursued has typically privileged short-term economic growth over environmental protection. Transnational corporations and international financial institutions have also contributed to the region's environmental decline.

AIR QUALITY

Air pollution is among the greatest environmental threats in Latin America today. This is true despite recent efforts to address the problem. Air quality standards have been established in most major urban areas and a number of countries tax gasoline on the basis of lead content. Some of the region's largest cities, including Mexico City, Santiago, and São Paulo, restrict vehicular use to certain times of the day or week and governments have instituted measures that encourage industries to utilize cleaner sources of energy.

Despite these initiatives, air quality continues to decline. Auto and industrial emissions of carbon dioxide, methane, sulfur oxide, and nitrogen oxide have increased dramatically over the course of the past two decades. Buenos Aires, Guatemala City, Lima, Mexico City, Rio de Janeiro, Santiago, and São Paulo are among the world's most polluted cities.[2] Such pollution causes thousands of premature deaths each year, especially among those suffering from respiratory disease or chronic bronchitis.[3] A large percentage of babies born in these cities have high levels of lead in their blood.

The consequences of air pollution extend well beyond the territorial borders of each nation. The combustion of carbon-based fossil fuels is contributing to a worldwide buildup of carbon dioxide, methane, sulfur oxide, and nitrogen oxide. While these gases allow sunlight to pass to the earth in the form of solar radiation, they are not as transparent to the heat that the Earth re-emits. Although most of this heat bounces back into space, some is reflected back to earth. This is thought to be raising the earth's surface temperature. Surface temperatures have risen nearly 1 degree Celsius since the early twentieth century and eleven of the twelve warmest years on record have occurred since 1995. If current trends continue, surface temperatures are expected to rise another 1.2–4.5 degrees Celsius by 2100.

The warming of the earth, it is argued, is causing the polar ice caps to melt and sea levels to rise. The UN's Inter-Governmental Panel on Climate Change forecasts that global warming over the next century will raise the world's seas by nearly 20 inches. Rising sea levels would likely cause coastal erosion, salinization of aquifers, and loss of coastal cropland. It could also lead to the flooding of cities and coastal areas, the submerging of small islands, the loss of wetlands, and the collapse of coral reefs. Nearly 20 percent of the world's population, as well as many of the most fragile ecosystems, would be vulnerable to coastal flooding. In other parts of the world, global warming could produce heat waves, droughts, and forest fires.[4]

WATER RESOURCES

Water pollution is also a major threat to the nations of Latin America.[5] Again, governments have taken some measures to protect freshwater and marine resources. This includes the installation of water quality monitoring and control systems and enhanced management of coastal and marine resources. Despite these efforts, water resources continue to deteriorate. The discharge of untreated wastes has damaged rivers, lakes, and watersheds. Some of this waste comes from the increased use of chemical pesticides, fertilizers, and herbicides in agriculture. Waste is also produced by the mining sector. Mining operations require intense purification before the ores are transported and this is typically done at the mine site, using chemicals such as mercury and cyanide. Wastes from these processes are then discharged directly into river systems. Industries also discharge toxic chemicals, heavy metals, solvents, and other hazardous wastes into lakes, rivers, and streams.

The major urban areas have seen a decline in water levels. Forty percent of Latin Americans live in areas that contain only ten percent of the region's water resources.[6] The supply of clean and safe water has not kept up with increased demand. Aquifers are being exploited at unsustainable rates and water tables are falling. Urban slums and shanty towns typically lack clean water, sanitation, waste collection, and drainage systems. Over 200 million people in the region dump their untreated wastewater directly into bodies of water.[7] Water pollution is a major cause of the spread of contagious diseases and other health problems.

Latin Americans have also witnessed the decline of their coastal and marine ecosystems. Sixty-one of the region's seventy-seven largest cities are located on the coast, and 60 percent of all people in the region live within 100 kilometers of the Atlantic or Pacific Ocean. This places considerable strain on coastal waters. Nearly 80 percent of the region's wastewater coming from land-based sources reaches the sea without being treated. Coastal pollution has also placed nearly half of the region's coral reefs at risk.

LAND USE

Latin America has also witnessed the loss of its most fertile cropland. 250 million hectares of land are now moderately or severely degraded. Again, this is largely due to the increased use of chemical pesticides, fertilizers, and herbicides in agriculture, especially as traditional farming for domestic consumption is replaced by large-scale, export-oriented agriculture. Most countries lack effective systems for managing and disposing of hazardous wastes.

When small farmers are pushed off fertile lands they often move to semi-arid regions, steep hillsides, or other marginal lands. Cultivation in these areas erodes fragile soils which are then increasingly vulnerable to wind and rain. Moreover, without a protective canopy of dense vegetation, tropical soils are unable to withstand the impact of the equatorial sun. Agricultural land becomes desert that is unfit for future cultivation.

FORESTS

While Latin America is home to the greatest expanse of tropical forests in the world, these forests are quickly being destroyed.[8] Such destruction continues despite the adoption of improved forest management practices.[9] Latin

America has the *fastest* rate of deforestation in the world with millions of hectares of tropical forests cleared each year.[10] At least 60 million hectares have been lost since 1990.[11] The Amazon, which constitutes one-third of the world's rainforests, loses 2 million hectares of trees annually. One-fifth of the Amazonian rainforest has now been destroyed. In Central America, one-half of the region's rainforests have been cleared or severely degraded since 1950.[12] In Haiti, forest cover has fallen from 50 percent of the territory a century ago to 2 percent today.

Deforestation causes multiple problems for Latin American nations. As noted earlier, the removal of forest cover leads to soil erosion. The root structure of trees holds soils in place and provides nutrients for ground cover. When trees are removed, these nutrients are lost. In addition, when trees are cleared, the thin soils of the tropical forest become vulnerable to erosion and soil depletion from heavy rainfall and intense heat. Because trees regulate the storage and release of rainwater, their removal often leads to droughts, floods, and mudslides.

Deforestation also threatens the biodiversity of Latin America. Diverse plant and animal life helps purify air and water, regulate climate cycles, regenerate soil, and absorb pollutants. Latin America has 178 eco-regions (regions with distinctive flora and fauna), 77 percent of which are currently endangered.[13] Five of the fifteen countries worldwide whose fauna is most threatened are in Latin America: Brazil, Colombia, Ecuador, Mexico, and Peru. Rainforests are among the world's richest ecosystems and the Amazon alone contains about 40 percent of the world's species of plants and animals. The loss of forest cover threatens the Amazon's extraordinary diversity of plant and animal life.

Deforestation also contributes to global warming. Tropical forests constitute an important source of carbon sequestration. The loss of forests reduces the absorption of carbon dioxide from the atmosphere. Moreover, when forests are burned they release large amounts of carbon dioxide.[14] After fossil fuel combustion, tropical deforestation is the second greatest source of carbon dioxide in the atmosphere

SOCIOECONOMIC CAUSES

A number of socioeconomic factors contribute to environmental decline in Latin America. Poverty is clearly a major part of the problem.[15] Because poor people depend heavily on natural resources for their daily survival, they often engage in environmentally destructive practices. The most impoverished countries and regions typically exhibit the greatest ecological damage.[16] The destructive practices of the poor clearly contribute to water pollution. Because impoverished urban neighborhoods do not have adequate sewage systems, people dispose of wastes in open drainage ditches. In the countryside, wastes are dumped into rivers, lakes, and coastal waterways.

Destructive practices also contribute to soil erosion. Since the colonial period, Latin America has been characterized by extreme inequalities in the distribution of land. Peasant farmers often have few alternatives other than to cultivate marginal lands, such as fragile mountain slopes or semi-arid regions. The soils in these areas have little long-term productivity and are easily damaged by improper or frequent cultivation. The poor also lack appropriate tools and technologies to practice more environmentally sustainable agriculture. Rather, they tend to farm the land until it is no longer productive and then move to new areas. This sometimes involves burning forest cover which in itself greatly reduces the fertility of the soil. Once this land is no longer fit for cultivation, peasant farmers replicate the same destructive practices elsewhere.

Latin America's environmental problems are compounded by continued population increases. As noted in chapter 3, population pressures in Latin America are not as great as other regions of the world. However, a steady increase in population has placed added pressures on water resources, coastal habitats, farmland, forests, and fragile ecosystems. Population growth contributes to the rapid consumption of natural resources. In the countryside, people are pushed onto increasingly marginal lands.

Population growth also contributes to urbanization. Because rural economies are unable to absorb all of the new entrants to the labor market, people move from the countryside to larger towns and cities. Urban populations in Latin America have increased dramatically during the past four decades. Since 1970 the region's urban population has grown by 240 percent, while its rural population has increased by just 6.5 percent.[17] Latin America is now the most urbanized region in the developing world with 78 percent of all people living in cities of at least 50,000 inhabitants. This figure is projected to reach 81 percent by 2015.[18] Most large cities, including Belo Horizonte, Bogota, Buenos Aires, Caracas, Guadalajara, Guatemala City, Lima, Managua, Manaus, Mexico City, Panama City, Porto Alegre, Recife, Rio de Janeiro, San Salvador, Santiago, Santo Domingo, São Paulo, and Tegucigalpa, have grown well beyond the size that can be adequately supported by the existing infrastructure.[19] Uncontrolled and unplanned urban growth places intense pressures on local environments and natural resources.[20]

POLITICAL CAUSES

The public sector has also contributed to environmental problems. Latin American governments have been slow to enact and enforce effective measures to protect natural environments. Rather, public officials have typically pursued a development model that relies on the intense exploitation of natural resources. The unwillingness of governments to prioritize the environment is, at least in part, a consequence of the long-term nature of environmental threats. Political leaders tend to have much shorter time horizons when setting national priorities and are inclined to address more immediate needs first, with economic growth generally prioritized over environmental preservation.[21]

Clearly governments have been slow to enact environmental protections. Most countries have few restrictions on emissions from vehicles and industries or the dumping of agricultural or industrial wastes into the groundwater or marine areas. Regulatory frameworks for water management are minimal. Governments have also failed to control land degradation or the use of chemical fertilizers, pesticides, and herbicides. Efforts to protect the region's tropical rainforests from logging and burning have been even less effective.

Although some environmental regulations have been adopted in recent years, they are poorly implemented and enforced. Governments rarely have sufficient capacity to monitor compliance. This is due not only to budgetary restrictions but also a lack of technical capacity among environmental agencies. Because the legal systems of most countries are weak, legal consequences of violations are frequently avoided through bribery or other forms of corruption.

Latin American governments have also been slow to institute proactive measures to protect their environments. Overall budgets for environmental programs are small and institutional frameworks to incorporate ecological considerations into public policy are limited. Most governments lack the capacity to plan, monitor, and manage programs for the conservation of natural resources or the protection of biodiversity.

The reluctance of governments to protect natural environments is evident in a number of respects. Few investments have been made in urban mass transit, with most cities relying on antiquated buses that emit high levels of carbon dioxide and other pollutants. Governments have also been slow to modernize and upgrade water treatment systems. On average, less than 10 percent of municipal sewage is treated. Few resources have been allocated to clean up fresh water and coastal areas, ensure the sustainable use of cropland, or protect tropical rainforests.

The development strategy adopted by many Latin American countries, which relies heavily on the exploitation of natural resources, has also contributed to environmental decline. The construction of roadways, such as the Trans-Amazonian Highway in Brazil, have been undertaken specifically to open up new areas for resource exploitation. Wherever roads are built, peasant farmers, miners, cattle ranchers, and loggers follow, all of whom place added pressures on water resources, land, and forests.

Rapid industrialization has long been a priority. As noted in chapter 3, by diversifying their economies, Latin American governments hope to increase economic growth and expand employment. Although this strategy has produced some economic benefits, the environmental costs have been considerable.[22] Not only do new industries consume nonrenewable natural resources, but they produce vast amounts of pollution and waste. The exploitation of natural resources is also evident in recent efforts to promote exports, especially in the mining and timber industries.

EXTERNAL CAUSES

External actors have also contributed to environmental decline in Latin America.[23] This is especially evident with respect to transnational corporations. Latin America often attracts foreign investment precisely because environmental regulations are minimal and poorly enforced. Shifting production to the region, especially for the most environmentally hazardous industries, is considered cost-effective. Businesses are able to avoid the added costs of pollution control equipment required in North America or Europe. A striking example of this phenomenon can be found along the United States-Mexican border region. A number of transnational corporations have established assembly plants on the Mexican side of the border where products are manufactured for sale in the United States. This practice has expanded considerably since the North American Free Trade Accord (NAFTA) took effect in 1994. While there are multiple reasons why companies prefer to produce in Mexico, including lower wage rates, lax environmental regulations are clearly a major incentive. Despite a side accord to NAFTA that addressed environmental concerns, companies operating in the border region continue to cause environmental damage through the emission of pollutants and the dumping of hazardous wastes.[24]

The environmental impact of transnational corporations can also be seen in other sectors. Large-scale agribusinesses producing for export markets generate more pollution than local farmers producing for domestic consumption.[25] The land used for export production is more intensively exploited through the use of chemical fertilizers, pesticides, and herbicides. An overdependence on chemicals reduces soil fertility and the capacity to yield good harvests in the future. Export agriculture is also highly dependent on irrigation, which taxes water resources. The large-scale export-oriented production of coffee, cotton, soybeans, and sugar cane has pushed peasant farmers in Central and South America onto increasingly marginal lands.

International mining operations also contribute to environmental decline. The rapid extraction of metal ores and petroleum by least-cost methods produces high levels of soil and water pollution. Denuded hills and sludge-filled rivers are the consequence of these operations. The dumping of mercury by mining interests has poisoned rivers throughout Latin America. Transnational logging and ranching interests also contribute to the region's environmental problems. Both sectors profit from the rapid destruction of rainforests. In the Amazon and Central America, the export beef industry has removed large parts of the tree cover to create areas for cattle grazing.

Environmental destruction can also be linked to the external debt crisis. As noted in chapter 3, the combined debt of Latin American countries today is US$750 billion. Countries throughout the region have depleted natural resources to earn the hard currency needed to service their debts. This has led to the over-cultivation and overgrazing of land, the depletion of non-renewable minerals, and accelerated deforestation.

International financial institutions have also played a role in environmental deterioration. The World Bank and the Inter-American Development Bank (IDB) have supported policies in Latin America, such as rapid industrialization and the development of large scale infrastructure, that have been environmentally hazardous. Although both institutions have adopted more environmentally safe lending policies in recent years, and now fund environmental preservation projects, the legacy of their past practices persists.

The structural adjustment programs (SAP) of the World Bank and International Monetary Fund have exacerbated environmental problems. As outlined in chapter 3, structural adjustment typically includes austerity, deregulation, privatization, and the liberalization of trade and investment regimes. Austerity has reduced the little public sector spending on environmental protections that existed and deregulation has lessened environmental regulations on the private sector. Through privatization, state owned lands have been opened for private development. The promotion of exports has also had an adverse environmental impact. As noted earlier, large-scale agribusinesses producing for export markets generate more pollution than local farmers producing for domestic consumption and the expansion in timber exports contributes to deforestation. Lastly, liberalization of foreign investment regimes often results in the reduction of environmental standards. Such investment in agriculture, mining, logging, ranching, and manufacturing have been highly destructive for the region's environment.[26]

CONCLUSION

This chapter reviewed environmental conditions in Latin America. Although the region is rich in natural resources, with extraordinary endowments of water, land, minerals, forests, and biodiversity, these resources are not well-protected. Latin America has some of the worst urban air pollution in the world, its rivers, streams, coastal waterways, and coral reefs are severely damaged, the productivity of agricultural land has declined, and deforestation accelerates each year.

Many of these environmental problems are interrelated with decline in one area exacerbating problems in other areas. Air pollution, for example, has damaged freshwater resources. As noted earlier, the burning of fossil fuels emits carbon dioxide, methane, sulfur oxide, and nitrogen oxide. Once in the atmosphere, these pollutants are converted to acid and returned to the earth's surface in rain water. Acid rain has damaged the ecosystems of lakes and rivers throughout the region. Acid rain also threatens forest areas. Excess acids absorb nutrients from forest soils and impair the ability of trees to effectively utilize the remaining nutrients. Declining water tables are a major cause of soil erosion and land degradation. Soils contaminated with fertilizers, pesticides, and herbicides damage freshwater and marine resources. The burning of forests causes both air pollution and soil erosion.

There are a number of forces that contribute to environmental decline in Latin America. Poverty is clearly part of the problem. Poor people depend heavily on natural resources for their basic survival and often engage in environmentally destructive practices. Environmental problems are compounded by continued population increases that jeopardize water resources, coastal habitats, farmland, and forests. Uncontrolled and unplanned urban growth places intense pressures on local resources and municipalities. Governments have pursued a development model that relies heavily on natural resource exploitation. Transnational corporations have also contributed to environmental problems. Excessive agriculture, mining, logging, and ranching operations have caused water pollution, soil erosion, and the loss of forest areas. Latin America often attracts foreign investment precisely because environmental regulations are minimal and poorly enforced. International financial institutions have supported policies, such as rapid industrialization, the development of large-scale infrastructure, and structural adjustment, that have privileged economic growth over environmental preservation.

Environmental problems undermine Latin America's long-term development prospects in a number of respects. Polluted environments produce serious health problems for local populations. Air pollution alone causes thousands of premature deaths among those suffering from bronchitis, pneumonia, and other respiratory diseases. Using polluted water for drinking and washing spreads infectious diseases such as cholera, diarrhea, gastroenteritis, and typhoid. A polluted environment can be especially damaging to the physical and intellectual development of children. Environmental decline also increases the destructive impact of natural disasters.[27] Soil erosion and the loss of vegetative cover in mountainous areas diminish the capacity to absorb heavy rainfall.[28] The region is thus more susceptible to landslides and flash floods, with poor people living on steep hillsides, river banks, ravines, or flood plains being the most vulnerable. Because water and waste management systems are easily damaged by natural disasters, the spread of cholera, dengue fever, and other infectious diseases is more likely.

Protecting natural resources and ecosystems is essential for the continued progress of Latin America. In recent years, the United Nations has become more heavily engaged in environmental preservation. UN agencies have worked to preserve air, water, land, and forest resources throughout the region, as well as enact policy and legal reforms to enhance overall environmental protections. These initiatives are described in the following chapter.

8 Preserving Natural Environments

The preceding chapter surveyed environmental conditions in Latin America. Despite some efforts to protect natural resources and ecosystems, the region continues to be plagued by high levels of air and water pollution, soil erosion, and forest loss. Emissions from factories and vehicles contribute to extensive air pollution and the dumping of untreated wastes damages freshwater and marine resources. Increased use of chemical fertilizers, pesticides, and herbicides is reducing the long-term productivity of agricultural land and deforestation accelerates with each passing year.

Continued progress in Latin America is not possible unless economic growth is more carefully balanced with environmental preservation. Healthy ecosystems are needed for economic growth to be sustainable. While this will largely depend on local governments and societal groups, most countries do not have the resources, technology, or managerial capacity needed to fully protect their natural environments and international assistance remains imperative.

This chapter reviews the environmental work of the UN. I begin with a brief chronology of the organization's general work in this area before turning to specific initiatives in Latin America during the past decade. UNEP has been at the center of these efforts. UNEP has a Regional Office for Latin America and the Caribbean (ROLAC) and most environmental projects supported by the UN have at least some UNEP involvement, either as the principal or a secondary sponsor.[1] UNDP has also worked to preserve natural environments in the region.

GENERAL WORK OF THE UNITED NATIONS

Unlike other issues reviewed in this volume, the global environment was *not* among the early priorities of the United Nations. In fact, during its first two decades of operations, environmental concerns were rarely acknowledged by the global body. Development was largely associated with fostering economic growth and improving basic living conditions. It was not until the late 1960s that environmental issues began to be addressed.[2] In 1968 the

Secretariat collected data on global environmental trends and General Assembly Resolution 2398, entitled *Problems of the Human Environment*, pointed to rapidly increasing air and water pollution, soil erosion, population growth, and urbanization.

The first international conference on environmental issues occurred in 1972. The United Nations Conference on the Human Environment, which took place in Stockholm, concluded with a declaration that included 26 principles for environmental governance and an action plan with 109 recommendations for better stewardship of the world's environment.[3] The plan called for establishing a permanent institution within the UN for the protection of the global environment. The United Nations Environmental Programme was created by the General Assembly later that same year.[4] At the 1976 Conference on Human Settlements the link between meeting basic human needs and protecting natural environments was reinforced. The following year the UN sponsored a conference on desertification and in 1979 completed work on a Convention on Long-Range Transboundary Air Pollution that addressed the problem of acid rain.

By 1980 global environmental management had become central to the work of the UN.[5] The General Assembly adopted a World Conservation Strategy that emphasized the importance of protecting natural life support systems. The UN also sponsored a major initiative to regulate use of the oceans. The United Nations Convention on the Law of the Sea (UNCLOS), which had been under negotiation for nearly a decade, was opened for signature in 1982.[6] The convention defined the rights and responsibilities of nations in their use of the oceans and set global standards to protect the marine environment. The convention also created a legal regime for controlling mineral resource exploitation in deep seabed areas, and an institution, the International Seabed Authority, to monitor compliance. In 1983 the General Assembly established a World Commission on Environment and Development (WCED).[7] The commission's final report *Our Common Future* defined sustainable development as "development that meets the needs of the present without compromising the ability of future generations to meet their own needs."[8] Economic growth and poverty eradication were closely linked with the need for environmental protection and conservation of nonrenewable resources.[9]

The UN has also sought to protect the earth's ozone layer—the atmospheric shield that prevents much of the sun's ultraviolet radiation from reaching the earth's surface.[10] The 1985 Vienna Convention for the Protection of the Ozone Layer sought to reduce emissions of chemical substances, especially chlorofluorocarbons (CFC), which cause the greatest damage to the ozone layer. Two years later, a second, more ambitious agreement was reached. Under the Montreal Protocol on Substances that Deplete the Ozone Layer, signatory nations agreed to reduce emissions of ozone-depleting substances to half their 1986 levels by the turn of the century.[11] Even further cuts were proposed later, and in 1990 an agreement was reached to rapidly eliminate CFCs altogether.[12]

Although leaders from the developing world were largely supportive of these environmental initiatives, they did not have the resources or technology needed to fully meet their national obligations. In 1991 the Global Environmental Facility (GEF) was established to provide grant and concessional funds to developing countries to support projects that protect natural environments. As noted in Chapter 2, GEF supports initiatives to reduce soil degradation, ocean pollution, hazardous wastes, ozone layer depletion, the loss of biodiversity, and climate change.

A second global conference on the environment took place in 1992 in Rio de Janeiro. The United Nations Conference on Environment and Development (UNCED), often referred to as the Earth Summit, coincided with the twentieth anniversary of the Stockholm conference. The Rio Declaration on the Environment and Development, which included 27 principles of sustainable development, called on states to conserve, protect, and restore the health of the Earth's ecosystem. The conference also adopted an action plan, Agenda 21, that covered just about every environmental issue imaginable, including protecting the atmosphere, managing land resources, combating deforestation and desertification, promoting sustainable agriculture, conserving biological diversity, protecting the oceans and coastal areas, managing toxic chemicals, and reducing hazardous wastes. Two legally binding conventions were opened for signature at UNCED. The *United Nations Framework Convention on Climate Change* committed industrialized countries to reducing emissions of carbon dioxide and other greenhouse gases[13] and the Convention on Biological Diversity obligated countries to protect their plant and animal species through various proactive measures including habitat preservation.[14] The Earth Summit also produced a Statement of Principles on the Management, Conservation and Sustainable Development of Forests.[15] A Commission on Sustainable Development (CSD) was established by the General Assembly to monitor national progress in meeting Agenda 21 obligations.[16]

The 1994 International Conference on Population and Development (ICPD) reinforced many of UNCED's basic principles. The conference's Programme of Action highlighted the relationship between population growth, economic development, and environmental threats. The document stated that "meeting the basic human needs of growing populations is dependent on a healthy environment"[17] and stressed that unsustainable consumption and production patterns deplete natural resources and degrade the environment. "Integrating population into economic and development strategies," the document added, "will both speed up the pace of sustainable development and poverty alleviation and contribute to the achievement of population objectives and an improved quality of life of the population."[18]

The *United Nations Framework Convention on Climate Change* was strengthened in 1997. The Kyoto Protocol to the convention committed

36 industrialized nations to reduce their emissions of carbon dioxide and five other greenhouse gases to 5 percent below 1990 levels by 2012. The protocol introduced market mechanisms to help countries meet their targeted reductions of greenhouse gases. Signatory nations receive "carbon credits" by simply purchasing emissions reductions from other countries that have a credit surplus or by making investments in another country that lead to emission reductions.[19] The protocol went into effect in February 2005.[20]

The global environment was also an important part of the 2000 Millennium Summit. As noted in chapter 2, the summit adopted eight Millennium Development Goals, one of which was to ensure environmental sustainability (see Appendix 5). The summit called for integrating the principles of sustainable development into national policies and reversing the loss of environmental resources. Benchmarks were established that included increasing the proportion of land area covered by forests and reducing energy use, carbon dioxide emissions, ozone-depleting substances, and greenhouse gases.

The 2002 World Summit on Sustainable Development (WSSD) in Johannesburg coincided with the tenth anniversary of the Earth Summit. The Johannesburg Declaration on Sustainable Development listed 37 principles to achieve sustainable development and the Johannesburg Plan of Implementation included quantifiable goals and targets. Countries agreed to phase out the production and use of chemicals that harm the environment. Additional commitments included preserving energy resources, combating desertification, protecting biodiversity, improving ecosystem management, restoring fisheries, establishing a network of marine protected areas, and altering unsustainable consumption and production patterns.

The 2005 World Summit reaffirmed the importance of environmental protection as one of three mutually reinforcing pillars of sustainable development, alongside economic and social development. It also highlighted "the need for more efficient environmental activities in the United Nations system, with enhanced coordination, improved policy advice and guidance . . . and better integration of environmental activities in the broader sustainable development framework."[21] In 2007 UNDP and UNEP launched a jointly-managed Poverty-Environment Initiative (PEI) to enhance the links between poverty reduction and environmental management. PEI provides financial and technical support for mainstreaming poverty-environment linkages into development planning.[22]

WORK IN LATIN AMERICA

United Nations efforts to preserve natural environments in Latin America have been consistent with the general principles and priorities outlined above. Particular attention is placed on reducing air pollution and promoting the use of renewable sources of energy. The UN also supports programs to safeguard freshwater and marine resources, expand land use planning, and improve forest management. UN agencies have worked with governments in the region to enhance institutional capacities to foster sustainable development. Emphasis is placed on undertaking environmental assessments, training government officials in environmental management, and strengthening environmental laws. The UN has also aided regional cooperation on common environmental threats.

PROTECTION OF NATURAL RESOURCES

United Nations efforts to combat air pollution have focused on replacing the combustion of fossil fuels with the use of renewable sources of energy. In Brazil, UNEP helped develop new enterprises that use clean, efficient, and sustainable energy technologies. Under the Rural Energy Enterprise Development Programme, entrepreneurs that shifted to sustainable energy sources received public financing and a range of support services.[23] UNEP also supported the production of sugar-based ethanol, which burns cleaner than gasoline and is less expensive to produce than corn-based ethanol.

Alternative energy projects were also supported in Mexico and Central America. In Mexico, UNEP helped develop biomass, photovoltaic solar, and wind energy.[24] Solar water heating technologies were also introduced in remote parts of the country. In rural areas of Ecuador, Honduras, and Nicaragua, UNEP promoted the use of renewable energy in agro-industrial processes.[25] UNDP helped formulate programs for the development of non-polluting sources of renewable energy in Panama and high-resolution wind energy resource maps in Belize, El Salvador, Guatemala, Honduras, and Nicaragua.[26]

UNEP also worked to improve public transportation systems. In Cartagena, Guatemala City, and Panama City, UNEP aided municipal governments establish Bus Rapid Transport (BRT) systems.[27] Technical assistance was also provided to Mexico City for the development of a hydrogen-based public transport system.[28] Hydrogen-fueled buses were later introduced in major cities throughout Brazil.

The UN also supported programs to preserve freshwater and marine resources. In Northeastern Brazil, UNEP supported training programs on the proper management of groundwater resources. These programs increased the understanding and adaptation of sound water management principles among the rural population and improved access to safe drinking water. A similar initiative was undertaken in Guatemala. Technical assistance was provided to train indigenous communities in the management of water resources.[29] In Panama, UNEP offered training in the maintenance and administration of aqueducts in over 200 rural communities. The UN also worked with local governments to establish ecosystem restoration zones in areas where river basins are prone to erosion. In Peru, WFP supported an integrated water resource management project.[30] The National Watershed Management and Soil Conservation Program introduced enhanced water management and conservation practices in 32 micro-watersheds throughout the country.[31] In Brazil, UNEP provided technical support to improve rural water quality. This included construction of an artificial marsh to filter waste water coming from a treatment facility that pours into the Bocaina River.[32] UNEP also promoted the sustainable management of transboundary water resources in the Amazon River Basin.[33]

Water management initiatives were also supported in the Andean region. This included a project that was jointly sponsored by the governments of Bolivia and Peru to better protect Lake Titicaca.[34] The project was designed by UNEP to evaluate the levels of waste water discharges and introduce measures to reduce contamination of the lake. UNEP also supported an integrated ecosystem management project in the Cotahuasi River Basin of southwestern Peru. The entire river basin was categorized into separate ecological zones with distinct management guidelines. Focus was placed on strengthening existing communal agricultural and resource management systems through environmental awareness and training. In Argentina and Uruguay, UNDP supported a project to lessen transboundary threats to the Rio de la Plata.[35] The project included preparation of a Strategic Action Program to ensure effective collaboration between both countries. Similarly, a UNDP project supported by the governments of Argentina, Bolivia, and Paraguay helped improve environmental management of the Pilcomayo River Basin.[36]

UNEP also worked to preserve coastal and marine ecosystems. In the Caribbean Basin, the programme designed regional action plans for the integrated protection and management of coastal areas.[37] National efforts to reduce the use of pesticides in agricultural activities were also supported. In Colombia, Costa Rica, Nicaragua, and Panama, UNEP introduced alternatives to the intensive use of pesticides and improved management practices to reduce runoff into coastal waterways. UNEP also sponsored training programs in the management of marine and coastal ecosystems. Over 450 professionals from across the region participated in the Marine Protected Area Training Programme that focused on environmental monitoring, reducing land-based sources of marine pollution, and regenerating coral reefs.[38]

UN agencies also worked to improve land use planning. UNEP projects helped decrease areas subject to erosion, salinization, and other soil degradation processes. This included establishing grazing systems in Argentina and Brazil that correspond to the carrying capacity of existing pastures.[39] In Paraguay, UNDP formulated a recovery plan for areas with high levels of salinization in parts of the western region of Chaco.[40] UNEP also promoted sustainable agricultural practices, such as terracing, organic production, and other traditional soil conservation practices in Bolivia, Ecuador, and Peru. In Nicaragua, UNEP worked with municipal authorities to formulate a national policy for the integrated management of municipal wastes.[41]

Similar policies were developed with municipal governments in El Salvador and Honduras. WFP has also been active in this area, often using food aid to encourage sustainable land use and soil conservation. Programme officials worked with local governments in Peru to prevent soil erosion by terracing hillsides, planting trees, and rotating crops. Food-for-Work projects in Guatemala and Nicaragua included the construction of micro-irrigation systems, nurseries, community gardens, and terraces. These projects were designed to improve land productivity, the availability of food, and water conservation.[42]

The preservation of forest resources was also prioritized. The UN sponsored a range of initiatives to improve forest management and promote reforestation. UNDP support for the Brazilian National Forestry Program helped establish sustainable forestry practices that were adapted to the specific ecological conditions of different forest systems.[43] UNEP also supported a multi-country effort to promote the sustainable development of the Amazon Basin. Working with the governments of Bolivia, Brazil, Colombia, Ecuador, Guyana, Peru, Suriname, and Venezuela, UNEP helped identify damaged ecosystems and implement measures for regeneration. UNDP also supported forest conservation projects in Mexico's Tehuantepec Moist Forest, Pacific Dry Tropical Forests, and Sierra Madre del Sur Pine-Oak Forest. Each forest provides a habitat for native fauna, acts as a carbon reservoir, and protects local watersheds. In Trinidad and Tobago, UNDP supported the National Parks and Protected Areas Project and helped revive the Civilian Conservation Corp to aid reforestation.[44] Assistance to Costa Rica and Honduras helped integrate sustainable forest management principles into existing efforts to protect water resources and preserve biodiversity.[45]

PUBLIC POLICY REFORM

The United Nations also worked to improve public sector capacity to foster sustainable development. These efforts typically began with an assessment of environmental conditions. The assessments provided Latin American governments with comprehensive descriptions of the major threats to natural resources and ecosystems. In fact, environmental assessments are now part of the Common Country Assessments (CCA) used to coordinate assistance to individual countries.[46] In Colombia, UNEP developed the National Capacity Needs Self-Assessment (NCSA) to identify threats to water, land, and forest resources. UNEP also aided Caribbean governments evaluate how population trends impact marine environments. Focus was placed on the interaction between the principal ecosystems of the region to determine the potential long-term costs of population growth. As noted in Chapter 6, UNFPA assisted a number of governments with assessment of population trends. These assessments produced databases on the interrelationship between population growth and environmental conditions.

UNDP also played a lead role in strengthening public sector capacity to promote sustainable development. Emphasis was placed on ensuring sustainability issues were incorporated into national economic and social planning. In Panama, UNDP helped develop and implement the National Environmental Strategy that was credited with reducing air, water, and soil pollution, increasing energy efficiency, and conserving protected zones.[47] UNDP contributed to the design of Mexico's "Green Plan" that introduced sustainable development planning procedures to government ministries. Support was also extended to the National Commission on Biosafety and Genetically Modified Organisms. In the Caribbean, UNDP strengthened administrative capacity to incorporate environmental and natural resources dimensions into socioeconomic development programs. Technical assistance and equipment was extended to the government of Paraguay to strengthen the Secretariat on the Environment.[48] Focus was placed on developing renewable energy sources, preventing soil erosion, and preserving biological diversity. In Haiti, UNDP improved the planning, coordination, and monitoring capacities of the Ministry of the Environment and the Ministry of the Interior.[49] This assistance led to development of a National Environmental Action Plan. In Argentina, UNDP helped incorporate environment and sustainability issues into national public policy. This involved strengthening the links between the environmental offices of the Ministry of Foreign Affairs, Ministry of Social Development, and the Administration of National Parks.[50] Assistance was extended to develop El Salvador's national strategy on biodiversity and to ensure effective implementation of a national environmental program.[51] UNDP helped mainstream environmental considerations in the formulation of public projects in Brazil and worked with national and local governments in Ecuador and Jamaica to introduce incentives for the conservation of natural resources.[52]

The UN also trained government officials in environmental planning and management. Such training was designed to broaden understanding of the importance of conserving natural resources and provide policy makers with the tools needed to incorporate environmental considerations into national development programs. Government officials were also trained on environmental law and multilateral environmental agreements.[53] UNDP's Sustainable Development and Human Settlements Division offered training programs to officials from environmental ministries. UNEP also established an Environmental Training Network for Latin America and the Caribbean to strengthen environmental education in the region.[54]

The UN also worked to improve environmental laws. Technical assistance was extended to strengthen existing legal frameworks and develop new regulations. UNEP assistance to Chile, Peru, and Suriname helped develop national legislation that meets multilateral environmental agreements. In Uruguay, UNDP aided the design of regulatory regimes in specific environmental areas, such as water resources, coastal zones, and unique ecosystems. In Brazil and Mexico, programme officials helped integrate international environmental commitments into national legislation.[55] UNDP also assisted most countries in the region prepare their national communications, as required by the *United Nations Framework Convention on Climate Change.* Under this convention, nations are required to provide data on sources of greenhouse gases, vulnerability to climate change, and prospective mitigation measures.

REGIONAL COOPERATION

The UN worked to promote cooperation among Latin American nations on environmental issues. UNEP serves as the secretariat for the Forum of Ministers of the Environment of Latin America and the Caribbean.[56] This forum, which helps coordinate environmental activities in the region, drafted the 2002 Latin American and Caribbean Initiative for Sustainable Development (ILAC) (see Appendix 6). This initiative, which constitutes the primary instrument for promoting sustainable development in the region, outlines a range of objectives, including increasing the use of renewable energy sources, improving the management of marine and coastal zones, increasing protected areas and forests, adopting regulatory frameworks for access to genetic resources, and implementing policies to reduce vulnerability to natural disasters.[57] UNEP also serves as the Technical Secretariat of the Environmental Commission of the Latin American Parliament (PARLATINO)

UN agencies also supported environmental initiatives in various subregions. In the Caribbean, UNEP assessed the major environmental threats and established a framework for regional cooperation. UNEP's Caribbean Environment Program (CEP) helped draft the *Convention for the Protection and Development of the Marine Environment of the Wider Caribbean Region.*[58] Programme officials also aided implementation of this convention through information exchange and environmental training.

UNEP also supported the efforts of regional and sub-regional networks to preserve coastal and marine areas. This included cooperative measures for the protection of endangered species and the harmonization of national policies for the management of wildlife, genetic resources, and natural habitats. It also included the strengthening of public sector capacities to develop or improve programs for water quality control in coastal areas. UNEP assisted Caribbean nations in the restoration of degraded coastal ecosystems, especially mangroves and coral reefs, as part of a broader environmental management plan.

Environmental cooperation in Central America was also prioritized.[59] UNDP's Programme of Sustainable Development Networks improved mechanisms for exchanging information on environmental issues among nations in the region. Programme officials worked with the Central American Bank for Economic Integration (CABEI) to reduce greenhouse gas emissions and promote renewable energy use in Belize, Costa Rica, El Salvador, Guatemala, Honduras, Nicaragua, and Panama. These efforts removed financial barriers that impeded the large-scale development of renewable energy projects in the region.[60] UNDP also supported indigenous communities in Central America that were engaged in integrated ecosystem management.[61]

UNDP also assisted the governments of Mexico and Central America in the design and implementation of the Meso-American Biological Corridor (MBC).[62] This corridor constitutes a common strategic framework for ensuring diverse habitats maintain their natural genetic dispersion.[63] UNEP also supported the Central American System of Protected Areas, the Central American Program for the Modernization of Environmental Management Systems, and the Meso-American Barrier Reef System Project.[64] In the Andean region, programme officials worked with leaders from the Andean Community to develop joint projects on biodiversity, climate change, and natural resource conservation. UNEP helped implement an Andean Biodiversity Strategy and supported the concerted efforts of Bolivia, Ecuador, and Peru to establish a regional biological corridor.

CONCLUSION

This chapter reviewed the environmental work of the UN in Latin America during the past decade. Particular emphasis was placed on reducing air pollution in the largest cities and promoting the use of renewable energies. The UN also supported programs to better protect freshwater and marine resources, expand land use planning, and improve forest management. Initiatives to improve public sector capacity included enhanced assessment of environmental conditions, the training of government officials in environmental management, and the strengthening of environmental laws and regulations. The UN also promoted regional cooperation to address common environmental threats, particularly among nations of the Caribbean, Central America, the Andes, and the Southern Cone.

UN initiatives advanced the cause of environmental conservation in Latin America. However, these initiatives have sometimes been compromised by weak oversight and monitoring. Part of the problem is simply the relative weakness of UNEP. Given limitations with respect to personnel and resources, the programme is not always able to closely monitor the performance of sponsored activities. A lack of support from local governments has also limited the impact of environmental initiatives. Because public sector actors typically operate with much shorter time horizons, environmental issues are generally not prioritized. Governments also feel fewer domestic pressures with respect to environmental issues. Although some environmental NGOs have emerged in recent years, overall environmental consciousness is fairly low among the general public. More immediate concerns typically outweigh the need to protect natural resources and ecosystems.

Environmental conservation and the sustainable use of natural resources are critical for the long-term development of Latin America. Societies depend on a well-functioning natural environment. When the environment is preserved and protected, each nation can more effectively use its resources to meet human needs. There are also fewer health problems among the general public. A well-preserved environment raises the attendance and performance of children in school and the capacity and productivity of adults in the workplace while reducing the destructive impact of natural disasters.

9   Aiding Development in the Americas

Latin American nations face enormous challenges. Most people in the region lack access to clean water, adequate nutrition, basic health care, and decent education. Poverty levels are especially high for women who continue to earn less income and have fewer productive resources than men. The region is also grappling with severe environmental problems as air and water pollution worsens each year, fragile soils are further degraded, and tropical rainforests are cleared at an accelerating pace.

The developmental imperative in Latin America is formidable: improving conditions for poor communities while simultaneously preserving natural resources and ecosystems. Meeting this challenge will largely depend on the people of the region. As I stressed in the introductory chapter, and reiterated throughout this book, economic, social, and environmental progress depends on the energy, skills, and determination of committed individuals within each nation. *Sustainable development is only possible if it is internally conceived and directed.* At the same time, domestic resources are not sufficient to achieve the broad-based change needed and there continues to be a role for external assistance. Such assistance can support and complement national efforts.

This book reviewed United Nations efforts to aid development in Latin America during the early years of the twenty-first century. Focus was placed on the work of five subsidiary agencies: the United Nations Development Programme, World Food Programme, United Nations Children's Fund, United Nations Populations Fund, and United Nations Environmental Programme. The work of these agencies was described in three areas critical for sustainable development: meeting basic human needs, promoting gender equity, and preserving natural environments.

This chapter considers the prospects for accelerating development in Latin America. It begins with a series of recommendations for meeting basic needs, improving women's lives, and protecting environments. I then consider various ways to strengthen the economic, social, and environmental work of the UN. The last section outlines the type of partnerships the UN must forge, both with governments and nongovernmental groups, to advance Latin American development in the years to come.

MEETING BASIC HUMAN NEEDS

Meeting basic human needs is critically important for the future of Latin America. Investments in nutrition, health care, and education create the foundation for genuine, equitable, and sustainable development. Expanding access to safe drinking water requires public investments in water purification and delivery systems, especially in poor urban neighborhoods and the countryside. Nutrition monitoring systems should be established to identify areas at risk in terms of malnutrition before its levels become critical. Special attention should be accorded the needs of children, pregnant and nursing women, the elderly, and other vulnerable groups. Women should be encouraged to breastfeed infants exclusively for at least six months and school meals, fortified with vitamin A, iodine, and iron, should be expanded. The provision of meals in schools not only enhances the nutritional status of children but improves school attendance and performance. Food-for-Work programs, that raise nutritional levels for the poor while simultaneously contributing to broader community improvements, should also be prioritized. When possible, food assistance should be procured locally as a means of aiding domestic farmers. Food production can be increased through expanded access to land, sustainable farming methods, high-yield seeds, and improved irrigation systems.

Ensuring access to affordable and quality health care is also imperative. This will require strengthening the institutional capabilities of public health systems and emphasizing preventative over curative care. Public spending could thus be directed away from expensive interventions toward more cost-effective health services. The construction and staffing of basic clinics, especially in remote areas, will also be necessary. Improving the management of public health expenditures will require enhanced mechanisms for assessing the health status of the general public, developing policies to address the most pressing needs, and assuring these policies are effectively implemented.

Universal vaccination against the most common childhood diseases should be prioritized. Immunizations are the most effective way of reducing the spread of infectious diseases. Carefully targeted provision of oral rehydration packets and vitamin A capsules would reduce infant mortality and child malnutrition. Expanding school-based health services would help reach children in poor communities who have the greatest needs yet the least access to regular care.

Improved health care will also require expanding health education. The general public must be well-informed on health issues, including the importance of regular physical examinations and the best methods for preventing the spread of infectious diseases. Education on sexually transmitted diseases, especially HIV/AIDS, should be included in middle and high school curriculums. Local media could also be utilized to communicate health information to the public.

Education systems should also be strengthened. This will require expanding access to public education and improving the quality of instruction with emphasis placed on reaching those communities with low enrollment rates. New initiatives could be established to encourage low income parents to enroll their children in school. School meal programs have been particularly effective in this respect. Incentives could also be developed to increase secondary school completion rates. Income transfers to poor households, for example, could be made contingent on school attendance. Greater parental and community involvement would enhance the performance and accountability of schools.

Special attention should be placed on recruiting high quality teachers. Improving salaries would lower the turnover rate, attract younger people to the profession, and enhance the morale, commitment, and professional status of teachers. Training programs are needed to ensure teachers are aware of, and have access to, the newest curricula, instructional materials, and methods for motivating young children and adolescents. Literacy programs for those adults who were unable to complete formal schooling are also needed.

Clearly meeting basic human needs is an essential prerequisite for sustainable development. In developing nutrition, health, and education programs, special efforts should be made to reach minority groups. Indigenous and Afro-Latino communities are among the poorest segments of the population and have historically benefitted the least from public sector programs. The appointment of minority nutritionists, health care providers, and teachers who have knowledge of local languages, customs, and cultures is critical. Minority perspectives should also be incorporated into the design of public services.

PROMOTING GENDER EQUITY

The continued development of Latin America will also require greater gender equity. Gender issues should be mainstreamed into the policy-making process, with all public sector activities evaluated on the basis of their differential impacts on women and men. Program indicators should be made gender-sensitive and gender-disaggregated databases should be a standard part of the assessment process. Gender-responsive budget analysis should be adopted to ensure women and men fare equally in the allocation of public resources.

It will be important to ensure that women have access to safe and affordable health care. This includes regular screening for breast and cervical cancer as well as the prevention, diagnosis, and treatment of sexually transmitted diseases. Adolescents should receive comprehensive sexuality education and women should have access to reproductive health care, including family planning and prenatal care. Safe childbirth involves skilled birth attendants and access to emergency obstetric care. Postpartum care to facilitate recovery from pregnancy and childbirth should be widely available. Special attention should be placed on expanding reproductive health services in remote, rural, and underserved areas.

New initiatives are also needed to ensure women enjoy the same rights and opportunities as men in the labor force. This includes training and vocational programs that strengthen women's entrepreneurial skills and capacity. Women should have greater access to productive assets, including land, capital, credit, and technology. Microcredit programs, which have an impressive record of empowering women and reducing family poverty, should be expanded in those areas where income generating opportunities for women are limited. Legal and regulatory frameworks should be altered to ensure women have the same employment and property rights as men. Informing women of their legal rights would reduce the potential for gender-based discrimination or mistreatment.

PRESERVING NATURAL ENVIRONMENTS

Preserving and protecting natural environments will also be essential for the long-term development of Latin America. Environmental issues should be mainstreamed into public sector activities and government officials trained in the sustainable management of natural resources. Environmental impact assessments should be included in project design and environmental monitoring undertaken throughout project implementation. Global information systems can be used to monitor changes in pollution levels, land use, and resource availability and regional monitoring programs employed to measure environmental threats that cross national borders. Tax systems can be structured to encourage environmentally safe consumption and production patterns and governments should play a proactive role in educating the public on environmental issues.

Reducing air pollution remains among the most pressing challenges for Latin American nations. To lessen fossil fuel consumption, governments will need to invest in clean, affordable, renewable, and locally available energy sources, such as solar, wind, geothermal, hydrogen, biofuel, and biomass energy. Greater availability of environmentally safe technologies such as fuel-efficient cooking stoves, water pumps, and solar generators would reduce the combustion of fossil fuels and other environmentally hazardous practices. Investments in public transportation would reduce air pollution and congestion in the major metropolitan areas.

Protecting water resources is also critically important. Investments should be made in technologies that enhance water management. This will necessitate modernizing and upgrading sewage and sanitation systems in urban areas. More consistent enforcement of environmental regulations would reduce the discharge of pollutants into watershed, freshwater, and marine resources. Governments should establish restoration zones in areas where river basins are prone to erosion and enhance protections of coastal ecosystems.

Improved land use planning should also be prioritized. This will require new measures to decrease erosion, salinization, and other forms of soil degradation. Environmentally safe agricultural methods, such as terracing hillsides, rotating crops, planting trees, and other traditional soil conservation practices, should be introduced to help replenish soils. Governments throughout the region will need to enhance systems for managing hazardous and other solid wastes.

Reversing deforestation should also be a top priority. Improved forest conservation and management will require sustainable practices adapted to the specific needs of different forest systems. This will necessitate expanding both protected areas and reforestation programs. Protection of the rainforest is closely tied to the goal of preserving biodiversity. Biodiversity conservation principles should be mainstreamed into the policy-making process.

As noted in chapter 7, the external debts of many Latin American nations contribute to environmental decline. Governments exploit their natural resources as a means of generating the foreign exchange needed to service their debts. It will be important to expand multinational mechanisms for restructuring and reducing these debts. The Heavily-Indebted Poor Countries (HIPC) initiative of the World Bank and International Monetary Fund is one such mechanism. Since HIPC was introduced, Bolivia, Guyana, Honduras, and Nicaragua have qualified for debt relief.[1] Such programs should be expanded to include other low and middle income countries with unsustainable debt burdens. Debt-for-nature swaps are also a promising option. Under these schemes, an international environmental group purchases a portion of a country's foreign debt at a discount. The debt is then sold back to the government in exchange for investments in the local environment, such as water management, soil conservation, reforestation, or biodiversity protection projects. This has the effect of simultaneously reducing external debts while preserving natural environments.[2]

Meeting basic human needs, improving women's lives, and protecting natural environments are essential for the continued development of Latin America in the twenty-first century. All three of these goals are interrelated as progress achieved in one area facilitates progress in other areas. Meeting basic needs, for example, helps combat gender inequalities, since women typically have less access than men to adequate nutrition and health care. Meeting basic needs also has a positive impact on natural environments. Because poverty engenders environmentally destructive practices, improving conditions for poor communities reduces pressures on natural resources and fragile ecosystems.

Reducing gender inequalities helps meet the basic needs of all people. Poor women are less able to provide for themselves and their children. As income levels increase, women are in a better position to meet their needs and the needs of their families. Natural environments also benefit from policies designed to combat patriarchy. For a variety of reasons, poor women generally have higher fertility rates. As women's educational and income levels improve they typically choose to have fewer children over the course of their reproductive years. Lower population growth reduces pressures on natural resources and ecosystems.

Lastly, preserving the environment helps meet basic human needs. Polluted environments contribute to a range of illnesses, especially in poor communities. As people gain access to clean water for drinking and washing, they are less susceptible to waterborne diseases. Similarly, as urban air quality improves, respiratory problems diminish. Preserving the environment also enhances the lives of women. Since women have higher poverty rates, they are more likely to suffer from polluted environments. As environmental conditions improve, the health and well-being of women also improve.

UNITED NATIONS REFORM

The preceding sections outlined an ambitious agenda for meeting basic needs, promoting gender equity, and protecting natural environments in Latin America. While the United Nations has contributed to progress in each of these areas, its effectiveness has sometimes been limited. To enhance the efficacy of UN efforts, a number of structural and policy weaknesses should be addressed.[3] It will be especially important to strengthen the subsidiary agencies, improve oversight and monitoring, and enhance interagency coordination.

Clearly the subsidiary agencies of the UN could be strengthened. These agencies operate with highly restricted budgets and their programs are rarely fully funded. Increasing the resources available to subsidiary agencies would enhance overall effectiveness. This could be achieved through the allocation of a greater share of the overall UN budget. These agencies could also develop more independent sources of revenue. At present, they are limited in raising their own resources and remain largely dependent upon the voluntary contributions of member states. A greater proportion of resources could come from private sources. While this would help alleviate budgetary shortfalls, it would be important to ensure outside donors do not exercise undue influence over the policies or programs of these agencies.

In fact, the subsidiary agencies should be able to exercise *greater* control over their agendas. The UN could structure its relationship with these agencies to more closely approximate its relationship with the specialized agencies. This would allow the funds and programs to select activities on the basis of their own resources and capabilities rather than simply responding to the mandates of the General Assembly or the Economic and Social

Council. Enhanced institutional and policy autonomy would also allow these agencies to more carefully structure their work to meet the specific needs of individual countries.

UN agencies could also strengthen oversight of their development projects.[4] Projects sometimes start out strong but decline over time and shortcomings are generally not detected until the project is seriously compromised. This is due, at least in part, to the tendency to focus on new projects rather than ensure the continued performance of existing projects. More effective auditing and monitoring procedures are needed to ensure progress is being made toward achieving desired outcomes.[5]

Improved coordination among UN agencies would also enhance the overall effectiveness of their work in Latin America.[6] *There are more than 30 funds, programs, and other institutions that are engaged in development activities.* Reducing the overlap of activities will necessitate merging or phasing out some of these agencies. It will also be important to more effectively share information, expertise, and resources among the different institutions. Joint programming and the use of common databases would help pool resources among agencies.

Poor coordination within the UN cannot be attributed to a lack of effort. A number of committees have been set up over the years with the express purpose of enhancing coordination. The Chief Executives Board for Coordination (CEB), which is composed of the directors of all of the major subsidiary and specialized agencies, is the principal coordinating mechanism within the UN. Chaired by the Secretary-General, CEB holds two sessions each year to share information and better coordinate sponsored activities.[7] Moreover, the United Nations Development Group (UNDG) was established to help all of the institutions engaged in development improve information sharing, strategic planning, and collaboration.[8] The Department of Economic and Social Affairs within the Secretariat has a Division of ECOSOC Support and Coordination that is also designed to aid coordination among the various subsidiary bodies. Moreover, an Executive Committee of Economic and Social Affairs (ECESA) was established under the Secretariat to coordinate the work of UN agencies. Through thematic clusters in areas such as trade, technology, finance, population, gender, the environment, and human settlements, ECESA is charged with facilitating joint strategic planning and program implementation.

In 2006 Secretary-General Kofi Annan established a High-level Panel on United Nations System-Wide Coherence in the areas of development, humanitarian assistance, and the environment. The panel's final report *Delivering as One* argued that the UN could improve its development operations if different institutions worked with one another in a more coherent manner.[9] A framework for unified operations was proposed that consolidated most country activities under one office, one country team leader, one budgetary framework, and one strategic program.

The UN has sought to coordinate its work in specific Latin American countries. Representatives of both UN agencies and local governments meet annually to establish a United Nations Development Assistance Framework (UNDAF). UNDAF is designed to harmonize the program cycles of different funds and programs. Country Strategy Notes also establish specific development priorities for each nation.[10] The various subsidiary agencies prepare Common Country Assessments (CCA) that identify the central challenges facing individual countries. The UNDP Resident Coordinator is responsible for coordinating all UN-sponsored development activities within each country.

ECOSOC has the greatest responsibility of coordinating the work of the various subsidiary and specialized agencies.[11] However, the council has often been unable to fully meet this responsibility. This is due, at least in part, to the relative weakness of ECOSOC itself. Given its limited authority with respect to the specialized agencies, the council is hardly in a position to coordinate their activities. Although ECOSOC has greater authority over the subsidiary funds and programs, coordination has also been difficult to achieve.

Strengthening ECOSOC would enhance the effectiveness of UN development activities.[12] The council would be in a stronger position to gain member country support for its initiatives and to advocate for economic, social, and environmental change. At present ECOSOC is under the authority of the General Assembly and has little decision-making autonomy. If ECOSOC was accorded the same institutional status as the Security Council, the UN would have two coequal branches, one focusing on political and security issues and the other focusing on economic, social, and environmental issues. It would be important to ensure ECOSOC remains more representative of UN member countries than is presently the case with the Security Council.

DOMESTIC PARTNERS

The United Nations will also need to strengthen relationships with both governments and nongovernmental organizations in Latin America. The success of international assistance depends, to a considerable extent, on local participation and stakeholder ownership. Both state actors and community groups should be engaged in project design, implementation, and evaluation.

It will be important to work with governments that are genuinely committed to economic and social progress. Public sector expenditures should be evaluated to determine the extent to which resources are directed toward meeting human needs. Resources should be channeled toward the poorest sectors of society, with special attention paid to the needs of ethnic minorities. In most cases, this will necessitate increased public expenditures in nutrition, health care, and education. Greater resource allocations in these areas would likely require adjustments in other budgetary areas. Since Latin American governments allocate a disproportionate amount of public resources to military and security forces, this is one area where reductions could be made. Public spending on human needs would lay a stronger foundation for long-term national development.

Governments will also need to address maldistributions of income and wealth. As noted in chapter 3, Latin America has the greatest inequalities of any region in the world. Economic growth in itself is not sufficient to ensure higher living standards. Rather, such growth must be broad-based and inclusive, expanding the income and productivity of poor communities. Even small reductions in inequality typically produce significant reductions in poverty.[13] However, this will require wider access to productive resources. The poor distribution of land is the single greatest cause of inequality in the region. Comprehensive land reform, especially in Central America and the Andean nations, is needed. Peasant farmers must also be granted greater access to the credit, training, and tools needed to enhance their operations. Progressive tax policies would also reduce inequalities. The increased revenues obtained through tax reform could be used to improve economic opportunities for the poor. At present, few countries have adopted genuinely redistributive tax policies.[14]

Latin American governments must also address gender inequalities. Public resources should be directed toward meeting the needs of women. Women must have access to affordable and safe health and reproductive care, including family planning services. Governments must also demonstrate a commitment to literacy and training programs that expand income and employment opportunities for women. Laws that discriminate against women should be revoked and new legislation that defends the rights of women should be adopted and enforced.

Latin American governments must also be committed to protecting their natural environments. Public resources should be directed toward reducing air pollution, preserving water resources, improving land management, and protecting forest resources. New private sector regulations, that internalize environmental costs, should be adopted. Governments must demonstrate a willingness to strengthen the agencies responsible for enforcing environmental laws and support regional environmental projects.

Lastly, Latin American leaders must be committed to good governance. As noted in the introductory chapter, sustainable development depends, to a considerable extent, on the quality of governance at home. Genuine development, which improves living conditions for poor communities, is unlikely without effective, inclusive, and impartial political institutions. It will be important to ensure public resources reach their intended beneficiaries. This necessitates civil service reform, improved budgeting, enhanced financial oversight, and stronger judicial systems.

The UN should also expand its partnerships with NGOs in Latin America. The UN has traditionally recognized the importance of working with civil society groups.[15] Its charter calls on ECOSOC to "make suitable arrangements for consultation with nongovernmental organizations."[16] Moreover, a nongovernmental liaison service was established to foster cooperation between the UN and NGOs on sustainable development issues and an interdepartmental working group on civil society meets regularly under the chairmanship of the Under Secretary-General for Political Affairs.[17] In 2003 Secretary-General Kofi Annan formed a panel to examine the relationship between the UN and civil society groups. The panel's 2004 report advanced a series of recommendations for improving relations with civil society.[18] The Outcome Document of the 2005 World Summit called for enhancing the participation of NGOs in the development process.[19] The United Nations Development Group also formed a working group on civil society to enhance the capacity of Resident Coordinators to engage nongovernmental groups at the country level.

Some of the subsidiary agencies have relatively strong records of working with NGOs. UNDP has a Civil Society Organizations Division and a Civil Society Advisory Committee that share responsibility for ensuring community groups are involved in all sponsored activities. Moreover, its Partners in Development Program provides direct assistance to community-based self-help initiatives. UNFPA involves civil society groups in the monitoring of reproductive health services and WFP includes community groups in the planning, management, and implementation of food assistance activities.[20] The Civil Society and NGOs Unit of UNEP was established to increase grassroots participation in environmental projects and research programs.

At the same time, UN agencies have not always maintained strong ties with societal groups.[21] Because these agencies operate at the request of host governments, and are required to work mainly through these governments, the nongovernmental sector is often underrepresented. Improving the involvement and participation of NGOs would enhance the effectiveness of development projects and programs. Although community groups have limited resources, they are remarkably successful in promoting grassroots development. In fact, NGOs typically operate with a better understanding of local needs and conditions, and are in a better position to reach intended beneficiaries, than governments. Over time it has become increasingly evident that projects that involve local communities have *higher* success rates and are *more* likely to continue after UN participation ends.[22]

Including civil society groups helps remove the economic, social, and political barriers that prevent people from achieving their full potential. As noted in the introductory chapter, capacity development is central to the development process: *poor people must be able to exercise greater control over their lives and the ability to direct the development process.* This will create more self-reliant communities that have the resources and skills necessary to meet their own needs on a long-term basis.

AIDING DEVELOPMENT

The challenge of development in Latin America is formidable. This book focused on three of the most pressing needs in the region: meeting basic human needs, ensuring gender equity, and protecting natural environments. Despite limited resources, the United Nations has played an important role in meeting these needs. While this may diverge from common perceptions of the UN, since institutional weaknesses, financial misdeeds, and failed projects receive much greater attention than every day achievements, it is reflected in the review presented in this volume.

Highlighting the significant and expanding influence of the UN in Latin America challenges traditional views of international affairs. Scholars in this field typically attribute global outcomes to sovereign nation-states pursuing unitary national interests in an anarchical system. Yet the world of the twenty-first century increasingly diverges from this image. We live in an era of declining sovereignty for nations and rising influence for international institutions.

Contrary to popular belief, this new world order does not constitute a threat to human freedom or progress. In fact, *political integration is necessary for both freedom and progress*. Because the most serious problems we face are transnational in nature, their effective resolution increasingly necessitates collective action by the community of nations. International institutions, most notably the UN, encourage and facilitate such collective action. The future progress of Latin America, and the wider world, requires a continued transition toward global governance.

Appendix 1
Universal Declaration of Human Rights

Adopted by General Assembly Resolution 217 A (III) of December 10, 1948

PREAMBLE

1.
Whereas recognition of the inherent dignity and of the equal and inalienable rights of all members of the human family is the foundation of freedom, justice and peace in the world,

Whereas disregard and contempt for human rights have resulted in barbarous acts which have outraged the conscience of mankind, and the advent of a world in which human beings shall enjoy freedom of speech and belief and freedom from fear and want has been proclaimed as the highest aspiration of the common people,

Whereas it is essential, if man is not to be compelled to have recourse, as a last resort, to rebellion against tyranny and oppression, that human rights should be protected by the rule of law,

Whereas it is essential to promote the development of friendly relations between nations,

Whereas the peoples of the United Nations have in the Charter reaffirmed their faith in fundamental human rights, in the dignity and worth of the human person and in the equal rights of men and women and have determined to promote social progress and better standards of life in larger freedom,

Whereas Member States have pledged themselves to achieve, in co-operation with the United Nations, the promotion of universal respect for and observance of human rights and fundamental freedoms,

Whereas a common understanding of these rights and freedoms is of the greatest importance for the full realization of this pledge,

Now, Therefore THE GENERAL ASSEMBLY proclaims THIS UNI-VERSAL DECLARATION OF HUMAN RIGHTS as a common standard of achievement for all peoples and all nations, to the end that every individual and every organ of society, keeping this Declaration constantly in mind, shall strive by teaching and education to promote respect for these rights and freedoms and by progressive measures, national and international, to secure their universal and effective recognition and observance, both among the peoples of Member States themselves and among the peoples of territories under their jurisdiction.

Article 1

All human beings are born free and equal in dignity and rights. They are endowed with reason and conscience and should act towards one another in a spirit of brotherhood.

Article 2

Everyone is entitled to all the rights and freedoms set forth in this Declaration, without distinction of any kind, such as race, colour, sex, language, religion, political or other opinion, national or social origin, property, birth or other status. Furthermore, no distinction shall be made on the basis of the political, jurisdictional or international status of the country or territory to which a person belongs, whether it be independent, trust, non-self-governing or under any other limitation of sovereignty.

Article 3

Everyone has the right to life, liberty and security of person.

Article 4

No one shall be held in slavery or servitude; slavery and the slave trade shall be prohibited in all their forms.

Article 5

No one shall be subjected to torture or to cruel, inhuman or degrading treatment or punishment.

Article 6

Everyone has the right to recognition everywhere as a person before the law.

Article 7

All are equal before the law and are entitled without any discrimination to equal protection of the law. All are entitled to equal protection against any discrimination in violation of this Declaration and against any incitement to such discrimination.

Article 8

Everyone has the right to an effective remedy by the competent national tribunals for acts violating the fundamental rights granted him by the constitution or by law.

Article 9

No one shall be subjected to arbitrary arrest, detention or exile.

Article 10

Everyone is entitled in full equality to a fair and public hearing by an independent and impartial tribunal, in the determination of his rights and obligations and of any criminal charge against him.

Article 11

(1) Everyone charged with a penal offence has the right to be presumed innocent until proved guilty according to law in a public trial at which he has had all the guarantees necessary for his defence.
(2) No one shall be held guilty of any penal offence on account of any act or omission which did not constitute a penal offence, under national or international law, at the time when it was committed. Nor shall a heavier penalty be imposed than the one that was applicable at the time the penal offence was committed.

Article 12

No one shall be subjected to arbitrary interference with his privacy, family, home or correspondence, nor to attacks upon his honour and reputation. Everyone has the right to the protection of the law against such interference or attacks.

Article 13

(1) Everyone has the right to freedom of movement and residence within the borders of each state.

(2) Everyone has the right to leave any country, including his own, and to return to his country.

Article 14

(1) Everyone has the right to seek and to enjoy in other countries asylum from persecution.
(2) This right may not be invoked in the case of prosecutions genuinely arising from non-political crimes or from acts contrary to the purposes and principles of the United Nations.

Article 15

(1) Everyone has the right to a nationality.
(2) No one shall be arbitrarily deprived of his nationality nor denied the right to change his nationality.

Article 16

(1) Men and women of full age, without any limitation due to race, nationality or religion, have the right to marry and to found a family. They are entitled to equal rights as to marriage, during marriage and at its dissolution.
(2) Marriage shall be entered into only with the free and full consent of the intending spouses.
(3) The family is the natural and fundamental group unit of society and is entitled to protection by society and the State.

Article 17

(1) Everyone has the right to own property alone as well as in association with others.
(2) No one shall be arbitrarily deprived of his property.

Article 18

Everyone has the right to freedom of thought, conscience and religion; this right includes freedom to change his religion or belief, and freedom, either alone or in community with others and in public or private, to manifest his religion or belief in teaching, practice, worship and observance.

Article 19

Everyone has the right to freedom of opinion and expression; this right includes freedom to hold opinions without interference and to seek, receive and impart information and ideas through any media and regardless of frontiers.

Article 20

(1) Everyone has the right to freedom of peaceful assembly and association.
(2) No one may be compelled to belong to an association.

Article 21

(1) Everyone has the right to take part in the government of his country, directly or through freely chosen representatives.
(2) Everyone has the right of equal access to public service in his country.
(3) The will of the people shall be the basis of the authority of government; this will shall be expressed in periodic and genuine elections which shall be by universal and equal suffrage and shall be held by secret vote or by equivalent free voting procedures.

Article 22

Everyone, as a member of society, has the right to social security and is entitled to realization, through national effort and international co-operation and in accordance with the organization and resources of each State, of the economic, social and cultural rights indispensable for his dignity and the free development of his personality.

Article 23

(1) Everyone has the right to work, to free choice of employment, to just and favourable conditions of work and to protection against unemployment.
(2) Everyone, without any discrimination, has the right to equal pay for equal work.
(3) Everyone who works has the right to just and favourable remuneration ensuring for himself and his family an existence worthy of human dignity, and supplemented, if necessary, by other means of social protection.
(4) Everyone has the right to form and to join trade unions for the protection of his interests.

Article 24

Everyone has the right to rest and leisure, including reasonable limitation of working hours and periodic holidays with pay.

Article 25

(1) Everyone has the right to a standard of living adequate for the health and well-being of himself and of his family, including food, clothing, housing and medical care and necessary social services, and the right to security in the event of unemployment, sickness, disability, widowhood, old age or other lack of livelihood in circumstances beyond his control.

(2) Motherhood and childhood are entitled to special care and assistance. All children, whether born in or out of wedlock, shall enjoy the same social protection.

Article 26

(1) Everyone has the right to education. Education shall be free, at least in the elementary and fundamental stages. Elementary education shall be compulsory. Technical and professional education shall be made generally available and higher education shall be equally accessible to all on the basis of merit.

(2) Education shall be directed to the full development of the human personality and to the strengthening of respect for human rights and fundamental freedoms. It shall promote understanding, tolerance and friendship among all nations, racial or religious groups, and shall further the activities of the United Nations for the maintenance of peace.

(3) Parents have a prior right to choose the kind of education that shall be given to their children.

Article 27

(1) Everyone has the right freely to participate in the cultural life of the community, to enjoy the arts and to share in scientific advancement and its benefits.

(2) Everyone has the right to the protection of the moral and material interests resulting from any scientific, literary or artistic production of which he is the author.

Article 28

Everyone is entitled to a social and international order in which the rights and freedoms set forth in this Declaration can be fully realized.

Article 29

(1) Everyone has duties to the community in which alone the free and full development of his personality is possible.

(2) In the exercise of his rights and freedoms, everyone shall be subject only

to such limitations as are determined by law solely for the purpose of securing due recognition and respect for the rights and freedoms of others and of meeting the just requirements of morality, public order and the general welfare in a democratic society.

(3) These rights and freedoms may in no case be exercised contrary to the purposes and principles of the United Nations.

Article 30

Nothing in this Declaration may be interpreted as implying for any State, group or person any right to engage in any activity or to perform any act aimed at the destruction of any of the rights and freedoms set forth herein.

Appendix 2

International Covenant on Economic, Social and Cultural Rights

Adopted by General Assembly Resolution 2200A (XXI), December 16, 1966.

PREAMBLE

The States Parties to the present Covenant,

Considering that, in accordance with the principles proclaimed in the Charter of the United Nations, recognition of the inherent dignity and of the equal and inalienable rights of all members of the human family is the foundation of freedom, justice and peace in the world,

Recognizing that these rights derive from the inherent dignity of the human person,

Recognizing that, in accordance with the Universal Declaration of Human Rights, the ideal of free human beings enjoying freedom from fear and want can only be achieved if conditions are created whereby everyone may enjoy his economic, social and cultural rights, as well as his civil and political rights,

Considering the obligation of States under the Charter of the United Nations to promote universal respect for, and observance of, human rights and freedoms,

Realizing that the individual, having duties to other individuals and to the community to which he belongs, is under a responsibility to strive for the promotion and observance of the rights recognized in the present Covenant,

Agree upon the following articles:

PART I

Article 1

1. All peoples have the right of self-determination. By virtue of that right they freely determine their political status and freely pursue their economic, social and cultural development.

2. All peoples may, for their own ends, freely dispose of their natural wealth and resources without prejudice to any obligations arising out of international economic co-operation, based upon the principle of mutual

benefit, and international law. In no case may a people be deprived of its own means of subsistence.

3. The States Parties to the present Covenant, including those having responsibility for the administration of Non-Self-Governing and Trust Territories, shall promote the realization of the right of self-determination, and shall respect that right, in conformity with the provisions of the Charter of the United Nations.

PART II

Article 2

1. Each State Party to the present Covenant undertakes to take steps, individually and through international assistance and co-operation, especially economic and technical, to the maximum of its available resources, with a view to achieving progressively the full realization of the rights recognized in the present Covenant by all appropriate means, including particularly the adoption of legislative measures.

2. The States Parties to the present Covenant undertake to guarantee that the rights enunciated in the present Covenant will be exercised without discrimination of any kind as to race, colour, sex, language, religion, political or other opinion, national or social origin, property, birth or other status.

3. Developing countries, with due regard to human rights and their national economy, may determine to what extent they would guarantee the economic rights recognized in the present Covenant to non-nationals.

Article 3

The States Parties to the present Covenant undertake to ensure the equal right of men and women to the enjoyment of all economic, social and cultural rights set forth in the present Covenant.

Article 4

The States Parties to the present Covenant recognize that, in the enjoyment of those rights provided by the State in conformity with the present Covenant, the State may subject such rights only to such limitations as are determined by law only in so far as this may be compatible with the nature of these rights and solely for the purpose of promoting the general welfare in a democratic society.

Article 5

1. Nothing in the present Covenant may be interpreted as implying for any State, group or person any right to engage in any activity or to perform any act aimed at the destruction of any of the rights or freedoms recognized herein, or at their limitation to a greater extent than is provided for in the present Covenant.

2. No restriction upon or derogation from any of the fundamental human rights recognized or existing in any country in virtue of law, conventions, regulations or custom shall be admitted on the pretext that the present Covenant does not recognize such rights or that it recognizes them to a lesser extent.

PART III

Article 6

1. The States Parties to the present Covenant recognize the right to work, which includes the right of everyone to the opportunity to gain his living by work which he freely chooses or accepts, and will take appropriate steps to safeguard this right.

2. The steps to be taken by a State Party to the present Covenant to achieve the full realization of this right shall include technical and vocational guidance and training programmes, policies and techniques to achieve steady economic, social and cultural development and full and productive employment under conditions safeguarding fundamental political and economic freedoms to the individual.

Article 7

The States Parties to the present Covenant recognize the right of everyone to the enjoyment of just and favourable conditions of work which ensure, in particular:

(a) Remuneration which provides all workers, as a minimum, with:

    (i) Fair wages and equal remuneration for work of equal value without distinction of any kind, in particular women being guaranteed conditions of work not inferior to those enjoyed by men, with equal pay for equal work;

    (ii) A decent living for themselves and their families in accordance with the provisions of the present Covenant;

(b) Safe and healthy working conditions;

(c) Equal opportunity for everyone to be promoted in his employment to an appropriate higher level, subject to no considerations other than those of seniority and competence;

(d) Rest, leisure and reasonable limitation of working hours and periodic holidays with pay, as well as remuneration for public holidays

Article 8

1. The States Parties to the present Covenant undertake to ensure:

(a) The right of everyone to form trade unions and join the trade union of his choice, subject only to the rules of the organization concerned, for the promotion and protection of his economic and social interests. No restrictions may be placed on the exercise of this right other than those prescribed by law and which are necessary in a democratic society in the interests of national security or public order or for the protection of the rights and freedoms of others;

(b) The right of trade unions to establish national federations or confederations and the right of the latter to form or join international trade-union organizations;

(c) The right of trade unions to function freely subject to no limitations other than those prescribed by law and which are necessary in a democratic society in the interests of national security or public order or for the protection of the rights and freedoms of others;

(d) The right to strike, provided that it is exercised in conformity with the laws of the particular country.

2. This article shall not prevent the imposition of lawful restrictions on the exercise of these rights by members of the armed forces or of the police or of the administration of the State.

3. Nothing in this article shall authorize States Parties to the International Labour Organisation Convention of 1948 concerning Freedom of Association and Protection of the Right to Organize to take legislative measures which would prejudice, or apply the law in such a manner as would prejudice, the guarantees provided for in that Convention.

Article 9

The States Parties to the present Covenant recognize the right of everyone to social security, including social insurance.

Article 10

The States Parties to the present Covenant recognize that:

1. The widest possible protection and assistance should be accorded to the family, which is the natural and fundamental group unit of society, particularly for its establishment and while it is responsible for the care and education of dependent children. Marriage must be entered into with the free consent of the intending spouses.

2. Special protection should be accorded to mothers during a reasonable period before and after childbirth. During such period working mothers should be accorded paid leave or leave with adequate social security benefits.

3. Special measures of protection and assistance should be taken on behalf of all children and young persons without any discrimination for reasons of parentage or other conditions. Children and young persons should be protected from economic and social exploitation. Their employment in work harmful to their morals or health or dangerous to life or likely to hamper their normal development should be punishable by law. States should also set age limits below which the paid employment of child labour should be prohibited and punishable by law.

Article 11

1. The States Parties to the present Covenant recognize the right of everyone to an adequate standard of living for himself and his family, including adequate food, clothing and housing, and to the continuous improvement of living conditions. The States Parties will take appropriate steps to ensure the realization of this right, recognizing to this effect the essential importance of international co-operation based on free consent.

2. The States Parties to the present Covenant, recognizing the fundamental right of everyone to be free from hunger, shall take, individually and through international co-operation, the measures, including specific programmes, which are needed:

(a) To improve methods of production, conservation and distribution of food by making full use of technical and scientific knowledge, by disseminating knowledge of the principles of nutrition and by developing or reforming agrarian systems in such a way as to achieve the most efficient development and utilization of natural resources;

(b) Taking into account the problems of both food-importing and food-exporting countries, to ensure an equitable distribution of world food supplies in relation to need.

Article 12

1. The States Parties to the present Covenant recognize the right of everyone to the enjoyment of the highest attainable standard of physical and mental health.

2. The steps to be taken by the States Parties to the present Covenant to achieve the full realization of this right shall include those necessary for:

(a) The provision for the reduction of the stillbirth-rate and of infant mortality and for the healthy development of the child;
(b) The improvement of all aspects of environmental and industrial hygiene;
(c) The prevention, treatment and control of epidemic, endemic, occupational and other diseases;
(d) The creation of conditions which would assure to all medical service and medical attention in the event of sickness.

Article 13

1. The States Parties to the present Covenant recognize the right of everyone to education. They agree that education shall be directed to the full development of the human personality and the sense of its dignity, and shall strengthen the respect for human rights and fundamental freedoms. They further agree that education shall enable all persons to participate effectively in a free society, promote understanding, tolerance and friendship among all nations and all racial, ethnic or religious groups, and further the activities of the United Nations for the maintenance of peace.

2. The States Parties to the present Covenant recognize that, with a view to achieving the full realization of this right:

(a) Primary education shall be compulsory and available free to all;
(b) Secondary education in its different forms, including technical and vocational secondary education, shall be made generally available and accessible to all by every appropriate means, and in particular by the progressive introduction of free education;
(c) Higher education shall be made equally accessible to all, on the basis of capacity, by every appropriate means, and in particular by the progressive introduction of free education;
(d) Fundamental education shall be encouraged or intensified as far as possible for those persons who have not received or completed the whole period of their primary education;
(e) The development of a system of schools at all levels shall be actively pursued, an adequate fellowship system shall be established, and the material conditions of teaching staff shall be continuously improved.

3. The States Parties to the present Covenant undertake to have respect for the liberty of parents and, when applicable, legal guardians to choose for their children schools, other than those established by the public authorities, which conform to such minimum educational standards as may be laid down or approved by the State and to ensure the religious and moral education of their children in conformity with their own convictions.

4. No part of this article shall be construed so as to interfere with the liberty of individuals and bodies to establish and direct educational institutions, subject always to the observance of the principles set forth in paragraph I of this article and to the requirement that the education given in such institutions shall conform to such minimum standards as may be laid down by the State.

Article 14

Each State Party to the present Covenant which, at the time of becoming a Party, has not been able to secure in its metropolitan territory or other territories under its jurisdiction compulsory primary education, free of charge, undertakes, within two years, to work out and adopt a detailed plan of action for the progressive implementation, within a reasonable number of years, to be fixed in the plan, of the principle of compulsory education free of charge for all.

Article 15

1. The States Parties to the present Covenant recognize the right of everyone:

    (a) To take part in cultural life;
    (b) To enjoy the benefits of scientific progress and its applications;
    (c) To benefit from the protection of the moral and material interests resulting from any scientific, literary or artistic production of which he is the author.

2. The steps to be taken by the States Parties to the present Covenant to achieve the full realization of this right shall include those necessary for the conservation, the development and the diffusion of science and culture.
3. The States Parties to the present Covenant undertake to respect the freedom indispensable for scientific research and creative activity.
4. The States Parties to the present Covenant recognize the benefits to be derived from the encouragement and development of international contacts and co-operation in the scientific and cultural fields.

PART IV

Article 16

1. The States Parties to the present Covenant undertake to submit in conformity with this part of the Covenant reports on the measures which they have adopted and the progress made in achieving the observance of the rights recognized herein.

2.

(a) All reports shall be submitted to the Secretary-General of the United Nations, who shall transmit copies to the Economic and Social Council for consideration in accordance with the provisions of the present Covenant;

(b) The Secretary-General of the United Nations shall also transmit to the specialized agencies copies of the reports, or any relevant parts therefrom, from States Parties to the present Covenant which are also members of these specialized agencies in so far as these reports, or parts therefrom, relate to any matters which fall within the responsibilities of the said agencies in accordance with their constitutional instruments.

Article 17

1. The States Parties to the present Covenant shall furnish their reports in stages, in accordance with a programme to be established by the Economic and Social Council within one year of the entry into force of the present Covenant after consultation with the States Parties and the specialized agencies concerned.

2. Reports may indicate factors and difficulties affecting the degree of fulfilment of obligations under the present Covenant.

3. Where relevant information has previously been furnished to the United Nations or to any specialized agency by any State Party to the present Covenant, it will not be necessary to reproduce that information, but a precise reference to the information so furnished will suffice.

Article 18

Pursuant to its responsibilities under the Charter of the United Nations in the field of human rights and fundamental freedoms, the Economic and Social Council may make arrangements with the specialized agencies in respect of their reporting to it on the progress made in achieving the observance of the provisions of the present Covenant falling within the scope of their activities. These reports may include particulars of decisions and recommendations on such implementation adopted by their competent organs.

Article 19

The Economic and Social Council may transmit to the Commission on Human Rights for study and general recommendation or, as appropriate, for information the reports concerning human rights submitted by States in accordance with articles 16 and 17, and those concerning human rights submitted by the specialized agencies in accordance with article 18.

Article 20

The States Parties to the present Covenant and the specialized agencies concerned may submit comments to the Economic and Social Council on any general recommendation under article 19 or reference to such general recommendation in any report of the Commission on Human Rights or any documentation referred to therein.

Article 21

The Economic and Social Council may submit from time to time to the General Assembly reports with recommendations of a general nature and a summary of the information received from the States Parties to the present Covenant and the specialized agencies on the measures taken and the progress made in achieving general observance of the rights recognized in the present Covenant.

Article 22

The Economic and Social Council may bring to the attention of other organs of the United Nations, their subsidiary organs and specialized agencies concerned with furnishing technical assistance any matters arising out of the reports referred to in this part of the present Covenant which may assist such bodies in deciding, each within its field of competence, on the advisability of international measures likely to contribute to the effective progressive implementation of the present Covenant.

Article 23

The States Parties to the present Covenant agree that international action for the achievement of the rights recognized in the present Covenant includes such methods as the conclusion of conventions, the adoption of recommendations, the furnishing of technical assistance and the holding of regional meetings and technical meetings for the purpose of consultation and study organized in conjunction with the Governments concerned.

Article 24

Nothing in the present Covenant shall be interpreted as impairing the provisions of the Charter of the United Nations and of the constitutions of the specialized agencies which define the respective responsibilities of the various organs of the United Nations and of the specialized agencies in regard to the matters dealt with in the present Covenant.

Article 25

Nothing in the present Covenant shall be interpreted as impairing the inherent right of all peoples to enjoy and utilize fully and freely their natural wealth and resources.

PART V

Article 26

1. The present Covenant is open for signature by any State Member of the United Nations or member of any of its specialized agencies, by any State Party to the Statute of the International Court of Justice, and by any other State which has been invited by the General Assembly of the United Nations to become a party to the present Covenant.

2. The present Covenant is subject to ratification. Instruments of ratification shall be deposited with the Secretary-General of the United Nations.

3. The present Covenant shall be open to accession by any State referred to in paragraph 1 of this article.

4. Accession shall be effected by the deposit of an instrument of accession with the Secretary-General of the United Nations.

5. The Secretary-General of the United Nations shall inform all States which have signed the present Covenant or acceded to it of the deposit of each instrument of ratification or accession.

Article 27

1. The present Covenant shall enter into force three months after the date of the deposit with the Secretary-General of the United Nations of the thirty-fifth instrument of ratification or instrument of accession.

2. For each State ratifying the present Covenant or acceding to it after the deposit of the thirty-fifth instrument of ratification or instrument of accession, the present Covenant shall enter into force three months after the date of the deposit of its own instrument of ratification or instrument of accession.

Article 28

The provisions of the present Covenant shall extend to all parts of federal States without any limitations or exceptions.

Article 29

1. Any State Party to the present Covenant may propose an amendment and file it with the Secretary-General of the United Nations. The Secretary-General shall thereupon communicate any proposed amendments to the States Parties to the present Covenant with a request that they notify him whether they favour a conference of States Parties for the purpose of considering and voting upon the proposals. In the event that at least one third of the States Parties favours such a conference, the Secretary-General shall convene the conference under the auspices of the United Nations. Any amendment adopted by a majority of the States Parties present and voting at the conference shall be submitted to the General Assembly of the United Nations for approval.

2. Amendments shall come into force when they have been approved by the General Assembly of the United Nations and accepted by a two-thirds majority of the States Parties to the present Covenant in accordance with their respective constitutional processes.

3. When amendments come into force they shall be binding on those States Parties which have accepted them, other States Parties still being bound by the provisions of the present Covenant and any earlier amendment which they have accepted.

Article 30

Irrespective of the notifications made under article 26, paragraph 5, the Secretary-General of the United Nations shall inform all States referred to in paragraph I of the same article of the following particulars:

(a) Signatures, ratifications and accessions under article 26;
(b) The date of the entry into force of the present Covenant under article 27 and the date of the entry into force of any amendments under article 29.

Article 31

1. The present Covenant, of which the Chinese, English, French, Russian and Spanish texts are equally authentic, shall be deposited in the archives of the United Nations.
2. The Secretary-General of the United Nations shall transmit certified copies of the present Covenant to all States referred to in article 26.

Appendix 3

Declaration on the Right to Development

Adopted by General Assembly resolution 41/128
of 4 December 1986

THE GENERAL ASSEMBLY

Bearing in mind the purposes and principles of the Charter of the United Nations relating to the achievement of international co-operation in solving international problems of an economic, social, cultural or humanitarian nature, and in promoting and encouraging respect for human rights and fundamental freedoms for all without distinction as to race, sex, language or religion,

Recognizing that development is a comprehensive economic, social, cultural and political process, which aims at the constant improvement of the well-being of the entire population and of all individuals on the basis of their active, free and meaningful participation in development and in the fair distribution of benefits resulting therefrom,

Considering that under the provisions of the Universal Declaration of Human Rights everyone is entitled to a social and international order in which the rights and freedoms set forth in that Declaration can be fully realized,

Recalling the provisions of the International Covenant on Economic, Social and Cultural Rights and of the International Covenant on Civil and Political Rights,

Recalling further the relevant agreements, conventions, resolutions, recommendations and other instruments of the United Nations and its specialized agencies concerning the integral development of the human being, economic and social progress and development of all peoples, including those instruments concerning decolonization, the prevention of discrimination, respect for and observance of, human rights and fundamental freedoms, the maintenance of international peace and security and the further promotion of friendly relations and co-operation among States in accordance with the Charter,

Recalling the right of peoples to self-determination, by virtue of which they have the right freely to determine their political status and to pursue their economic, social and cultural development,

Recalling also the right of peoples to exercise, subject to the relevant provisions of both International Covenants on Human Rights, full and complete sovereignty over all their natural wealth and resources,

Mindful of the obligation of States under the Charter to promote universal respect for and observance of human rights and fundamental freedoms for all without distinction of any kind such as race, colour, sex, language, religion, political or other opinion, national or social origin, property, birth or other status,

Considering that the elimination of the massive and flagrant violations of the human rights of the peoples and individuals affected by situations such as those resulting from colonialism, neo-colonialism, apartheid, all forms of racism and racial discrimination, foreign domination and occupation, aggression and threats against national sovereignty, national unity and territorial integrity and threats of war would contribute to the establishment of circumstances propitious to the development of a great part of mankind,

Concerned at the existence of serious obstacles to development, as well as to the complete fulfilment of human beings and of peoples, constituted, inter alia, by the denial of civil, political, economic, social and cultural rights, and considering that all human rights and fundamental freedoms are indivisible and interdependent and that, in order to promote development, equal attention and urgent consideration should be given to the implementation, promotion and protection of civil, political, economic, social and cultural rights and that, accordingly, the promotion of, respect for and enjoyment of certain human rights and fundamental freedoms cannot justify the denial of other human rights and fundamental freedoms,

Considering that international peace and security are essential elements for the realization of the right to development,

Reaffirming that there is a close relationship between disarmament and development and that progress in the field of disarmament would considerably promote progress in the field of development and that resources released through disarmament measures should be devoted to the economic and social development and well-being of all peoples and, in particular, those of the developing countries,

Recognizing that the human person is the central subject of the development process and that development policy should therefore make the human being the main participant and beneficiary of development,

Recognizing that the creation of conditions favourable to the development of peoples and individuals is the primary responsibility of their States,

Aware that efforts at the international level to promote and protect human rights should be accompanied by efforts to establish a new international economic order,

Confirming that the right to development is an inalienable human right and that equality of opportunity for development is a prerogative both of nations and of individuals who make up nations,

Proclaims the following Declaration on the Right to Development:

ARTICLE 1

1. The right to development is an inalienable human right by virtue of which every human person and all peoples are entitled to participate in, contribute to, and enjoy economic, social, cultural and political development, in which all human rights and fundamental freedoms can be fully realized.

2. The human right to development also implies the full realization of the right of peoples to self-determination, which includes, subject to the relevant provisions of both International Covenants on Human Rights, the exercise of their inalienable right to full sovereignty over all their natural wealth and resources.

ARTICLE 2

1. The human person is the central subject of development and should be the active participant and beneficiary of the right to development.

2. All human beings have a responsibility for development, individually and collectively, taking into account the need for full respect for their human rights and fundamental freedoms as well as their duties to the community, which alone can ensure the free and complete fulfilment of the human being, and they should therefore promote and protect an appropriate political, social and economic order for development.

3. States have the right and the duty to formulate appropriate national development policies that aim at the constant improvement of the well-being of the entire population and of all individuals, on the basis of their active, free and meaningful participation in development and in the fair distribution of the benefits resulting therefrom.

ARTICLE 3

1. States have the primary responsibility for the creation of national and international conditions favourable to the realization of the right to development.

2. The realization of the right to development requires full respect for the principles of international law concerning friendly relations and co-operation among States in accordance with the Charter of the United Nations.

3. States have the duty to co-operate with each other in ensuring development and eliminating obstacles to development. States should realize their rights

and fulfil their duties in such a manner as to promote a new international economic order based on sovereign equality, interdependence, mutual interest and co-operation among all States, as well as to encourage the observance and realization of human rights.

ARTICLE 4

1. States have the duty to take steps, individually and collectively, to formulate international development policies with a view to facilitating the full realization of the right to development.

2. Sustained action is required to promote more rapid development of developing countries. As a complement to the efforts of developing countries, effective international co-operation is essential in providing these countries with appropriate means and facilities to foster their comprehensive development.

ARTICLE 5

States shall take resolute steps to eliminate the massive and flagrant violations of the human rights of peoples and human beings affected by situations such as those resulting from apartheid, all forms of racism and racial discrimination, colonialism, foreign domination and occupation, aggression, foreign interference and threats against national sovereignty, national unity and territorial integrity, threats of war and refusal to recognize the fundamental right of peoples to self-determination.

ARTICLE 6

1. All States should co-operate with a view to promoting, encouraging and strengthening universal respect for and observance of all human rights and fundamental freedoms for all without any distinction as to race, sex, language or religion.

2. All human rights and fundamental freedoms are indivisible and interdependent; equal attention and urgent consideration should be given to the implementation, promotion and protection of civil, political, economic, social and cultural rights.

3. States should take steps to eliminate obstacles to development resulting from failure to observe civil and political rights, as well as economic social and cultural rights.

ARTICLE 7

All States should promote the establishment, maintenance and strengthening of international peace and security and, to that end, should do their utmost to achieve general and complete disarmament under effective international control, as well as to ensure that the resources released by effective disarmament measures are used for comprehensive development, in particular that of the developing countries.

ARTICLE 8

1. States should undertake, at the national level, all necessary measures for the realization of the right to development and shall ensure, inter alia, equality of opportunity for all in their access to basic resources, education, health services, food, housing, employment and the fair distribution of income. Effective measures should be undertaken to ensure that women have an active role in the development process. Appropriate economic and social reforms should be carried out with a view to eradicating all social injustices.

2. States should encourage popular participation in all spheres as an important factor in development and in the full realization of all human rights.

ARTICLE 9

1. All the aspects of the right to development set forth in the present Declaration are indivisible and interdependent and each of them should be considered in the context of the whole.

2. Nothing in the present Declaration shall be construed as being contrary to the purposes and principles of the United Nations, or as implying that any State, group or person has a right to engage in any activity or to perform any act aimed at the violation of the rights set forth in the Universal Declaration of Human Rights and in the International Covenants on Human Rights.

ARTICLE 10

Steps should be taken to ensure the full exercise and progressive enhancement of the right to development, including the formulation, adoption and implementation of policy, legislative and other measures at the national and international levels.

Appendix 4
United Nations Millennium Declaration

Adopted by the United Nations General Assembly Resolution 55/2 on September 18, 2000

UNITED NATIONS MILLENNIUM DECLARATION

I. Values and principles

1. We, heads of State and Government, have gathered at United Nations Headquarters in New York from 6 to 8 September 2000, at the dawn of a new millennium, to reaffirm our faith in the Organization and its Charter as indispensable foundations of a more peaceful, prosperous and just world.

2. We recognize that, in addition to our separate responsibilities to our individual societies, we have a collective responsibility to uphold the principles of human dignity, equality and equity at the global level. As leaders we have a duty therefore to all the world's people, especially the most vulnerable and, in particular, the children of the world, to whom the future belongs.

3. We reaffirm our commitment to the purposes and principles of the Charter of the United Nations, which have proved timeless and universal. Indeed, their relevance and capacity to inspire have increased, as nations and peoples have become increasingly interconnected and interdependent.

4. We are determined to establish a just and lasting peace all over the world in accordance with the purposes and principles of the Charter. We rededicate ourselves to support all efforts to uphold the sovereign equality of all States, respect for their territorial integrity and political independence, resolution of disputes by peaceful means and in conformity with the principles of justice and international law, the right to self-determination of peoples which remain under colonial domination and foreign occupation, non-interference in the internal affairs of States, respect for human rights and fundamental freedoms, respect for the equal rights of all without distinction as to race, sex, language or religion and international cooperation in solving international problems of an economic, social, cultural or humanitarian character.

5. We believe that the central challenge we face today is to ensure that globalization becomes a positive force for all the world's people. For while globalization offers great opportunities, at present its benefits are very unevenly shared, while its costs are unevenly distributed. We recognize that developing countries and countries with economies in transition face special difficulties in responding to this central challenge. Thus, only through broad and sustained efforts to create a shared future, based upon our common humanity in all its diversity, can globalization be made fully inclusive and equitable. These efforts must include policies and measures, at the global level, which correspond to the needs of developing countries and economies in transition and are formulated and implemented with their effective participation.

6. We consider certain fundamental values to be essential to international relations in the twenty-first century. These include:

- **Freedom.** Men and women have the right to live their lives and raise their children in dignity, free from hunger and from the fear of violence, oppression or injustice. Democratic and participatory governance based on the will of the people best assures these rights.
- **Equality.** No individual and no nation must be denied the opportunity to benefit from development. The equal rights and opportunities of women and men must be assured.
- **Solidarity.** Global challenges must be managed in a way that distributes the costs and burdens fairly in accordance with basic principles of equity and social justice. Those who suffer or who benefit least deserve help from those who benefit most.
- **Tolerance.** Human beings must respect one other, in all their diversity of belief, culture and language. Differences within and between societies should be neither feared nor repressed, but cherished as a precious asset of humanity. A culture of peace and dialogue among all civilizations should be actively promoted.
- **Respect for nature.** Prudence must be shown in the management of all living species and natural resources, in accordance with the precepts of sustainable development. Only in this way can the immeasurable riches provided to us by nature be preserved and passed on to our descendants. The current unsustainable patterns of production and consumption must be changed in the interest of our future welfare and that of our descendants.
- **Shared responsibility.** Responsibility for managing worldwide economic and social development, as well as threats to international peace and security, must be shared among the nations of the world and should be exercised multilaterally. As the most universal and most representative organization in the world, the United Nations must play the central role.

7. In order to translate these shared values into actions, we have identified key objectives to which we assign special significance.

II. Peace, security and disarmament

8. We will spare no effort to free our peoples from the scourge of war, whether within or between States, which has claimed more than 5 million lives in the past decade. We will also seek to eliminate the dangers posed by weapons of mass destruction.

9. We resolve therefore:

- To strengthen respect for the rule of law in international as in national affairs and, in particular, to ensure compliance by Member States with the decisions of the International Court of Justice, in compliance with the Charter of the United Nations, in cases to which they are parties.
- To make the United Nations more effective in maintaining peace and security by giving it the resources and tools it needs for conflict prevention, peaceful resolution of disputes, peacekeeping, post-conflict peace-building and reconstruction. In this context, we take note of the report of the Panel on United Nations Peace Operations and request the General Assembly to consider its recommendations expeditiously.
- To strengthen cooperation between the United Nations and regional organizations, in accordance with the provisions of Chapter VIII of the Charter.
- To ensure the implementation, by States Parties, of treaties in areas such as arms control and disarmament and of international humanitarian law and human rights law, and call upon all States to consider signing and ratifying the Rome Statute of the International Criminal Court.
- To take concerted action against international terrorism, and to accede as soon as possible to all the relevant international conventions.
- To redouble our efforts to implement our commitment to counter the world drug problem.
- To intensify our efforts to fight transnational crime in all its dimensions, including trafficking as well as smuggling in human beings and money laundering.
- To minimize the adverse effects of United Nations economic sanctions on innocent populations, to subject such sanctions regimes to regular reviews and to eliminate the adverse effects of sanctions on third parties.
- To strive for the elimination of weapons of mass destruction, particularly nuclear weapons, and to keep all options open for achieving this aim, including the possibility of convening an international conference to identify ways of eliminating nuclear dangers.
- To take concerted action to end illicit traffic in small arms and light weapons, especially by making arms transfers more transparent and

supporting regional disarmament measures, taking account of all the recommendations of the forthcoming United Nations Conference on Illicit Trade in Small Arms and Light Weapons.

- To call on all States to consider acceding to the Convention on the Prohibition of the Use, Stockpiling, Production and Transfer of Anti-personnel Mines and on Their Destruction, as well as the amended mines protocol to the Convention on conventional weapons.

10. We urge Member States to observe the Olympic Truce, individually and collectively, now and in the future, and to support the International Olympic Committee in its efforts to promote peace and human understanding through sport and the Olympic Ideal.

III. Development and poverty eradication

11. We will spare no effort to free our fellow men, women and children from the abject and dehumanizing conditions of extreme poverty, to which more than a billion of them are currently subjected. We are committed to making the right to development a reality for everyone and to freeing the entire human race from want.

12. We resolve therefore to create an environment – at the national and global levels alike – which is conducive to development and to the elimination of poverty.

13. Success in meeting these objectives depends, *inter alia*, on good governance within each country. It also depends on good governance at the international level and on transparency in the financial, monetary and trading systems. We are committed to an open, equitable, rule-based, predictable and non-discriminatory multilateral trading and financial system.

14. We are concerned about the obstacles developing countries face in mobilizing the resources needed to finance their sustained development. We will therefore make every effort to ensure the success of the High-level International and Intergovernmental Event on Financing for Development, to be held in 2001.

15. We also undertake to address the special needs of the least developed countries. In this context, we welcome the Third United Nations Conference on the Least Developed Countries to be held in May 2001 and will endeavour to ensure its success. We call on the industrialized countries:

- To adopt, preferably by the time of that Conference, a policy of duty- and quota-free access for essentially all exports from the least developed countries;

- To implement the enhanced programme of debt relief for the heavily indebted poor countries without further delay and to agree to cancel all official bilateral debts of those countries in return for their making demonstrable commitments to poverty reduction; and
- To grant more generous development assistance, especially to countries that are genuinely making an effort to apply their resources to poverty reduction.

16. We are also determined to deal comprehensively and effectively with the debt problems of low- and middle-income developing countries, through various national and international measures designed to make their debt sustainable in the long term.

17. We also resolve to address the special needs of small island developing States, by implementing the Barbados Programme of Action and the outcome of the twenty-second special session of the General Assembly rapidly and in full. We urge the international community to ensure that, in the development of a vulnerability index, the special needs of small island developing States are taken into account.

18. We recognize the special needs and problems of the landlocked developing countries, and urge both bilateral and multilateral donors to increase financial and technical assistance to this group of countries to meet their special development needs and to help them overcome the impediments of geography by improving their transit transport systems.

19. We resolve further:

- To halve, by the year 2015, the proportion of the world's people whose income is less than one dollar a day and the proportion of people who suffer from hunger and, by the same date, to halve the proportion of people who are unable to reach or to afford safe drinking water.
- To ensure that, by the same date, children everywhere, boys and girls alike, will be able to complete a full course of primary schooling and that girls and boys will have equal access to all levels of education.
- By the same date, to have reduced maternal mortality by three quarters, and under-five child mortality by two thirds, of their current rates.
- To have, by then, halted, and begun to reverse, the spread of HIV/AIDS, the scourge of malaria and other major diseases that afflict humanity.
- To provide special assistance to children orphaned by HIV/AIDS.
- By 2020, to have achieved a significant improvement in the lives of at least 100 million slum dwellers as proposed in the "Cities Without Slums" initiative.

20. We also resolve:

- To promote gender equality and the empowerment of women as effective ways to combat poverty, hunger and disease and to stimulate development that is truly sustainable.
- To develop and implement strategies that give young people everywhere a real chance to find decent and productive work.
- To encourage the pharmaceutical industry to make essential drugs more widely available and affordable by all who need them in developing countries.
- To develop strong partnerships with the private sector and with civil society organizations in pursuit of development and poverty eradication.
- To ensure that the benefits of new technologies, especially information and communication technologies, in conformity with recommendations contained in the ECOSOC 2000 Ministerial Declaration, are available to all.

IV. Protecting our common environment

21. We must spare no effort to free all of humanity, and above all our children and grandchildren, from the threat of living on a planet irredeemably spoilt by human activities, and whose resources would no longer be sufficient for their needs.

22. We reaffirm our support for the principles of sustainable development, including those set out in Agenda 21, agreed upon at the United Nations Conference on Environment and Development.

23. We resolve therefore to adopt in all our environmental actions a new ethic of conservation and stewardship and, as first steps, we resolve:

- To make every effort to ensure the entry into force of the Kyoto Protocol, preferably by the tenth anniversary of the United Nations Conference on Environment and Development in 2002, and to embark on the required reduction in emissions of greenhouse gases.
- To intensify our collective efforts for the management, conservation and sustainable development of all types of forests.
- To press for the full implementation of the Convention on Biological Diversity and the Convention to Combat Desertification in those Countries Experiencing Serious Drought and/or Desertification, particularly in Africa.
- To stop the unsustainable exploitation of water resources by developing water management strategies at the regional, national and local levels, which promote both equitable access and adequate supplies.
- To intensify cooperation to reduce the number and effects of natural and man-made disasters.
- To ensure free access to information on the human genome sequence.

V. Human rights, democracy and good governance

24. We will spare no effort to promote democracy and strengthen the rule of law, as well as respect for all internationally recognized human rights and fundamental freedoms, including the right to development.

25. We resolve therefore:

- To respect fully and uphold the Universal Declaration of Human Rights.
- To strive for the full protection and promotion in all our countries of civil, political, economic, social and cultural rights for all.
- To strengthen the capacity of all our countries to implement the principles and practices of democracy and respect for human rights, including minority rights.
- To combat all forms of violence against women and to implement the Convention on the Elimination of All Forms of Discrimination against Women.
- To take measures to ensure respect for and protection of the human rights of migrants, migrant workers and their families, to eliminate the increasing acts of racism and xenophobia in many societies and to promote greater harmony and tolerance in all societies.
- To work collectively for more inclusive political processes, allowing genuine participation by all citizens in all our countries.
- To ensure the freedom of the media to perform their essential role and the right of the public to have access to information.

VI. Protecting the vulnerable

26. We will spare no effort to ensure that children and all civilian populations that suffer disproportionately the consequences of natural disasters, genocide, armed conflicts and other humanitarian emergencies are given every assistance and protection so that they can resume normal life as soon as possible.

We resolve therefore:

- To expand and strengthen the protection of civilians in complex emergencies, in conformity with international humanitarian law.
- To strengthen international cooperation, including burden sharing in, and the coordination of humanitarian assistance to, countries hosting refugees and to help all refugees and displaced persons to return voluntarily to their homes, in safety and dignity and to be smoothly reintegrated into their societies.
- To encourage the ratification and full implementation of the Convention on the Rights of the Child and its optional protocols on the involvement of children in armed conflict and on the sale of children, child prostitution and child pornography.

VII. Meeting the special needs of Africa

27. We will support the consolidation of democracy in Africa and assist Africans in their struggle for lasting peace, poverty eradication and sustainable development, thereby bringing Africa into the mainstream of the world economy.

28. We resolve therefore:

- To give full support to the political and institutional structures of emerging democracies in Africa.
- To encourage and sustain regional and subregional mechanisms for preventing conflict and promoting political stability, and to ensure a reliable flow of resources for peacekeeping operations on the continent.
- To take special measures to address the challenges of poverty eradication and sustainable development in Africa, including debt cancellation, improved market access, enhanced Official Development Assistance and increased flows of Foreign Direct Investment, as well as transfers of technology.
- To help Africa build up its capacity to tackle the spread of the HIV/AIDS pandemic and other infectious diseases.

VIII. Strengthening the United Nations

29. We will spare no effort to make the United Nations a more effective instrument for pursuing all of these priorities: the fight for development for all the peoples of the world, the fight against poverty, ignorance and disease; the fight against injustice; the fight against violence, terror and crime; and the fight against the degradation and destruction of our common home.

30. We resolve therefore:

- To reaffirm the central position of the General Assembly as the chief deliberative, policy-making and representative organ of the United Nations, and to enable it to play that role effectively.
- To intensify our efforts to achieve a comprehensive reform of the Security Council in all its aspects.
- To strengthen further the Economic and Social Council, building on its recent achievements, to help it fulfil the role ascribed to it in the Charter.
- To strengthen the International Court of Justice, in order to ensure justice and the rule of law in international affairs.
- To encourage regular consultations and coordination among the principal organs of the United Nations in pursuit of their functions.
- To ensure that the Organization is provided on a timely and predictable basis with the resources it needs to carry out its mandates.

- To urge the Secretariat to make the best use of those resources, in accordance with clear rules and procedures agreed by the General Assembly, in the interests of all Member States, by adopting the best management practices and technologies available and by concentrating on those tasks that reflect the agreed priorities of Member States.
- To promote adherence to the Convention on the Safety of United Nations and Associated Personnel.
- To ensure greater policy coherence and better cooperation between the United Nations, its agencies, the Bretton Woods Institutions and the World Trade Organization, as well as other multilateral bodies, with a view to achieving a fully coordinated approach to the problems of peace and development.
- To strengthen further cooperation between the United Nations and national parliaments through their world organization, the Inter-Parliamentary Union, in various fields, including peace and security, economic and social development, international law and human rights and democracy and gender issues.
- To give greater opportunities to the private sector, non-governmental organizations and civil society, in general, to contribute to the realization of the Organization's goals and programmes.

31. We request the General Assembly to review on a regular basis the progress made in implementing the provisions of this Declaration, and ask the Secretary-General to issue periodic reports for consideration by the General Assembly and as a basis for further action.

32. We solemnly reaffirm, on this historic occasion, that the United Nations is the indispensable common house of the entire human family, through which we will seek to realize our universal aspirations for peace, cooperation and development. We therefore pledge our unstinting support for these common objectives and our determination to achieve them.

8th plenary meeting
8 September 2000

Appendix 5
Millennium Development Goals

Adopted at the United Nations Millennium Summit, September 2000 (Goals, Targets, and Indicators)

GOAL 1. ERADICATE EXTREME POVERTY AND HUNGER

Target 1. Halve, between 1990 and 2015, the proportion of people whose income is less than one dollar a day

1. Proportion of population below $1 per day
2. Poverty gap ratio (incidence x depth of poverty)
3. Share of poorest quintile in national consumption

Target 2. Halve, between 1990 and 2015, the proportion of people who suffer from hunger

4. Prevalence of underweight children (under five years of age)
5. Proportion of population below minimum level of dietary energy consumption

GOAL 2. ACHIEVE UNIVERSAL PRIMARY EDUCATION

Target 2. Ensure that, by 2015, children everywhere, boys and girls alike, will be able to complete a full course of primary schooling

6. Net enrolment ratio in primary education
7. Proportion of pupils starting grade 1 who reach grade 5
8. Literacy rate of 15–24-year-olds

GOAL 3. PROMOTE GENDER EQUALITY AND EMPOWER WOMEN

Target 4. Eliminate gender disparity in primary and secondary education, preferably by 2005, and to all levels of education no later than 2015

9. Ratio of girls to boys in primary, secondary and tertiary education
10. Ratio of literate females to males of 15–24-year-olds
11. Share of women in wage employment in the non-agricultural sector
12. Proportion of seats held by women in national parliament

GOAL 4. REDUCE CHILD MORTALITY

Target 5. Reduce by two-thirds, between 1990 and 2015, the under-five mortality rate

13. Under-five mortality rate
14. Infant mortality rate
15. Proportion of 1-year-old children immunized against measles

GOAL 5. IMPROVE MATERNAL HEALTH

Target 6. Reduce by three-quarters, between 1990 and 2015, the maternal mortality ratio

16. Maternal mortality ratio
17. Proportion of births attended by skilled health personnel

GOAL 6. COMBAT HIV/AIDS, MALARIA AND OTHER DISEASES

Target 7. Have halted by 2015 and begun to reverse the spread of HIV/AIDS

18. HIV prevalence among 15–24-year-old pregnant women
19. Contraceptive prevalence rate
20. Number of children orphaned by HIV/AIDS

Target 8. Have halted by 2015 and begun to reverse the incidence of malaria and other major diseases

21. Prevalence and death rates associated with malaria
22. Proportion of population in malaria-risk areas using effective malaria prevention and treatment measures
23. Prevalence and death rates associated with tuberculosis
24. Proportion of tuberculosis cases detected and cured under directly observed treatment short course.

GOAL 7. ENSURE ENVIRONMENTAL SUSTAINABILITY

Target 9. Integrate the principles of sustainable development into country policies and programmes and reverse the loss of environmental resources

25. Proportion of land area covered by forest
26. Land area protected to maintain biological diversity
27. GDP per unit of energy use (as proxy for energy efficiency)
28. Carbon dioxide emissions (per capita)

[Plus two figures of global atmospheric pollution: ozone depletion and the accumulation of global warming gases]

Target 10. Halve by 2015 the proportion of people without sustainable access to safe drinking water

29. Proportion of population with sustainable access to an improved water source

Target 11. By 2020 to have achieved a significant improvement in the lives of at least 100 million slum dwellers

30. Proportion of people with access to improved sanitation
31. Proportion of people with access to secure tenure

GOAL 8. DEVELOP A GLOBAL PARTNERSHIP FOR DEVELOPMENT

Target 12. Develop further an open, rule-based, predictable, non-discriminatory trading and financial system

Includes a commitment to good governance, development, and poverty reduction – both nationally and internationally

Target 13. Address the special needs of the least developed countries

Includes: tariff- and quota-free access for least developed countries' exports; enhanced programme of debt relief for HIPCs and cancellation of official bilateral debt; and more generous ODA for countries committed to poverty reduction

Target 14. Address the special needs of landlocked countries and small island developing States

(through the Programme of Action for the Sustainable Development of Small Island Developing States and the outcome of the twenty-second special session of the General Assembly)

Target 15. Deal comprehensively with the debt problems of developing countries through national and international measures in order to make debt sustainable in the long term

Official development assistance

32. Net ODA as percentage of OECD/DAC donors' gross national product (targets of 0.7% in total and 0.15% for LDCs)
33. Proportion of ODA to basic social services (basic education, primary health care, nutrition, safe water and sanitation)
34. Proportion of ODA that is untied
35. Proportion of ODA for environment in small island developing States
36. Proportion of ODA for transport sector in landlocked countries

Market access

37. Proportion of exports (by value and excluding arms) admitted free of duties and quotas
38. Average tariffs and quotas on agricultural products and textiles and clothing
39. Domestic and export agricultural subsidies in OECD countries
40. Proportion of ODA provided to help build trade capacity

Debt sustainability

41. Proportion of official bilateral HIPC debt cancelled
42. Debt service as a percentage of exports of goods and services
43. Proportion of ODA provided as debt relief
44. Number of countries reaching HIPC decision and completion points

Target 16. In cooperation with developing countries, develop and implement strategies for decent and productive work for youth

45. Unemployment rate of 15–24-year-olds

Target 17. In cooperation with pharmaceutical companies, provide access to affordable essential drugs in developing countries

46. Proportion of population with access to affordable essential drugs on a sustainable basis

Target 18. In cooperation with the private sector, make available the benefits of new technologies, especially information and communications

47. Telephone lines per 1,000 people
48. Personal computers per 1,000 people

Appendix 6

Latin American and Caribbean Initiative for Sustainable Development

Approved at the Seventh Meeting of the Inter-Sessional Committee of the Forum of Ministers of the Environment of Latin America and the Caribbean, May 15–17, 2002, São Paulo, Brazil.

I. BACKGROUND

1. The Rio Conference of 1992 was convened upon the acknowledgement that patterns of production and consumption, especially in developed countries, had reached unsustainable levels, jeopardizing the stability of several environmental goods and services that guarantee not only the continuity of productive activities but also the quality of life itself, with the intention to pave the way to revert this situation in the benefit of the world.

2. Ten years after Rio-92, the governments of Latin America and the Caribbean recognized that significant progress was made in some areas, especially in awareness building and the entry into force of national and international legal norms. There remain, however, important challenges and new imperatives have emerged to turn sustainable development into a reality and to materialize the necessary changes in the current development models. It is indispensable to revert the current tendencies of degradation of both the natural and urban environment and, in particular, eliminate at a vigorous rhythm poverty and inequity – together with their impacts – that afflict the countries of the region.

3. This initiative recognizes the importance of regional action to promote sustainable development in Latin America and the Caribbean, especially in the framework of the Platform for Action on the Road to Johannesburg 2002, approved in Rio de Janeiro, Brazil, in October 2001. The launching of a Latin American and Caribbean Initiative is justified by the need to give a practical direction to the World Summit on Sustainable Development and reflect the unique characteristics, visions and goals of the region, taking into account, above all, the validity of the principle of common but differentiated responsibilities of the States.

4. The peoples and countries in the region see the World Summit on Sustainable Development as a unique opportunity to proceed to the evaluation of progress achieved at all levels in fulfilling the commitments undertaken in Rio-92 and to adopt effective actions in the search for solutions to the new challenges of sustainable development. The Summit is, moreover, a historic opportunity to assume that it is not only possible but necessary to give response to the economic and social roots of environmental problems and to ensure financing redirected towards a new globalization that will ensure sustainable, equitable and inclusive development. It should also promote the adoption of concrete actions through the cooperation of developed countries, multilateral and regional organizations, including financing institutions, and through the strengthening of South-South cooperation.

5. The task at hand consists in identifying programmes and projects aimed at the attainment of these goals. This initiative implies adjustments to the current international situation, and takes into account the social, economic and environmental dimensions and, on the foundation of an ethical basis, makes sustainable development a priority for social and economic political programmes for countries in Latin America and the Caribbean.

II. OBJECTIVES

6. The objectives of the Latin American and Caribbean Initiative are the following:

(a) Consolidating and continuing the efforts of Latin American and the Caribbean, at the different levels of Government and civil society, in order to overcome obstacles in the implementation of programmes and projects of interest to the region in implementing the recommendations of Agenda 21 emphasizing effective implementation and the development of participatory mechanisms in the Caribbean;

(b) Developing actions in selected areas that, based on the political will of States, stimulate the participation of the private sector and of civil society in order to promote investments that may generate sustainable productive activities and, at the same time, allow for the conservation and sustainable use of environmental goods and services essential to life;

(c) Promoting the implementation of sustainable development models on the foundation of an ethical basis that are competitive and supported by public policies devoted to fomenting science and technology, financing, human resource capacity-building, institutional development, valuation of goods and services and development of sustainable indicators adapted to the social, economic, environmental and political conditions of each country or to the needs of sub-regional groups of countries; and

(d) Contributing, as a political framework, to identifying and prioritising financial, technical and institutional mechanisms for the effective implementation of Agenda 21, facilitating the transfer of, access to and development of technology and knowledge and promoting the adoption of suitable regulatory frameworks.

7. This initiative will also identify topics that are suitable for articulation and cooperation with proposals by other regions, such as the New Partnership for Africa's Development (NEPAD).

III. OPERATIVE GUIDELINES FOR THE INITIATIVE

8. The operative guidelines for this Initiative are:

a) **Reinforcing positions consolidated after Rio 1992:**

  i)   To ratify the commitment to devote 0.7 % of the GDP of industrialized countries to official development assistance, as approved in Agenda 21;

  ii) To fulfill the commitments contained in the Doha Declaration and in the Consensus of Monterrey to ensure access to the market and the availability of the financial resources required to achieve sustainable development goals, particularly in support for the efforts of developing countries;

  iii) To provide guidance for the creation of new financial mechanisms, including cancellation of the debt of developing countries and particularly the least developed countries, and the creation of a contingency fund for natural disasters;

  iv) To fully apply the principle of common but differentiated responsibilities of the States and the respect for the sovereign right of each country over its natural resources;

  (v) To reiterate commitment to the precautionary principle, in accordance with the definition that appears in the Rio Declaration, as a key component of environmental policy, so as to safeguard our natural and social heritage;

  vi) To give priority to the interests of countries in the Caribbean, especially in compliance with the Barbados Action Plan;

  vii) To enhance participation of non-governmental agents and transparency in decision-making processes, strengthening initiatives such as National Councils on Sustainable Development and the elaboration of national and local Agendas 21.

  viii) To promote the construction of a new ethical practice for sustainable development that takes into account the processes developed so far, such as the Earth Charter.

  ix) To implement the Guidelines on Sustainable Consumption approved by the United Nations Commission on Sustainable Development in 1999.

b) Operative guidelines:

The programmes and projects intended to face the challenges of sustainable development in the region should follow these operative guidelines within an ethical framework:

i.   Promoting sustainable economic growth and the definition of mechanisms and instruments to face new sources of instability promoting internal savings capacity and private capital flows.

ii. Supporting the implementation of public policies aimed at reducing poverty and social inequality, creating jobs and promoting sustainable development with justice, equity and social inclusion.

iii) Implementing integrated human health and environmental measures to ensure that the health and well-being of the people of the region are increasingly recognized and systematically translated into policies and programmes.

iv) Underlining the existing links between unsustainable patterns of consumption and the internationalisation of production patterns, in particular the growing importance of the awareness of consumers and enterprises for the application of concepts regarding social and environmental responsibilities.

v)   Developing new sustainable bases of competitiveness for the productive structure of countries in the region in order to strengthen their insertion in the world economy, proposing strategies that seek to achieve the effective opening of external markets, above all in the developed countries, a *sine qua non* condition for obtaining the objective of sustainable development in the region.

vi) Creating and strengthening economic, tax and fiscal instruments for the promotion of sustainable development.

vii) Stimulating the adoption by governments and the productive sector of voluntary instruments (certifications, ISO 14000, certification for sustainable tourism, etc.) applicable to the sustainable development process.

viii) Initiating or continuing the processes for valuation of the environment and natural resources to take advantage of the region's comparative advantages, incorporating indicators in the field of environmental liabilities and assets to allow their inclusion in the national accounting systems.

ix) Supporting regional actions and sub-regional efforts, in particular those of the Caribbean (SIDS), the Amazon Countries (TCA), the Andean sub-region (CAN), of MERCOSUR and Central America (ALIDES).

x)   Strengthening regional, sub-regional and national institutions, as well as the sub-national mechanisms, for the implementation, follow up and monitoring of policies, programmes and projects deriving from this Initiative.

xi) Formulating strategies for the absorption, transfer and development of technology that should be supported through the mobilization and expansion of resources from existing financial institutions.

xii) Improving or adapting existing systems of sustainability indicators that respond to the social, economic and political characteristics of the region, or build such systems.

xiii) Developing South-South cooperation activities that will favour the use of the developing countries' strengths and opportunities on the basis of the sustainable development of the nations in the region.

xiv) Promoting the development of *sui generis* systems to protect traditional knowledge, based on instruments and mechanisms of various nature and encouraging that the current systems of intellectual property take into account the traditional knowledge associated with biological diversity in the evaluation of patent requests and other related rights.

IV. ACTION PRIORITIES

A. Priority Themes

9. On the occasion of the XIII Meeting of the Foreign Ministers of the Environment of Latin America and the Caribbean and the Regional Preparatory Conference for the World Summit on Sustainable Development, held in October 2001, the countries of the region agreed to identify actions that could focus the efforts for the implementation of this Initiative.

10. Among them, priority actions are adopted that address, among others, eradication of poverty and social inequalities; expansion of the environmental education dimension in all economic and social endeavours; sustainable management of water resources; sustainable generation of energy and the increasing participation of renewable sources; management of protected areas for the sustainable use of biodiversity; adaptation to impacts caused by climate change and sustainable management of urban and rural areas, with special emphasis on health, environmental sanitation and minimization of risks and vulnerability to natural disasters. Actions to promote scientific and technological innovation, the strengthening of research and development institutions and the increasing of existing sources of financing are also relevant. In this context, centres of excellence in research and development should promote the building of a solid scientific alliance through, among others, activities of scientific exchange, establishment of interdisciplinary information networks and formulation of joint research projects.

11. The countries of the region should act together so that cooperation and financial multilateral institutions, as well as regional and sub-regional organizations, provide support to programmes of action and projects identified in this Initiative.

12. They should also promote inter-regional cooperation actions with a view to reinforcing technical and scientific cooperation between Latin American and the Caribbean and Africa.

13. Finally, countries of the region should strengthen public-private sector partnerships for the promotion of scientific and technical progress based on the conservation and sustainable use of natural resources.

14. The countries of the region should advocate concrete activities to promote an ethic for sustainable development in the discussions conducted at international forums, consistent with the Rio de Janeiro Platform of Action of October 2001.

15. The implementation of the guiding goals and indicative purposes at the regional level will be reviewed every five years.

16. The action proposals identified in this Initiative constitute the intentions for future action by the Latin American and Caribbean countries in terms of the imperatives of sustainable development. The region recognizes that, to achieve these goals, means of implementation and possible partnerships still need to be determined; and it underscores the need for a favourable international scenario, basically a scenario of peace and solidarity, enhanced by the effective commitment of the developed countries to the transfer and adaptation of technologies, the provision of new and sufficient additional resources, the elimination of subsidies and greater openness of their markets, among others.

B. Guiding Goals and Indicative Purposes

1) *Biological Diversity*

–Increase of the forest area.

  i)   ensure the sustainable management of forest resources in the region, significantly reducing the present deforestation rates.

–Territory included in protected areas.

  i)   Increase significantly the territory in the region under protected area regimes, considering in their definition buffer zones and biological corridors.

−Genetic resources − Equitable sharing of benefits.

i)   Adopt regulatory frameworks for access to genetic resources, as well as for fair and equitable sharing of the benefits derived from their utilization, compatible with the Convention on Biological Diversity.

2) *Water Resources Management*

−Watershed management.

i)   Improve and strengthen the institutional arrangements for the integrated management of water basins and aquifers through, among other measures, the establishment of water basin committees with the participation of all sub-national levels of government, civil society, the private sector and all involved stakeholders.

−Management of marine and coastal areas and their resources.

i)   Implement national and regional environmental action plans for the integrated management of the coastal zone, with particular attention to the Small Island Developing States.

−Better quality of inland waters.

i)   Improve the quality of effluents and reduce the discharge of pollutants into surface water bodies, groundwater and coastal areas.

3) *Vulnerability, Human Settlements and Sustainable Cities*

−Land-use planning.

i)   implement plans and policies for land-use planning from a sustainable development approach.

ii) incorporate instruments for risk management in land-use planning

−Areas affected by degradation processes.

i)   Reduce significantly the areas of the regional territory subject to erosion, salinization and other soil degradation processes.

−Air pollution.

i)   Reduce the concentration of polluting emissions in the air.

−Water Pollution.

i)   Increase the coverage of drinking water services and wastewater treatment.

–Solid wastes.

i)   Reduce significantly solid waste generation (domestic and industrial) and promote, among others, recycling and reuse.

ii) Implement integrated management of solid wastes (domestic and industrial), including appropriate treatment and final disposal.

–Vulnerability to anthropogenic disasters and those caused by natural phenomena.

i)   Implement and strengthen regional cooperation mechanisms for the risk management and the mitigation of anthropogenic disasters and those caused by natural phenomena, including the formulation of a regional early-warning system and the formation of immediate response groups.

4) Social Issues, Including Health, Inequity and Poverty

–Health and environment.

i)   Implement policies and plans to reduce environmental risks which cause health damages, in particular those transmitted by water, vectors, air pollution and exposure to chemical substances.

ii) Expand the proportion of green and healthy areas per inhabitant.

–Environment and job creation.

i)   Promote the formulation and implementation of sustainable development projects and programmes that will contribute to job creation and avoid migration and displacement.

–Poverty and inequity.

i)   Reduce drastically the poverty rates in the countries of the region.

5) Economic Issues, Including Competitiveness, Trade and Production and Consumption Patterns (Energy)

–Energy.

i)   Increase renewable energy use in the region to, at least, 10% of total energy consumption in the region by the year 2010.

–Cleaner production.

i)   Install cleaner production centres in all the countries of the region.

ii) Incorporate the concept of cleaner production in a significant number of the main industries, with emphasis on small and medium-sized industries.

–*Economic instruments.*

i) Establish a system of economic incentives for productive and industrial processing projects that will save natural resources and energy and finally reduce the amount of effluents discharged into water, land and the air.

6. Institutional Arrangements

–*Environmental education.*

i. Improve and strengthen the incorporation of the environmental dimension in formal and non-formal education, in the economy and in society.

–*Training and capacity building of human resources.*

i) Eradicate illiteracy and universalise registration in primary and secondary education.
ii) Establish programmes for capacity building in sustainable development management for the public and private sectors and the community.

–*Evaluation and indicators.*

i) Develop and implement an assessment process to monitor the progress made towards attaining sustainable development objectives, adopting sustainability indicator systems at the national and regional levels, that respond to the unique social, economic and political features of the region.

–*Participation of society.*

i) Create and strengthen participation mechanisms in sustainable development issues, with government, non-government and major groups representation in all countries of the region.

Notes

1. Introduction

1. See Gylfason 1999; Rodrik 2003; Scott 1991; Thirlwall 2006; and Van Den Berg 2001 for an analysis of the centrality of economic growth to the development process.
2. United Nations Economic Commission for Latin America and the Caribbean 2005b, p. 10.
3. Emphasis on basic human needs is reflected in the works of Leipziger 1980; McHale and McHale 1979; Moon 1991; and Streeten 1982.
4. The most widely utilized index for measuring a nation's physical quality of life is the Human Development Index (HDI) that was devised by the UNDP.
5. See Alsop et al. 2005; Friedman 1992; Narayan 2002; Stern, Dethier, and Rogers 2006; and Titi and Singh 1997 for an analysis of the link between development and empowerment.
6. UNDP devised a "capacity" measurement to reflect this broader definition of development. Capacity is considered the ability of individuals, institutions, and societies to perform functions, solve problems, and achieve objectives in a sustainable manner. See United Nations Development Programme 2005a, 2006a, 2007a, and 2008.
7. This definition of sustainability can be found in the 1987 report of the World Commission on Environment and Development, p. 43. The importance of sustainability to the development process is also reflected in Blewitt 2008; Cooper and Vargas 2004; Glasbergen Biermann, and Mol 2008; Hettne 2008; López 2004; López and Toman 2006; Sachs 2008; Soubbotina 2004; United Nations 2006d; United Nations Development Programme 1997c; and Wood and Roberts 2005.
8. Although scholarship on the economic, social, and environmental work of the UN is limited, prominent examples include Bhouraskar 2006; Hill 2008; Jones and Coleman 2004; Singer 2001; and Toye and Toye 2004.
9. This figure refers to the subsidiary funds and programs directly administered by the UN and does not include the specialized agencies or peacekeeping operations.
10. The importance the UN places on democratic political reform, which became especially evident in the mid-1990s, is reflected in Boutros-Ghali 1995, 1996; United Nations 1997a, 1997b; and United Nations Development Programme 1997b. More recently, the 2005 World Summit Outcome Document stated that "good governance and the rule of law at the national and international levels are essential for sustained economic growth, sustainable development and the eradication of poverty and hunger." United Nations 2005a, p. 2.

11. See, for example, Adams 2003; Burnell 2000; Carothers 1999; Crawford 2001; Forsythe 1996; and White 2000.
12. It should be noted that WFP is somewhat of an exception in this respect since it is co-managed by FAO which is a specialized agency of the UN.

2. The United Nations and Development

1. Preamble to the *Charter of the United Nations*, United Nations 1945.
2. As noted in the UN charter, "[C]onditions of stability and well-being ... are necessary for peaceful and friendly relations among nations." United Nations 1945, Chapter 9, Article 55.
3. The Secretary-General is recommended by the Security Council and appointed on a two-thirds vote of the General Assembly for a renewable five-year term.
4. About half of the Secretariat's staff members are under the regular budget and the other half are paid through special funding.
5. DESA was created by consolidating the Department for Policy Coordination and Sustainable Development, Department for Economic and Social Information and Policy Analysis, and Department for Development Support and Management Services.
6. It should be noted that the Secretariat also has an Office for the Coordination of Humanitarian Affairs (OCHA) that focuses on emergency relief efforts, especially at times of natural disaster. The office has less direct involvement in the promotion of long-term development.
7. The six main committees of the General Assembly are Disarmament and International Security; Economic and Financial; Social, Humanitarian and Cultural; Special Political and Decolonization; Administrative and Budgetary; and Legal. The General Assembly also oversees the work of various specialized commissions.
8. Because ECOSOC is under the authority and supervision of the General Assembly it does not enjoy the same institutional autonomy as the other principal organs.
9. United Nations 1945, Chapter 19, Article 62. ECOSOC receives administrative support from DESA of the UN Secretariat.
10. ECOSOC, which was originally composed of 18 member states, was expanded to 27 member states in 1965 and 54 member states in 1973. The member states are elected by the General Assembly for overlapping three-year terms. Seats on the council are distributed on the basis of geographic representation, with 14 seats allocated to African states, 11 to Asian states, 6 to Eastern European states, 10 to Latin American and Caribbean states, and 13 to Western European and other states. The five permanent members of the Security Council are usually members of ECOSOC. Retiring members are eligible for immediate re-election and decisions are based on majority vote. See United Nations 1945, Chapter 10, Article 61.
11. There are also a number of standing and ad hoc committees that report to ECOSOC. These committees focus on such areas as energy, forests, human settlements, development policy, and indigenous issues.
12. The regional commissions include the United Nations Economic Commission for Latin America and the Caribbean (UNECLAC), founded in 1948 and based in Santiago; United Nations Economic Commission for Europe (UNECE), founded in 1947 and based in Geneva; United Nations Economic and Social Commission for Asia and the Pacific (UNESCAP), founded in 1947 and based in Bangkok; United Nations Economic Commission for Africa (UNECA), founded in 1958 and based in Addis Ababa; and United Nations Economic and Social

Commission for Western Asia (UNESCWA), founded in 1974 and based in Beirut.

13. Berthelot 2004 offers a comprehensive review of the regional commissions.

14. Formal relationships with the specialized agencies are negotiated by ECOSOC and approved by the General Assembly.

15. For detailed analyses of the UNDP see Klingebiel 1999; Mandeville 2009; and Murphy 2006.

16. The one exception here is countries that are hosting peacekeeping operations. In these cases the country team is led by a special representative of the Secretary-General.

17. UNDP currently has staff from 152 nations and territories. Within Latin American and the Caribbean, UNDP maintains 24 country offices which support programs in 44 countries and territories.

18. Additional factors may also be considered in the allocation of resources, such as geographic disadvantages or sudden economic difficulties.

19. United Nations Economic and Social Council 1997, Chapter 4, Section I. A.

20. The Policy and Program Manual highlights a number of areas, including health care, education, agriculture, food production, and handicrafts, where gender mainstreaming should be prioritized.

21. United Nations Development Programme 2006a, p. 33.

22. UNDP also administers the United Nations Office to Combat Desertification and Drought.

23. United Nations Development Programme 2007a, p. 17.

24. In responding to natural disasters UNDP typically works with the Department of Humanitarian Affairs of the Secretariat.

25. United Nations Development Programme 2006a, p. 28.

26. UNDP also developed a Human Poverty Index (HPI) that measures deprivation through the use of such indicators as lack of access to safe water, malnutrition, poor health care, and illiteracy.

27. For a comprehensive description of the work of the World Food Programme see Shaw 2001.

28. UNICEF replaced the United Nations Relief and Rehabilitation Administration, which had been the principal relief organization for Europe.

29. Some of these private funds are generated by National Committees for UNICEF, which undertake fund raising in 37 countries. These national committees collectively raise almost a third of UNICEF's annual income. United Nations Children's Fund 2007a, p. 26.

30. Under the Global Polio Eradication Initiative, UNICEF has dramatically reduced the transmission of polio. The fund also has a *Global Measles Strategic Plan* to help contain the spread of this disease.

31. The widespread introduction of ORT has helped reduce the number of children in the developing world dying from dehydration by 50 percent since 1968.

32. Historical reviews of the work of the UNFPA can be found in Mousky 2002 and Sadik 2002.

33. The Executive Board of UNFPA is composed of eight representatives from Africa, seven from Asia and the Pacific, four from Eastern Europe, five from Latin America and the Caribbean, and twelve from Western Europe and Other States. The board is under the authority of ECOSOC.

34. See Sanwal 2007 for the role of UNEP in the evolution of global environmental governance.

35. The *Nairobi Declaration on the Role and Mandate of UNEP* (United Nations Environmental Programme 1997) and the *Bali Strategic Plan* (United Nations Environmental Programme 2005b), which were both adopted by the Governing Council, further define the institutional mission of UNEP.

36. The Governing Council of UNEP reports to the General Assembly through ECOSOC.
37. A regional formula is used to determine the composition of UNEP's Governing Council. Sixteen seats are allocated to Africa, thirteen to Asia, six to Eastern Europe, ten to Latin America and the Caribbean, and thirteen to Western Europe and Other States.
38. UNEP resources derive from the regular UN budget and from the voluntary contributions of member states.
39. A small Environmental Fund was established within UNEP to assist UN agencies incorporate environmental concerns into their economic and social programs.
40. UNEP provides the secretariat for various environmental conventions, including the Convention on International Trade in Endangered Species, the Convention on Biological Diversity, the Convention on Migratory Species, the Basel Convention on the Transboundary Movement of Hazardous Wastes, and the Stockholm Convention on Persistent Organic Pollutants.
41. See United Nations Environmental Programme 2007e.
42. A number of scholars have examined the broad development agenda of the UN. See especially Bhouraskar 2006; Fomerand 2004; Jeong 1998; Jolly et al. 2004; and Singer 2001. Such a review can also be found in the following institutional documents: United Nations 2006c, 2007b.
43. United Nations 1945, Chapter 1, Article 1.
44. United Nations 1945, Chapter 9, Article 55.
45. United Nations 1948b, Article 25.
46. United Nations 1948b, Article 26.
47. United Nations 1966b, Part 3, Articles 11–12.
48. United Nations 1966b, Part 2, Article 2.
49. The Committee on Economic, Social and Cultural Rights is made up of 18 individual experts and may include no more than one citizen from any single country. Membership must reflect different social and legal systems and ensure equitable geographic representation.
50. This request was included in General Assembly Resolution 200. See United Nations 1948a.
51. A Technical Assistance Committee was established as a standing body of ECOSOC to review and approve EPTA activities and a Technical Assistance Board was established to coordinate technical assistance activities.
52. Although its name reflects the original number of member countries, the Group of 77 has since grown to 125 countries.
53. This request was made via General Assembly Resolution 1710. See United Nations 1961.
54. See United Nations 1962, p. 1.
55. See Jackson 1969.
56. This report was officially entitled *A United Nations Structure for Global Economic Cooperation*, though commonly referred to as the Gardner Report. See United Nations 1975a.
57. See Brandt Commission 1980.
58. The *Bertrand Report* was officially entitled *Some Reflections on Reform of the United Nations*. See Bertrand 1985.
59. See United Nations 1986, Article 1, Paragraph 1.
60. United Nations 1986, Article 2, Paragraph 3.
61. United Nations 1986, Article 4, Paragraph 2.
62. United Nations 1995b, "Introduction," p. 1.
63. Secretary-General Kofi Annan prepared a report in advance of the summit outlining the central challenges for the global community in the new millennium. See Annan 2000.

64. A total of 191 member nations were represented at the Millennium Summit, including 147 heads of state or government.
65. See United Nations 2001 and United Nations Development Programme 2002o.
66. For application of the Millennium Development Goals to the Latin American and Caribbean context see Inter-American Development Bank 2003; United Nations Development Programme 2004c; and United Nations Economic Commission for Latin America and the Caribbean 2003b. See also United Nations Development Programme 2005c for an assessment of further measures needed to achieve the Millennium Development Goals.
67. United Nations 2005a, p. 2.
68. Critical studies of the UN that have appeared in recent years include Alleyne 2003; Ameri 2003; Babbin 2004; Gold 2005; Schaefer 2006; and Shawn 2006.
69. As an example of redundancy within the UN, there are 29 different agencies and departments that have food and agricultural programs.
70. It should be noted that the UN has recently adopted a number of reforms to enhance financial transparency and accountability, including introducing whistleblower protections, strengthening the Office of Internal Oversight Services, establishing a new ethics office, and enhancing accounting and disclosure standards. A Procurement Task Force was also established to investigate allegations of corruption in purchasing practices.
71. Ameri 2003, p. 7.
72. While many of the concerns raised about the UN are valid, it is important to recognize that some of the harshest critics tend to oppose international organizations and multilateralism in general.
73. See United Nations 2005b for an internal assessment of the perennial difficulties generating sufficient resources for economic and social development programs.

3. Poverty in the Americas

1. Detailed studies of economic and social conditions in Latin America can be found in Gindling 2005; Machinea and Sierra 2007; Olave 2001; Sahn and Younger 2005; Sojo and Uthoff 2007; United Nations Development Programme 2004c; and United Nations Economic Commission for Latin America and the Caribbean 2005b; 2006c; 2007b; 2008a; 2008c; 2008d.
2. United Nations Economic Commission for Latin America and the Caribbean 2007a, p. 7. See also United Nations Environmental Programme 2008a, p. 42.
3. The FAO defines food insecurity as "[a] situation that exists when people lack secure access to sufficient amounts of safe and nutritious food for normal growth and development and an active and healthy life." Food insecurity may be caused by "the unavailability of food, insufficient purchasing power, inappropriate distribution, or inadequate use of food at the household level." Food and Agriculture Organization 2008, p. 2.
4. United Nations Children's Fund 2008b and United Nations Economic Commission for Latin America and the Caribbean 2005b, 2007c survey nutritional levels for children in Latin America.
5. A recent overview of general health conditions in Latin America can be found in United Nations Economic Commission for Latin America and the Caribbean 2008b. See also Savedoff 2009and World Health Organization 2003.
6. The IMR reflects the number of infants who die before their first birthday out of 1000 births. It should be noted that IMRs vary considerably throughout Latin America. Some countries, such as Cuba (5) and Chile (7) are quite low while other countries, such as Bolivia (46) and Haiti (49) are much higher.

7. The CMR reflects the number of children who die before their fifth birthday out of 1000 births. Again, considerable variation exists among Latin American countries. In the higher income countries the CMR is 10–12, in the middle income countries the rate is 35–40, and in the lower income countries the rate is 80–85. See United Nations Children's Fund 2007b.

8. The highest life expectancies are in the Southern Cone of South America, Cuba, and Costa Rica, while the lowest life expectancies are in Haiti, the Central American region, and the Andean nations.

9. A report by the Pan American Health Organization (2004) offers a comprehensive assessment of the exclusive nature of health care in Latin America. See also Belizan et al. 2007 and Cruces and Titelman 2007.

10. See Aggleton 2003; Smallman 2007; United Nations Development Programme 2004c; and United Nations Economic Commission for Latin America and the Caribbean 2005b for detailed information on the HIV/AIDS pandemic in Latin America and the Caribbean.

11. Although HIV was initially spread through blood transfusions, hospitals and clinics have since instituted enhanced screening practices and such transmissions are now exceedingly rare.

12. See United Nations Education, Scientific and Cultural Organization 2004 for an assessment of primary education in the region.

13. Inter-American Development Bank 2008, p. 4.

14. For a detailed review of education systems in Latin America see Moura Castro, Carnoy and Wolff 2000; United Nations Economic Commission for Latin America and the Caribbean 2005b; Wolff 2001; Wolff and Moura Castro 2000; and Wolff, Schiefelbein, and Schiefelbein 2002.

15. The nations with the highest rates of adult illiteracy are Bolivia, Guatemala, Nicaragua, and Peru while the countries with the lowest rates are Argentina, Chile, Colombia, Costa Rica, and Uruguay.

16. There are substantial differences between public and private schools. Middle and upper income parents typically send their children to private schools where the quality of education is significantly higher than in the public schools. See especially Wolff 2001.

17. Inter-American Development Bank 2008, p. 4.

18. It is important to recognize, however, that conditions vary considerably throughout the region. The Southern cone nations of Argentina, Chile, and Uruguay, for example, are clearly better off. Costa Rica and some Caribbean nations, such as the Bahamas, Barbados, and Cuba have also achieved higher living standards. Middle income countries in the region include Brazil, Colombia, the Dominican Republic, Mexico, Panama, Paraguay, and Venezuela. The poorest nations tend to be in Central American, especially El Salvador, Guatemala, Honduras, and Nicaragua, and the Andean nations of Bolivia, Ecuador, and Peru. Nearly half of the population in these countries live in poverty. Haiti is by far the most destitute with 80 percent of its population living in poverty.

19. There is an extensive literature on inequality in Latin America. Among the most comprehensive works includes Berry 1997; Borda and Masi 2001; Gasparini 2004; Grynspan 2004; Hoffman and Centeno 2003; Jubany and Meltzer 2004; Korzeniewicz and Smith 1999; Oxhorn 2003; Oxhorn and Ducatenzeiler 1998; Thorp 1998; United Nations Economic Commission for Latin America and the Caribbean 2003b; World Bank 2004; and Ziccardi 2001. The Gini Coefficient for the region as a whole is 0.51.

20. Tokman 2007 offers an overview of the informal economy in Latin America.

21. There is also an extensive literature on ethnicity and ethnic exclusion in Latin America. See especially Applebaum, MacPherson, and Rosemblatt 2007; Branche 2008; Busso, Cicowiez, and Gasparini 2005; Eakin 2007; Ñopo,

Saavedra, and Torero 2007; United Nations Economic Commission for Latin America and the Caribbean 2005b; and Wade 1997.

22. The plight of indigenous peoples has been extensively studied. See Hall and Patrimos 2006; Postero and Zamosc 2004; Sieder 2002; United Nations Economic Commission for Latin America and the Caribbean 2005b; Webber 2007; and Yashar 2005.

23. Today there are almost 50 million indigenous people in Latin America, roughly 9 percent of the total population, divided into roughly 400 linguistic groups. While most of these people are highland Indians, there are also indigenous groups in the Amazonian regions of Brazil, Colombia, Ecuador, Guyana, Peru, and Venezuela.

24. Middle America refers to Mexico and the Central American countries. Nearly half of the population of Guatemala is indigenous. In the Andean nations of Bolivia, Ecuador, and Peru the indigenous population constitutes one-third to one-half of the total population.

25. There are roughly 120 million people of African descent in Latin America today. For general description of the lives of Afro-Latinos see Andrews 2004; Davis 2006; Morrison 2007; and United Nations Economic Commission for Latin America and the Caribbean 2005b.

26. Demographic transition is the process in which societies move from a stage of high fertility and mortality through a phase of rapid population growth (as mortality declines but fertility remains high) to a state of low population growth as fertility also declines.

27. The only Latin American countries where population size clearly outstrips resource endowments are El Salvador and Haiti.

28. United Nations Economic Commission for Latin America and the Caribbean 2005b, p. 9.

29. United Nations Economic Commission for Latin America and the Caribbean 2005b. The countries with the highest population growth include Belize, Bolivia, Guatemala, Haiti, Nicaragua, and Paraguay. Women in these countries have, on average, four children during their reproductive years. The lowest population growth rates are in Chile, Cuba, Uruguay, and some of the English-speaking Caribbean countries. There are also important differences among ethnic groups, with fertility rates generally higher among indigenous and Afro-Latina women.

30. See Jaspers-Faijer 2007 and Machinea 2007 for an analysis of population trends in Latin America.

31. United Nations Economic Commission for Latin America and the Caribbean 2005b, p. 185.

32. Berg 2004; Klasen and Nowak-Lehmann 2008; Pellegrino 2003; and Solimano 2006 consider the impact of emigration on countries of origin in Latin America. It should be noted that migration also occurs within the region. Argentina, Brazil, Chile, Costa Rica, Mexico, and Venezuela have been primary destinations for migrants from neighboring countries. Both professionals and manual laborers tend to move from lower income to higher income countries.

33. It is estimated that in the absence of these family remittances, the extreme poverty rate in Latin America would be 2–3 percent higher. United Nations Economic Commission for Latin America and the Caribbean 2005b, p. 29. See also Acosta 2007; Acosta et al. 2006; Fajnzylber and López 2007, 2008; and Inter-American Development Bank 2004.

34. See Solimano and Allendes 2008 and United Nations Economic Commission for Latin America and the Caribbean 2006a; 2006b. Nearly 90 percent of all Latin Americans who leave their home countries emigrate to the United States.

35. The countries that receive the greatest remittances from abroad are Brazil, Colombia, and Mexico. In Haiti, Jamaica, and Nicaragua, remittances exceed 20 percent of Gross National Product. See Solimano and Allendes 2008.

36. Scholarly literature on the poor quality of governance in Latin America, especially with respect to economic and social challenges, is extensive. See especially Blake 2004; Elvira and Davila 2005; Haber 2000; Vanden and Prevost 2008; and Wiarda and Kline 2006.
37. This argument can be found in Adams 2003; Landman 1999; Lowenthal 2000; and Wodon 2000.
38. Bulmer-Thomas 1994; Buxton and Phillips 1999; and Haber 2000 offer historical reviews of economic policy making in Latin America.
39. State-owned corporations were especially prevalent in utilities, transportation, and the energy sector.
40. This argument is reflected in Bulmer-Thomas 1994 and Franko 2007.
41. González 2004; Kay 2005; and Siegle and Gudeman 2004 offer comprehensive reviews of the decline of rural economies in Latin America.
42. Such a characterization of Latin American political systems is reflected in Haber 2002 and Vanden and Prevost 2008.
43. Public sector corruption in Latin America has been extensively studied. See especially Blake and Morris 2009; González 2008; Haber 2002; and Tulchin and Espach 2000. Public officials have also been implicated in narcotics trafficking not only in drug-producing countries of the Andean region but in the "transit" countries of Middle America and the Caribbean.
44. For scholarship representative of this tradition see especially Keeling 2004; Kumar Saha and Parker 2002; Robinson 2008; and Stirton Weaver 2000.
45. For critical analyses of structural adjustment reforms in Latin America see Barra and Dello Buono 2009; Brooks 2008; Burdick, Oxhorn, and Roberts 2009; Segura-Ubiergo 2007; and Wise and Roett 2003.
46. This argument is reflected in the following scholarship: Hershberg and Rosen 2006; Lustig 1995; Massey, Sanchez, and Behrman 2006; Ocampo 2004; Oxhorn and Ducatenzeiler 1998; Portes 1997; Portes and Hoffman 2003; Roberts 2002; Robinson 1999; and Smith and Korzeniewicz 1997.
47. See Sierra Castro 2000.
48. This argument is an oversimplification since the impact of foreign investment can vary according to the nature, scope, and size of such investment. There are important differences, for example, between investments that are primarily extractive, industrial, or service-oriented. See United Nations Economic Commission for Latin America and the Caribbean 2007d for a recent survey of foreign investment in Latin America and the Caribbean.

4. Meeting Basic Human Needs

1. United Nations 1948b, Article 25.
2. United Nations 1966b, Part 3, Article 11.
3. United Nations 1974c, p. 2.
4. While the World Food Council met from 1974 to 1996, its functions have since been incorporated into the annual work of the FAO.
5. Food and Agriculture Organization, 1996, *Preamble* to the World Food Summit *Plan of Action*, paragraph 7.
6. United Nations, 1948a, Article 25.
7. United Nations 1966b, Part 3, Article 12.
8. United Nations 1978, Article 1.
9. United Nations 1978, Article 8.
10. This conference was a special session of the United Nations General Assembly in 1999.

11. This partnership was a combined effort of UNFPA, UNICEF, WHO, and the World Bank.

12. United Nations 1948b, Article 26.

13. United Nations 1966b, Part 3, Article 13.

14. United Nations Education, Scientific and Cultural Organization 1990.

15. The International Consultative Forum on Education for All, with its secretariat located at the UNESCO headquarters in Paris, was established as an interagency body to guide and monitor follow-up actions to the World Conference on Education for All.

16. The forum set 2015 as the deadline for achieving these goals. See United Nations Education, Scientific and Cultural Organization 2000.

17. United Nations 2005a, p. 11.

18. World Food Programme 2007e, pp. 8–9.

19. World Food Programme 2001b, p. 8. Anemia affects 27 percent of pregnant women in Cuba and approximately 30 percent of women of childbearing age.

20. WFP efforts to support breast feeding are typically undertaken in collaboration with UNICEF and UNFPA. See United Nations Children's Fund 2004, p. 6.

21. World Food Programme 2006a.

22. World Food Programme 2006a, p. 33; 2007a, p. 37; 2008b, p. 10.

23. World Food Programme 2007c, p. 10.

24. World Food Programme 2007e, pp. 9–10.

25. World Food Programme 2001a, p. 12.

26. World Food Programme 2006b, p. 9.

27. World Food Programme 2006b, p. 9.

28. World Food Programme 2007d, p. 8.

29. World Food Programme 2008b, pp. 10–11. Colombia has the second largest number of internally displaced people in the world, with most people fleeing rural areas for larger towns and cities.

30. World Food Programme 2001a, pp. 6–8.

31. World Food Programme 2001b, pp. 8–9.

32. World Food Programme 2007f, p. 10.

33. World Food Programme 2008a, p. 27.

34. World Food Programme 2007c, pp. 9–10.

35. World Food Programme 2007a.

36. World Food Programme 2007c, pp. 9–10.

37. This section does not review reproductive health programs since these programs are described in considerable detail in chapter 6.

38. United Nations Children's Fund 2008a, p. 5.

39. United Nations Children's Fund 2005, p. 23.

40. The purchase of medicines and health supplies has been an important component of UNICEF's Integrated Management of Childhood Illness Initiative in Haiti.

41. Much of this work is coordinated by the Joint United Nations Programme on HIV/AIDS (UNAIDS). UNAIDS, which was established in 1999, is made up of the following co-sponsoring agencies: UNDP, UNFPA, UNICEF, WFP, UNESCO, UNHCR, WHO, and the World Bank. See also United Nations Development Programme 2000, 2002e. UN efforts to combat the spread of HIV/AIDS in Latin America are also coordinated with the Pan-American Health Organization (PAHO) which serves as the regional office of WHO.

42. This initiative was later extended to 39 local and provincial governments throughout the country. United Nations Development Programme 2007a, p. 18.

43. United Nations Development Programme 2002n, p. 4.

44. United Nations Population Fund 2001c, p. 9.

45. United Nations Population Fund 2006c, pp. 4–5.

46. United Nations Population Fund 2006d, pp. 3–5; 2006f, pp. 3–5.

47. United Nations Population Fund 2000b, p. 7; 2002d, pp. 3–4.
48. United Nations Population Fund 2001a, p. 9; 2006c, p. 4; 2007d, p. 4.
49. United Nations Population Fund 2001c, p. 9.
50. United Nations Population Fund 2007c, pp. 3–5.
51. United Nations Population Fund 2001a, pp. 8–9; 2001c, p. 8.
52. United Nations Population Fund 2007c, p. 4.
53. World Food Programme 2005a, p. 33.
54. United Nations Population Fund 2005a, p. 9. See also United Nations Population Fund 2006e, pp. 3–5.
55. The work of UNFPA in this area is carried out in partnership with the Inter-American Institute of Human Rights (IIHR), the Central American Council of Human Rights Lawyers, and the International Labor Organization (ILO).
56. United Nations Children's Fund 2006a, p. 10.
57. The work of UNDP in this area is typically carried out in collaboration with the United Nations Economic Commission for Latin America and the Caribbean (UNECLAC), the Inter-American Development Bank (IDB), and the World Bank.
58. United Nations Population Fund 2006e, p. 5.
59. United Nations Development Programme 2002n, p. 4.
60. United Nations Development Programme 2002d, p. 4; 2002l, p. 5; 2002m, p. 8; 2005b, p. 4.
61. United Nations Development Programme 2001d, p. 7.
62. United Nations Population Fund 2004, p. 5. See also United Nations Development Programme 2001c, p. 4; 2004b, pp. 4–6.
63. United Nations Population Fund 2001a, p. 10.
64. United Nations Population Fund 2007b, p. 4.
65. United Nations Population Fund 2006b, pp. 4–5.
66. United Nations Development Programme 2004a, p. 10.
67. United Nations Development Programme 2001f, p. 9.
68. United Nations Development Programme 2002b, p. 4; 2002m, p. 8.
69. United Nations Development Programme 2002h, p. 4.
70. United Nations Development Programme 2002l, p. 5.
71. United Nations Development Programme 2002i, p. 5.
72. United Nations Development Programme 2002c, p. 3.
73. United Nations Development Programme 2001d, p. 8.

5. Women in the Americas

1. The link between gender equity and sustainable development is now commonly acknowledged by both scholars and practitioners. As stated in the Outcome Document of the 2005 World Summit "progress for women is progress for all." United Nations 2005a, Part 2, Article 58. Such a perspective is reflected in Blue 2005; Boserup 2007; Heyzer 2002; InterAction 2005; Jackson and Pearson 1998; Jaquette and Summerfield 2006; Mokate 2004; Nussbaum 2001; and Parpart, Connelly, and Barriteau 2000. See also United Nations Children's Fund 2006b; United Nations Development Programme 2006a; United Nations Economic Commission for Latin America and the Caribbean 2005b; and United Nations Population Fund 2005c, 2005d, 2006h, 2008b.
2. For a general assessment of gender inequality in Latin America see Caulfield 2001; Godoy and Montaño 2004; Gorlier and Gwzik 2002; Htun 1999; Montaño 2005, 2007, and United Nations Economic Commission for Latin America and the Caribbean 2005b.
3. Buvinic 2002 and Levine, Glassman, and Schneidman 2001 consider gender

inequalities in the provision of health care in Latin America at the beginning of the twenty-first century.
4. United Nations Economic Commission for Latin America and the Caribbean 2005b, pp. 149–54 and United Nations Population Fund 2005a, p. 10.
5. The differential impact of the HIV/AIDS pandemic on men and women in Latin America is examined in Gupta 2003.
6. See Shepard 2006 for a review of the obstacles Latin American women face in obtaining adequate reproductive health care.
7. Abortion is illegal in most Latin American countries except to save the life of the mother or if the pregnancy resulted from rape. The strictest laws are in Chile, El Salvador, and Nicaragua where abortion is not allowed under any circumstances while Barbados, Cuba, and Guyana have more liberal abortion laws.
8. In Latin America, 18 percent of births are not attended by skilled health personnel. This figure is considerably higher in Bolivia, Colombia, Ecuador, Guatemala, Haiti, Nicaragua, Paraguay, and Peru.
9. United Nations Economic Commission for Latin America and the Caribbean 2005b, p. 145. Maternal mortality rates are highest in Bolivia, Haiti, and Peru.
10. At the same time, gender disparities in education continue to exist among the region's poor. See Duryea et al. 2007 and United Nations Economic Commission for Latin America and the Caribbean 2005b. Poor families tend to prioritize their son's education, assuming the long-term financial return will be greater. This is especially true in some of the poorest countries, such as Bolivia, El Salvador, Guatemala, and Peru that have not yet achieved gender parity in public schools.
11. Changes in the labor force participation rates of Latin American women are reviewed in Abramo and Valenzuela 2005; Piras 2004; United Nations Economic Commission for Latin America and the Caribbean 2005b; and United States Agency for International Development 2003.
12. See Deere and León 2001.
13. For an overview of economic conditions for Latin American women see Buvinic 2002; Gálvez 2001; Hite and Viterna 2005; and United Nations Economic Commission for Latin America and the Caribbean 2004, 2005b.
14. United Nations Economic Commission for Latin America and the Caribbean 2005b, p. 44.
15. Women also spend twice as much time as men on unpaid work, especially when home and child care are considered, and thus have less time to participate in paid employment.
16. Chile, Cuba, Mexico, and Venezuela are the exceptions in this respect and have fewer restrictions on female employment.
17. See Salzinger 2003.
18. See also Abramo and Valenzuela 2005; Tokman 2007; and Vuletin 2008 for recent analyses of informal economies in Latin America.
19. Deere 2005 offers detailed analysis of the feminization of agriculture in Latin America.
20. At the same time, the status of women varies considerably between and within countries. Some countries, especially those in the Southern Cone, along with Costa Rica, Cuba, and Venezuela, have made greater progress in improving the rights and opportunities of women while other countries, especially Brazil, the Central American countries, and the Andean countries, have made less progress. Differences also exist with respect to socioeconomic position. Middle and upper-income women obviously have better access to quality health care, education, and other basic services than poor women and are more likely to obtain higher-paid positions in the labor market. Ethnicity is also a crucial factor, with women of European background typically enjoying higher incomes than indigenous or Afro-Latino women. See Poggio and Sagot 2000.

21. See Socolow 2000, 2005.
22. See Craske 1999; Deere and León 2001; Del Campo 2005; and Dore and Molyneux 2000 for an assessment of male privilege in public sector programs.
23. Htun 1999.
24. It is important to recognize divisions within the Catholic Church in Latin America. Traditional and charismatic Catholic churches adopt more conservative positions on gender roles while churches that are more sympathetic to Liberation Theology tend to challenge long-standing practices and promote stronger roles for women. See Gandolfo 2007.
25. The expansion of evangelical protestant churches is most evident in Central America. Twenty-five percent of all people in Guatemala and almost 20 percent of people in El Salvador and Nicaragua are members of such churches. There are also large numbers of evangelical Protestants in Argentina, Brazil, and Chile. See Freston 2008; Shaull and Cesar 2001; Steigenga and Cleary 2008; and Westmeier 2000.
26. While most members of evangelical protestant churches are poor, there are an increasing number of middle and even upper income members.
27. It is sometimes argued that evangelical protestant churches, where women typically constitute two-thirds of the membership, help women exercise greater control over their lives. These churches have sometimes demonstrated greater acceptance of women in leadership roles than traditional Catholic churches. See Grudem 2006.
28. For analysis of the evolution and complexity of gender roles in Latin America see Caulfield 2001, French and Bliss 2007, and González-Lopez 2006.
29. The changing nature of gender relations in Latin America and the emergence of feminist movements have been the focus of extensive scholarship. See especially Abbassi and Lutjens 2002; Barrig 2001; Burton 2004; Cagan 2000; Chant and Craske 2003; Craske and Molyneux 2002; Femenías and Oliver 2007; Navarro and Korrol 1999; Smith, Troutner, and Hunefeldt 2007; Stromquist 2007; Tiano 2001; and Weinstein 2006.
30. It is important to recognize that both the World Bank and IDB have adopted more progressive gender policies in recent years. Both have established gender divisions to evaluate the likely impact of project proposals on women and increased support for programs that directly benefit women. See World Bank 2001.
31. Critical assessments of the impact of structural adjustment reforms on Latin American women can be found in Ball 2004; Hite and Viterna 2005; León 2000; Razavi 2009; Sparr 1994; and Thorin 2001.

6. Promoting Gender Equity

1. See Pietilä and Vickers 1998 for a review of UN's efforts to promote the rights of women.
2. Although the CSW was initially under the Commission on Human Rights, it was soon granted institutional autonomy as one of six functional commissions of ECOSOC.
3. The Commission on the Status of Women can also receive communications from individuals and groups concerning specific cases of discrimination against women.
4. United Nations 1948b, Article 2.
5. United Nations 1967, Article 2. The *Declaration on the Elimination of Discrimination against Women* was drafted by the CSW.

6. The official name of this conference was the World Conference of the International Women's Year.
7. This declaration also called for combating the trafficking of women, prostitution, child and sexual abuse, and domestic violence.
8. INSTRAW is an autonomous body of the UN and governed an 11-member board of trustees.
9. UNIFEM also works to ensure that gender considerations are included in international policies concerning refugees and displaced persons, human rights, and the environment.
10. United Nations 1979. The *Convention on the Elimination of All Forms of Discrimination against Women* was also drafted by the Commission on the Status of Women. The convention came into force in September 1981 following ratification by 20 member states.
11. United Nations 1979, Part 1, Article 1.
12. The composition of the Committee on the Elimination of Discrimination against Women is designed to represent the different geographical areas and legal systems of the world.
13. The Committee on the Elimination of Discrimination against Women has not been especially powerful. In 1999, the General Assembly adopted the Optional Protocol of the *Convention on the Elimination of All Forms of Discrimination against Women* that allows individual women or groups to bring national violations of CEDAW directly to a Committee of Experts.
14. The official name of this conference was the World Conference of the United Nations Decade for Women.
15. The official name of this conference was the World Conference to Review and Appraise the Achievements of the United Nations Decade for Women.
16. The *Plan of Action* was officially called the *Nairobi Forward-Looking Strategies for the Advancement of Women*. See United Nations 1985. The Commission on the Status of Women was charged with monitoring implementation of the *Plan of Action*.
17. United Nations 1986, Article 8, Paragraph 1.
18. A recent assessment of UN efforts to mainstream gender issues into all institutional policies and programs can be found in United Nations Economic and Social Council 2005.
19. The Division for the Advancement of Women also acts as the secretariat for the UN Commission on the Status of Women.
20. United Nations Environmental Programme 1992, Chapter 24, entitled "Global Action for Women toward Sustainable and Equitable Development."
21. United Nations 1994. UNFPA was designated the lead agency for the follow-up and implementation of the *Program of Action* of the Cairo conference.
22. United Nations 1995b, p 1, paragraph 7.
23. United Nations 1995a.
24. United Nations 2000, Part 3, Article 20.
25. United Nations 2005a, Part 1, Article 12.
26. United Nations Population Fund 2000c, pp. 7–8; 2005b, pp. 3–4.
27. United Nations Population Fund 2007a, p. 6; 2007b, p. 4.
28. United Nations Population Fund 2007c, pp. 3–5.
29. United Nations Population Fund 2006b, p. 4.
30. United Nations Population Fund 2007e, p. 4.
31. United Nations Population Fund 2007f, pp. 3–5. See also United Nations Population Fund 2001e, pp. 6–9.
32. United Nations Population Fund 2006f, pp. 3–4.
33. United Nations Population Fund 2002d, p. 5; 2003b, pp. 4–5.
34. United Nations Population Fund 2007b, p. 4.

164   *Notes*

35. United Nations Population Fund 2001d, p. 9; 2006e, pp. 3–5.
36. United Nations Population Fund 2002a, pp. 3–5; 2007b, p. 3.
37. United Nations Population Fund 2001b, p. 9.
38. United Nations Population Fund 2001d, p. 10; 2006e, pp. 4–5.
39. United Nations Population Fund 2000c, pp. 8–9; 2005b, p. 4; 2007g, pp. 3–4.
40. United Nations Population Fund 1995, p. 11; 2007d, pp. 3–5.
41. United Nations Population Fund 2001f, pp. 7–8; 2003a, pp. 3–5.
42. United Nations Population Fund 2003b, p. 4.
43. United Nations Population Fund 2006a, p. 3; 2007g, p. 4.
44. United Nations Population Fund 2001a, pp. 8–9.
45. United Nations Population Fund 2000b, p. 8; 2004, p. 4.
46. United Nations Population Fund 2006c, p. 4; 2006d, p. 4.
47. United Nations Population Fund 2008a, p. 8.
48. United Nations Population Fund 2000a, pp. 7–8.
49. United Nations Population Fund 2002a, pp. 4–5.
50. United Nations Population Fund 2006a, p. 18.
51. World Food Programme 2007d, p. 7.
52. World Food Programme 2001a, p. 16.
53. World Food Programme 2000, pp. 7–9.
54. The Gender Empowerment Measure (GEM) focuses on the percentage of women in administrative and managerial positions, professional and technical jobs, and high offices in the public sector.
55. United Nations Population Fund 2004, p. 5.
56. United Nations Population Fund 2007b, p. 4.
57. United Nations Population Fund 2007d, p. 4.
58. United Nations Population Fund 2000a, pp. 9–10; 2003b, p. 5.
59. United Nations Population Fund 2001d, p. 10; 2006e, p. 5.
60. United Nations Population Fund 2002e, pp. 3–5.
61. United Nations Development Programme 2003b, 2006a, p. 21.
62. United Nations Development Programme 2001b, pp. 7–8.
63. United Nations Development Programme 2001a, p. 5.
64. United Nations Population Fund 2007d, p. 5.
65. United Nations Population Fund 2001a, p. 10.
66. United Nations Population Fund 1998, p. 9; 2001g, pp. 9–10; 2002b, pp. 4–5; 2006g, p. 4. See also United Nations Development Programme 2002g, p. 3.
67. United Nations Population Fund 2006f, pp. 4–5.
68. United Nations Population Fund 2004, p. 4.
69. United Nations Population Fund 2007g, pp. 3–5.
70. United Nations Population Fund 2000a, p. 8; 2003b, p. 4.
71. United Nations Population Fund 2002c, pp. 3–5; 2006d, pp. 3–5.
72. United Nations Population Fund 2002d, pp. 4–5.
73. United Nations Population Fund 1998, p. 8; 2007c, pp. 3–5.
74. United Nations Population Fund 2000c, pp. 7–8; 2005b, pp. 3–5.
75. United Nations Population Fund 2001d, pp. 8–10.
76. United Nations Population Fund 2001a, pp. 8–9; 2006e, pp. 3–4.
77. United Nations Population Fund 2001b, pp. 8–9.
78. United Nations Population Fund 2001c, p. 10.
79. United Nations Population Fund 2001d, p. 11.
80. United Nations Population Fund 2007b, p. 5.

7. Ecology of the Americas

1. For a general survey of environmental conditions in Latin America see Hillstrom and Hillstrom 2003; Miller 2007; Roberts and Parks 2004; Romero and West 2005; United Nations Economic Commission for Latin America and the Caribbean 2005b; and Villarroel 2006.
2. Air pollution in Mexico City and Santiago can be life threatening. Both cities experience thermal inversions and a lack of air circulation due to their geographic setting and altitude.
3. The ill health effects of air pollution in Mexico City lead to the loss of approximately 65 million working days each year. United Nations Economic Commission for Latin America and the Caribbean 2005b, p. 188. See also Cifuenten 2005 for analysis of the extent to which air pollution threatens human health in Latin America and the Caribbean.
4. The potential impact of climate change on Latin American nations is considered in Fajnzylber and Nash 2008; Moreno 2006; Simms and Reid 2006; and United Nations Environmental Programme 2007g, pp. 40–43. See also United Nations Development Programme 2007b.
5. Escobar 2002 and United Nations Economic Commission for Latin America and the Caribbean 2006d offer comprehensive assessments of both freshwater and marine resources in Latin America.
6. United Nations Environmental Programme 2008a, p. 42.
7. Only 14 percent of the region's wastewater is treated before being dumped into bodies of water. United Nations Economic Commission for Latin America and the Caribbean 2005b, p. 173.
8. Latin America has a higher proportion of land area covered by forests than any other region in the world and Brazil alone contains 26 percent of the world's tropical forests. United Nations Economic Commission for Latin America and the Caribbean 2005b, p. 176.
9. Most countries have crafted plans for forest management. The Amazon Region Protected Areas program in Brazil, for example, includes protection of 46 national forests. Similarly, Costa Rica's Forest Law designates more than 10 percent of the country as a protected area. Reforestation programs have been undertaken in Brazil, Costa Rica, Ecuador, Peru, and Venezuela. See Ros-Tonen 2006.
10. Forty percent of the world's loss of natural forest in the last 30 years has been in Latin America.
11. Around 4.3 million hectares of forests in Latin America were cleared annually between 2000 and 2005 and deforestation rates have increased by almost 17 percent since 2000.
12. In Central America, deforestation is most evident in Guatemala where 65 percent of original forest cover has been destroyed in the last three decades. At current rates, the remainder of this nation's forests will disappear within 25 years.
13. United Nations Economic Commission for Latin America and the Caribbean 2005b, p. 177.
14. Brazil is the world's fourth largest producer of greenhouse gases with roughly 75 percent of those emissions resulting from deforestation.
15. This concept is more fully developed in Swinton, Escobar, and Reardon 2003. See also Carruthers 2008.
16. United Nations Development Programme 2006a, p. 14; 2007a, p. 4.
17. United Nations Economic Commission for Latin America and the Caribbean 2005b, p. 185. See also González 2005.
18. United Nations Economic Commission for Latin America and the Caribbean 2005a; 2005b, p. 185; and United Nations Environmental Programme 2008b,

p. 16. The percent of total population living in urban areas is highest in Argentina (88), Uruguay (86), Chile (86), Venezuela (82), Brazil (79), and Cuba (78) and lowest is Panama (52), Bolivia (56), Costa Rica (58), El Salvador (54), Guatemala (43), Honduras (51), and Paraguay (44).

19. A recent World Bank report describes conditions for the urban poor in Latin America. See Fay 2005. See also Sánchez-Rodríguez and Bonilla 2007.

20. United Nations Population Fund 2007h.

21. It is important to recognize that some countries have been more committed to preserving their natural environments than other countries. Argentina, Belize, Chile, and Costa Rica have fairly strong environmental records. This is reflected in public sector support for environmental projects, the expansion of nature preserves, and consistent enforcement of environmental laws. Other countries, especially in Central America and the Andes, have been less committed to protecting natural resources and ecosystems. Brazil, with the largest forest area and greatest biodiversity, has instituted some measures to better protect its environment in recent years, though its overall record remains relatively weak.

22. For an assessment of the environmental costs of industrialization in Latin America see Jenkins 2001.

23. The link between external forces and environmental decline in Latin America is examined in Aide and Grau 2004 and Roberts and Thanos 2003.

24. Gamper-Rabindran 2006 surveys the environmental consequences of NAFTA.

25. See Schatán 1999, 2000 for an analysis of the environmental impact of export agriculture in Latin America.

26. The link between neoliberalism and environmental decline is more fully examined in Heynen 2007; Liverman and Vilas 2006; and López 2006.

27. United Nations Economic Commission for Latin America and the Caribbean 2003a, 2005a. Latin America is highly vulnerable to droughts, earthquakes, floods, hurricanes, and volcanic eruptions. With an average of 40 major natural disasters a year, the region ranks second to Asia in terms of the frequency of such disasters. In the last ten years, natural disasters killed more than 45,000 people and caused over US$20 billion in direct damages.

28. For example, Hurricane Mitch, which struck Central America in October 1998, came after decades of deforestation and the cultivation of marginal lands without soil conservation measures or adequate watershed management. Because the soil was unable to absorb the prolonged rains, the hurricane produced much more serious flooding and mudslides than would otherwise have been the case. Three million people, or about *one-tenth* of the entire population of Central America, were left homeless.

8. Preserving Natural Environments

1. UNEP's Regional Office for Latin America and the Caribbean is based in Panama City, Panama.

2. Initial attention to environmental issues by the UN was due, at least in part, to the emergence of grassroots environmental movements in a number of member countries.

3. United Nations 1973.

4. United Nations 1972b.

5. See Mische and Ribeiro 1998 for an assessment of the environmental work of the United Nations.

6. UNCLOS entered into force in 1994 and currently has 154 state parties.

7. This commission was more commonly known as the Brundtland Commission after its chairperson, former Norwegian prime minister Gro Harlem Brundtland.

8. World Commission on Environment and Development 1987, p. 43.
9. Elsewhere the report defined sustainable development as "a process of change in which the exploitation of resources, the direction of investments, the orientation of technological development, and institutional change are all in harmony and enhance both current and future potential to meet human needs and aspirations." World Commission on Environment and Development 1987, 46.
10. Exposure to ultra-violet radiation can cause serious health problems, including skin cancer, cataracts, and damage to the immune system. Such radiation can also disrupt agricultural production and reduce crop yields.
11. Although the UN was not officially involved in drafting the Montreal Protocol, UNEP provided technical assistance and advice throughout the negotiation process.
12. The UN has also worked to limit the interstate transport of toxic wastes. The 1989 Basel Convention on the Control of Transboundary Movements of Hazardous Wastes, which is administered by UNEP, restricts the export of toxic wastes to developing countries.
13. The *United Nations Framework Convention on Climate Change* drew upon the work of the United Nations Inter-Governmental Panel on Climate Change. The panel's initial report in 1988 forecast serious consequences if global warming is not reversed, including desertification, the disruption of agricultural systems, and shoreline erosion.
14. The Convention on Biological Diversity is administered by UNEP.
15. This document listed 17 nonbinding recommendations for forest conservation and reforestation. Within three years an Intergovernmental Panel on Forests was established to monitor forest use and devise policies to protect forest areas.
16. The Commission on Sustainable Development, which is a functional commission of ECOSOC, meets annually to review the progress achieved by all countries and propose policy guidelines for future action.
17. United Nations 1994, Chapter III, Section C, 3.24.
18. United Nations 1994, Chapter III, Section A, 3.3.
19. In July 2001 additional mechanisms for obtaining carbon credits were added to the Kyoto Protocol. Nations could obtain such credits for carbon sequestration and reforestation projects.
20. Subsequent efforts at the Hague (2000), Berlin (2001), and Marrakesh (2001) to translate the Kyoto Protocol into a detailed, enforceable treaty, and establish penalties for noncompliance, were largely unsuccessful. However, climate change conferences in Nairobi (2006) and Bali (2007) did establish timetables for negotiating further reductions of greenhouse gas emissions. The United Nations is currently negotiating a new climate change treaty to take effect after the Kyoto Protocol expires in 2012. See United Nations Development Programme 2007b.
21. United Nations 2005a, p. 39.
22. United Nations Environmental Programme 2006, p. 12; 2007a, p. 10; and 2008a, p. 55.
23. United Nations Environmental Programme 2007g, p. 43.
24. United Nations Development Programme 2002k, p. 6.
25. United Nations Development Programme 2002j, p. 8; 2002l, p. 5; 2003a, p. 6.
26. United Nations Development Programme 2002a, p. 4; United Nations Environmental Programme 2007g, p. 44.
27. United Nations Environmental Programme 2008a, p. 16.
28. United Nations Development Programme 2002k, p. 6.
29. United Nations Environmental Programme 2007f, p. 16.
30. Integrated water resource management refers to coordinated management and development of water resources in order to maximize use without compromising sustainability.

31. World Food Programme 2000, pp. 6–9.
32. United Nations Environmental Programme 2007f, p. 16.
33. United Nations Environmental Programme 2006, p. 68–69; 2008a, p. 42.
34. United Nations Development Programme 2001e, p. 5; United Nations Environmental Programme 2007f, p. 16.
35. United Nations Development Programme 2001f, pp. 10–11.
36. United Nations Development Programme 2002m, p. 10.
37. United Nations Environmental Programme 2007f, p. 18.
38. United Nations Environmental Programme 2007f, p. 18.
39. UNEP supported the National Plan to Combat Desertification and the Effects of Drought in Brazil.
40. United Nations Development Programme 2002m, p. 10.
41. United Nations Environmental Programme 2007f, p. 20.
42. World Food Programme 2007e, p. 10.
43. UNDP also supported the Pilot Programme for the Conservation of the Brazilian Rainforest, one of the largest multilateral programs for the sustainable use of tropical forests.
44. United Nations Development Programme 2002n, pp. 4–5.
45. United Nations Development Programme 2002j, p. 8.
46. In preparing these Common Country Assessments, UNEP employs the methodologies developed by its Global Environmental Outlook (GEO) project.
47. United Nations Development Programme 2002a, p. 4.
48. United Nations Development Programme 2002m, p. 10.
49. United Nations Development Programme 2001d, p. 8.
50. United Nations Development Programme 2002f, p. 5.
51. United Nations Development Programme 2002i, p. 9.
52. United Nations Development Programme 2001a, p. 5; 2006b, p. 7; 2006c, pp. 4–6.
53. United Nations Environmental Programme 2007f, p. 18.
54. The UN has also sponsored training programs for civil society groups. UNEP established an Environmental Training Network for Latin America and the Caribbean to provide community-based training in environmental management.
55. United Nations Development Programme 2001a, p. 8.
56. United Nations Environmental Programme 2005a, p. 35. See also United Nations Environmental Programme 2007b, 2007c, 2007d.
57. For a five year assessment of the Latin American and Caribbean Initiative for Sustainable Development see United Nations Environmental Programme 2008b.
58. This convention is also known as the *Cartegena Convention.*
59. Cooperation on the environment in Central America can be traced to December 1989 when the nations of this region signed the Agreement for the Protection of the Environment in Central America and established the Central American Commission on Environment and Development of the Central American Integration System. Member countries include Belize, Costa Rica, El Salvador, Guatemala, Honduras, Nicaragua, and Panama.
60. UNEP also supported the Central American Environment and Development Fund (FOCADES).
61. For example, UNDP supported the Central American Indigenous and Peasant Coordination Association for Community Agroforestry.
62. United Nations Development Programme 2002i, p. 6. The Meso-American Biological Corridor includes the nations of Belize, Costa Rica, El Salvador, Guatemala, Honduras, Nicaragua, Panama, and five states in Southeastern Mexico (Campeche, Chiapas, Quintana Roo, Tabasco, and Yucatán).
63. Roughly US$100 million has been invested for biodiversity conservation in the Meso-American Biological Corridor by the GEF.

64. UNDP also supported six biological corridors in the southeastern Mexico. The corridors help mainstream biodiversity conservation and sustainable management of natural resources into local development processes.

9. Aiding Development in the Americas

1. United Nations Economic Commission for Latin America and the Caribbean 2005b, p. 285.
2. Bolivia, Costa Rica, and Ecuador have all participated in debt-for-nature swaps with international environmental organizations.
3. This perspective follows a long line of scholarship on UN reform. In recent years, such scholarship is reflected in the works of Idris and Bartolo 2000; Kennedy 2006; Krasno 2004; Magariños 2005; Mingst and Karns 2000; Muravchik 2005; and Taylor and Groom 2000. See also the following institutional assessments: United Nations 2002c, 2006a.
4. UN activities are subject to a range of audit and review boards, including the Board of Auditors, the Joint Inspection Unit, and the Office of Internal Oversight Services.
5. It is important to acknowledge that some of the subsidiary agencies have a strong record with respect to oversight and monitoring. The UNDP's Office of Evaluation conducts fairly rigorous program and policy evaluations. In 1999 UNDP introduced a Multi-Year Funding Framework (MYFF) where financial contributions are linked to program performance. See United Nations Development Programme 2006a, pp. 32–33. Similarly, the WFP undertakes a midterm review, final review, and special evaluation reports to ensure regular feedback on each country program.
6. The 2002 International Conference on Financing for Development recognized that building a global alliance for development necessitates greater cooperation among existing institutions. See United Nations 2003. Hill 2008 also highlights the need for more effectively coordinating the economic and social work of the UN.
7. CEB has three main committees responsible for administrative concerns along with numerous subcommittees that focus on more specific issues.
8. United Nations 2002c. UNDG is led by an executive committee, chaired by the Administrator of UNDP, and supported by the Development Group Office, an interagency unit administered by UNDP.
9. United Nations 2006a. See also United Nations Development Programme 2006a, p. 30 and 2007a, p. 7.
10. Country Strategy Notes are prepared in consultation with UN specialized agencies, subsidiary funds and programs, and local governments.
11. The 2005 World Summit mandated that ECOSOC hold Annual Ministerial Reviews (AMR) and a biennial Development Cooperation Forum (DCF). The objective of the AMR is to assess progress in achieving the development goals that emerged from major UN conferences while the DCF is designed to enhance coordination among different development partners. The DCF meets within the framework of the High-Level Segment of ECOSOC. United Nations 2005a, p. 34.
12. The Outcome Document of the 2005 World Summit called for strengthening the existing capabilities of ECOSOC and expanding its mandate. See United Nations 2005a, pp. 33–34. Taylor 2000 also offers proposals for strengthening ECOSOC.
13. As noted by United Nations Economic Commission for Latin America and the Caribbean, a slight decline in the Gini Coefficient produces the same reduction in

poverty as many years of positive economic growth. United Nations Economic Commission for Latin America and the Caribbean 2005b, p. 53. This argument is also advanced by Jubany and Meltzer 2004, p. 3.

14. The Latin American countries with the most progressive tax systems are Chile, Costa Rica, and Uruguay. See Jubany and Meltzer 2004, p. 6.

15. See Otto 1996, Sollis 1996, and Weiss and Gordenker 1996 for an analysis of the UN experience working with civil society organizations.

16. United Nations 1945, Chapter 10, Article 71. At present, over 2100 NGOs have obtained consultative status with ECOSOC. Consultative status is awarded by the Committee on Nongovernmental Organizations which meets biennially.

17. The Conference on Nongovernmental Organizations in Consultative Relationship with the United Nations (CONGO) helps ensure civil society groups are involved in the formulation of UN-sponsored development projects and programs.

18. United Nations 2004.

19. United Nations 2005a, p. 5. See also United Nations 2002c, pp. 24–25.

20. World Food Programme 2007a, p. 52; 2007b, pp. 22–23. Roughly half of WFP assistance is distributed through civil society partners.

21. *The United Nations Millennium Declaration* called on member states to afford greater opportunities to nongovernmental organizations and civil society. See United Nations 2000.

22. There is an extensive literature on the importance of civil society participation in the development process. Donnelly-Roark 1991 offers an early institutional assessment of NGO involvement in UNDP projects. More recently, this tradition is reflected in Bebbington, Hickey, and Mitlin 2008; Brinkerhoff, Smith, and Teegen 2007; Domike 2008; Eade 2000; Lewis and Wallace 2000; Rugendyke 2007; and Stahler-Sholk, Kuecker, and Vanden 2008.

Bibliography

Abbassi, Jennifer, and Sheryl L. Lutjens, eds. 2002. *Rereading Women in Latin America and the Caribbean*. Lanham, MD: Rowman and Littlefield.

Abramo, Laís, and María Elena Valenzuela. 2005. "Women's Labour Force Participation Rates in Latin America." *International Labor Review* 144 (4): 369–99.

Acosta, Pablo. 2007. *What is the Impact of Remittances on Poverty and Inequality in Latin America?* Washington, DC: World Bank, Latin America and Caribbean Region.

Acosta, Pablo, Cesar Calderón, Pablo Fajnzylber, and Humberto López. 2006. "Remittances and Development in Latin America." *The World Economy* 29 (7): 957–87.

Adams, Francis. 2003. *Deepening Democracy: Global Governance and Political Reform in Latin America*. Westport, CT: Praeger.

Aggleton, Peter. 2003. *Stigma, Discrimination and HIV/AIDS in Latin America and the Caribbean*. Washington, DC: Inter-American Development Bank, Sustainable Development Department.

Aide, T. Mitchell, and H. Ricardo Grau. 2004. "Globalization, Migration and Latin American Ecosystems." *Science* 305 (5692, September): 1915–16.

Alleyne, Mark D. 2003. *Global Lies? Propaganda, the United Nations, and World Order*. New York: Palgrave Macmillan.

Alsop, Ruth, Mette Bertelsen, and Jeremy Holland. 2005. *Empowerment in Practise: From Analysis to Implementation*. Washington, DC: World Bank.

Ameri, Houshang. 2003. *Fraud, Waste and Abuse: Aspects of United Nations Management and Personnel Policies*. Lanham: University Press of America.

Andrews, George Reid. 2004. *Afro-Latin America: 1800–2000*. Oxford: Oxford University Press.

Annan, Kofi. 2000. *We the Peoples: The Role of the United Nations in the Twenty-first Century*. New York: United Nations.

Applebaum, Nancy P., Anne S. MacPherson, and Karin Alejandra Rosemblatt. 2007. *Race and Nation in Modern Latin America*. Chapel Hill: University of North Carolina Press.

Babbin, Jed. 2004. *Inside the Asylum: Why the United Nations and Old Europe are Worse than You Think*. Washington, DC: Regnery Publishers.

Ball, Jennifer A. 2004. "The Effects of Neoliberal Structural Adjustment on Women's Relative Employment in Latin America." *International Journal of Social Economics* 31 (10): 976–90.

Barra, Ximena de la, and Richard Alan Dello Buono. 2009. *Latin America after the Neoliberal Debacle*. Lanham, MD: Rowman and Littlefield.

Barrig, Maruja. 2001. "Latin American Feminism: Gains, Loses, and Hard Times." *NACLA Report on the Americas* 34 (5, March/April): 29–45.

Bebbington, Anthony, Samuel Hickey, and Diana C. Mitlin, eds. 2008. *Can NGOs Make a Difference: The Challenge of Development Alternatives*. London: Zed Books.

Belizan, J. M., M. L. Cafferata, M. Belizan, and F. Althabe. 2007. "Health Inequality in Latin America." *The Lancet* 370 (9599): 1599–1600.

Berg, Mette Louise. 2004. *Migration and Development in Latin America and the Caribbean*. Oxford: Center on Migration, Policy and Society.

Berry, Albert. 1997. "The Inequality Threat in Latin America." *Latin American Research Review* 32 (2): 3–40.

Berthelot, Yves, ed. 2004. *Unity and Diversity in Development Ideas: Perspectives from the United Nations Regional Commissions*. Bloomington: Indiana University Press.

Bertrand, Maurice. 1985. *Some Reflections on Reform of the United Nations* (Bertrand Report). Geneva: United Nations Joint Inspection Unit, JIU/REP/85/9, December.

Bhouraskar, Digambar. 2006. *United Nations Development Aid: A Study in History and Politics*. New Delhi: Academic Foundation.

Blake, Charles H. 2004. *Politics in Latin America: The Quests for Development, Liberty and Governance*. Boston: Houghton Mifflin.

Blake, Charles H., and Stephen D. Morris, eds. 2009. *Corruption and Democracy in Latin America*. Pittsburgh: University of Pittsburgh Press.

Blewitt, John. 2008. *Understanding Sustainable Development*. London: Earthscan.

Blue, Sarah. 2005. "Including Women in Development." *Latin American Perspectives* 32 (5): 101–17.

Borda, Dionisio, and Fernado Masi, eds. 2001. *Pobreza, Desigualdad, y Política Social en América Latina*. Asuncion: Centro de Análisis y Difusión de la Economía Paraguaya.

Boserup, Ester. 2007. *Women's Role in Economic Development*. London: Earthscan.

Boutros-Ghali, Boutros. 1992. *An Agenda for Peace: Report of the Secretary-General*. A/47/277–S/24111. New York: United Nations, June 17.

———. 1994. *An Agenda for Development: Report of the Secretary-General*. A/48/935. New York: United Nations, May 6.

———. 1995. "Democracy: A Newly Recognized Imperative." *Global Governance* 1: 3–11.

———. 1996. *An Agenda for Democratization*. Report of the Secretary-General to the General Assembly. UN Doc A/51/761. New York: United Nations, December 20.

Branche, Jerome. 2008. *Race, Colonialism and Social Transformation in Latin America and the Caribbean*. Gainesville: University Press of Florida.

Brandt Commission. 1980. *North-South: A Program for Survival*. London: Pan Books.

Brinkerhoff, Jennifer, Stephen C. Smith, and Hildy Teegen, eds. 2007. *NGOs and the Millennium Development Goals: Citizen Action to Reduce Poverty*. New York: Palgrave Macmillan.

Brooks, Sarah M. 2008. *Social Protection and the Market in Latin America:*

The Transformation of Social Security Institutions. Cambridge: Cambridge University Press.

Bulmer-Thomas, Victor. 1994. *The Economic History of Latin America since Independence.* Cambridge: Cambridge University Press.

Burdick, John, Philip Oxhorn, and Kenneth M. Roberts. 2009. *Beyond Neoliberalism in Latin America? Societies and Politics at the Crossroads.* New York: Palgrave Macmillan.

Burnell, Peter, ed. 2000. *Democracy Assistance: International Cooperation for Democratization.* London: Frank Cass.

Burton, Barbara. 2004. "The Transmigration of Rights: Women, Movement and the Grassroots in Latin American and Caribbean Communities." *Development and Change* 35 (4, September): 773–98.

Busso, Matias, Martin Cicowiez, and Leonardo Gasparini. 2005. *Ethnicity and the Millennium Development Goals.* Santiago: United Nations Economic Commission for Latin America and the Caribbean.

Buvinic, Mayra. 2002. *Gender Inequality in Health and Work: The Case of Latin America and the Caribbean.* Washington, DC: Inter-American Development Bank.

Buxton, Julie, and Nicola Phillips, eds. 1999. *Developments in Latin American Political Economy: States, Markets and Actors.* Manchester: Manchester University Press.

Cagan, Elizabeth. 2000. *Women and Democratization: Lessons from Latin America.* Stamford: JAI Press.

Carothers, Thomas. 1999. *Aiding Democracy Abroad.* Washington, DC: Carnegie Endowment for International Peace.

Carruthers, David V., ed. 2008. *Environmental Justice in Latin America: Problems, Promise and Practice.* Cambridge: Massachusetts Institute of Technology Press.

Caulfield, Sueann. 2001. "The History of Gender in the Historiography of Latin America." *Hispanic American Historical Review* 81 (3–4): 449–90.

Chant, Sylvia H., and Nikki Craske. 2003. *Gender in Latin America.* New Brunswick: Rutgers University Press.

Cifuenten, Luis A. 2005. *Urban Air Quality and Human Health in Latin America and the Caribbean.* Santiago: Centro de Economía Aplicada, Universidad de Chile.

Cooper, Phillip J., and Claudia María Vargas. 2004. *Implementing Sustainable Development: From Global Policy to Local Action.* Lanham, MD: Rowman and Littlefield.

Craske, Nikki. 1999. *Women and Politics in Latin America.* New Brunswick: Rutgers University Press.

Craske, Nikki, and Maxine Molyneux, eds. 2002. *Gender and the Politics of Rights and Democracy in Latin America.* New York: Palgrave.

Crawford, Gordon. 2001. *Foreign Aid and Political Reform: A Comparative Analysis of Democratic Assistance and Political Conditionality.* New York: Palgrave.

Cruces, Guillermo and Daniel Titelman. 2007. "Challenges for Health and Social Protection in Latin America." *Global Social Policy* 7 (2): 136–39.

Davis, Darien J. 2006. *Beyond Slavery: The Multilayered Legacy of Africans in Latin America and the Caribbean.* Lanham, MD: Rowman and Littlefield.

Deere, Carmen Diana. 2005. *The Feminization of Agriculture? Economic*

Restructuring in Rural Latin America. Geneva: United Nations Research Institute for Social Development.

Deere, Carmen Diana, and Magdalena León. 2001. *Empowering Women: Land and Property Rights in Latin America.* Pittsburgh: University of Pittsburgh Press.

Del Campo, Esther. 2005. "Women and Politics in Latin America: Perspectives and Limits of the Institutional Aspects of Women's Political Representation." *Social Forces* 83 (4, June): 1697–1725.

Domike, Arthur L. 2008. *Civil Society and Social Movements: Building Sustainable Democracies in Latin America.* Washington, DC: Inter-American Development Bank.

Donnelly-Roark, Paula. 1991. *Grassroots Participation: Defining New Realities and Operationalizing New Strategies,* UNDP Discussion Paper. New York: United Nations Development Programme.

Dore, Elizabeth, and Maxine Molyneux, eds. 2000. *Hidden Histories of Gender and the State in Latin America.* Durham: Duke University Press.

Duryea, Suzanne, Alejandra Cox Edwards, and Manuelita Ureta. 2003. *Women in the Latin American Labor Market.* Washington, DC: Inter-American Development Bank, Sustainable Development Department.

Duryea, Suzanne, Sebastian Galiani, Hugo Ñopo, and Claudia Piras. 2007. *The Education Gender Gap in Latin America and the Caribbean.* Working Paper 600. Washington, DC: Inter-American Development Bank.

Eade, Deborah. 2000. *Development, NGOs and Civil Society.* Williamsburg, MA: Kumarian Press.

Eakin, Marshall C. 2007. *The History of Latin America: Collision of Cultures.* New York: Palgrave Macmillan.

Elvira, Marta M., and Anabella Davila, eds. 2005. *Managing Human Resources in Latin America.* New York: Routledge.

Escobar, Jairo. 2002. *La Contaminación de los Ríos y sus Efectos en las Áreas Costeras y el Mar.* Santiago: United Nations Economic Commission for Latin America and the Caribbean, División de Recursos Naturales y Infraestructura.

Fajnzylber, Pablo, and J. Humberto López, eds. 2007. *Close to Home: The Development Impact of Remittances in Latin America.* Washington, DC: World Bank.

——. 2008. *Remittances and Development: Lessons from Latin America.* Washington, DC: World Bank.

Fajnzylber, Pablo, and John Nash. 2008. *Climate Change in Latin America: Impact and Policy Challenges.* Washington, DC: World Bank.

Fay, Marianne, ed. 2005. *The Urban Poor in Latin America.* Washington, DC: World Bank.

Femenías, María Luisa, and Amy Oliver, eds. 2007. *Feminist Philosophy in Latin America and Spain.* New York: Rodopi.

Food and Agriculture Organization. 1996. *Rome Declaration on World Food Security and World Food Summit Plan of Action.* WFS 98/REP, adopted at the World Food Summit, November 13–17, 1996, Rome, Italy. Rome: Food and Agriculture Organization.

——. 2008. *State of Food Insecurity in the World 2008.* Rome: Food and Agriculture Organization.

Fomerand, Jacques. 2004. "Agent of Change: The United Nations and Development." In *The United Nations: Confronting the Challenges of Global Security,* edited by Jean E. Krasno, 163–92. Boulder: Lynne Rienner.

Forsythe, David P. 1996. "The United Nations, Democracy and the Americas." In *Beyond Sovereignty: Collectively Defending Democracy in the Americas*, edited by Tom F. Farer, 107–31. Baltimore: Johns Hopkins University Press.

Franko, Patrice. 2007. *The Puzzle of Latin American Economic Development*. Lanham, MD: Rowman and Littlefield.

French, William E., and Katherine Elaine Bliss, eds. 2007. *Gender, Sexuality and Power in Latin America since Independence*. Lanham, MD: Rowman and Littlefield.

Freston, Paul. 2008. *Evangelical Christianity and Democracy in Latin America*. Oxford: Oxford University Press.

Friedman, John. 1992. *Empowerment: The Politics of Alternative Development*. Cambridge, MA: Basil Blackwell.

Gálvez, Thelma. 2001. *Aspectos Económicos de la Equidad de Género*. Women and Development Series No. 35. Santiago: United Nations Economic Commission for Latin America and the Caribbean.

Gamper-Rabindran, Shanti. 2006. "NAFTA and the Environment: What Can the Data Tell Us." *Economic Development and Cultural Change* 54 (3): 605–35.

Gandolfo, Elizabeth O'Donnell. 2007. "Women and Martyrdom: Feminist Liberation Theology in Dialog with the Latin American Paradigm." *Horizons* 34 (1): 26–54.

Gasparini, Leonardo. 2004. "Different Lives: Inequality in Latin America and the Caribbean." In *Inequality in Latin America and the Caribbean: Breaking with History?* edited by David de Ferranti, Guillermo E. Perry, Francisco H. G. Ferreira, and Michael Walton, 35–76. Washington, DC: World Bank.

Gindling, Tim H. 2005. "Poverty in Latin America." *Latin American Research Review* 40 (1): 207–22.

Glasbergen, Pieter, Frank Biermann, and Arthur P. J. Mol. 2008. *Partnerships, Governance and Sustainable Development: Reflections on Theory and Practice*. Cheltenham: Edward Elgar Publishing.

Godoy, Lorena, and Sonia Montaño. 2004. *Understanding Poverty from a Gender Perspective*. Santiago: United Nations Economic Commission for Latin America and the Caribbean.

Gold, Dore. 2005. *Tower of Babble: How the United Nations has Fueled Global Chaos*. New York: Random House.

González, Andres. 2008. *Governance for the Twenty-first Century: The Fight against Corruption in Latin America*. Hamburg: Lit Verlag.

González, Daniela. 2005. *América Latina: Urbanización y Evolución de la Poplación Urbana 1950–2000*. Santiago: Centro Latinoamericano y Caribeño de Demografia.

González, Diana Alarcon. 2004. *Priorities and Strategies in Rural Poverty Reduction: Experiences from Latin America and Asia*. Washington, DC: Inter-American Development Bank.

González-Lopez, Gloria. 2006. "Gender and Sexuality in Las Americas." *Latin American Research Review* 41 (2): 187–98.

Gorlier, Juan Carlos, and Keith Gwzik. 2002. *La Política de Género en América Latina: Debates, Theorías, Metodologías y Estudios de Caso*. La Plata, Argentina: Ediciones al Margen.

Grudem, Wayne. 2006. *Evangelical Feminism: A New Path to Liberalism*. Wheaton, IL: Crossway Books.

Grynspan, Rebeca. 2004. "Economic and Social Trends in Latin America: The Bases for Social Discontent." *International Review of Administrative Sciences* 70 (4): 693–709.

Gupta, Geeta Rao. 2003. *Vulnerability and Resilience: Gender and HIV/AIDS in Latin America and the Caribbean*. Washington, DC: Inter-American Development Bank, Sustainable Development Department.

Gylfason, Thorvaldur. 1999. *Principles of Economic Growth*. Oxford: Oxford University Press.

Haber, Stephen, ed. 2000. *Political Institutions and Economic Growth in Latin America*. Stanford: Hoover Institution Press.

——. 2002. *Crony Capitalism and Economic Growth in Latin America*. Stanford: Hoover Institution Press.

Hall, Gillette, and Harry Anthony Patrimos, eds. 2006. *Indigenous Peoples, Poverty and Human Development in Latin America*. New York: Palgrave Macmillan.

Hershberg, Eric, and Fred Rosen. 2006. *Latin America after Neoliberalism: Turning the Tide in the Twenty-first Century*. New York: New Press.

Hettne, Björn, ed. 2008. *Sustainable Development in a Globalized World*. New York: Palgrave Macmillan.

Heynen, Nik, ed. 2007. *Neoliberal Environments: False Promises and Unnatural Consequences*. New York: Routledge.

Heyzer, Noeleen. 2002. "Women are the Key to Development." In *An Agenda for People: The UNFPA Through Three Decades*, edited by Nafis Sadik, 81–94. New York: New York University Press.

Hill, Martin. 2008. *The United Nations System: Coordinating its Economic and Social Work*. Cambridge: Cambridge University Press.

Hillstrom, Kevin, and Laurie Hillstron. 2003. *Latin America and the Caribbean: A Continental Overview of Environmental Issues*. Santa Barbara, CA: ABC-CLIO.

Hite, Amy Bellone, and Jocelyn S. Viterna. 2005. "Gendering Class in Latin America: How Women Effect and Experience Change in the Class Structure." *Latin American Research Review* 40 (2, June): 50–82.

Hoffman, Kelly, and Miguel Angel Centeno. 2003. "The Lopsided Continent: Inequality in Latin America." *Annual Review of Sociology* 29: 363–90.

Htun, Mala. 1999. "Women in Latin America: Unequal Progress toward Equality." *Current History* (March): 133–38.

Idris, Kamil, and Michael Bartolo. 2000. *A Better United Nations for the New Millennium*. The Hague: Kluwer Law International.

InterAction. 2005. *Tapping the Power of Equal Opportunity for Women and Men: A Proven Strategy for Effective Foreign Assistance*. Washington, DC: InterAction.

Inter-American Development Bank. 2003. *Los Objetivos de Desarrollo del Milenio en América Latina y el Caribe*. Washington, DC: Inter-American Development Bank.

——. 2004. *Sending Money Home: Remittances to Latin America and the Caribbean*. Washington, DC: Inter-American Development Bank.

——. 2008. "The Education Paradox: High Opinions, Low Scores." In *Ideas for Development in the Americas*, September-December, 4–5. Washington, DC: Inter-American Development Bank.

Jackson, Cecile, and Ruth Pearson, eds. 1998. *Feminist Visions of Development: Gender Analysis and Policy*. London: Routledge.

Jackson, Robert G. A. 1969. *Study of the Capacity of the United Nations Development System* (Jackson Report). 2 vols. Geneva: United Nations.

Jaquette, Jane S., and Gale Summerfield, eds. 2006. *Women and Gender Equity in Development Theory and Practice: Institutions, Resources and Mobilization.* Durham: Duke University Press.

Jaspers-Faijer, Dirk. 2007. "A New Look at the Population Pyramid." *ECLAC Notes* 53 (July): 7–8.

Jenkins, Rhys, ed. 2001. *Industry and Environment in Latin America.* New York: Routledge.

Jeong, Ho-Won. 1998. "The Struggle in the United Nations System for Wider Participation in Forming Global Economic Policies." In *The Future of the United Nations System: Potential for the Twenty-first Century*, edited by Chadwick F. Alger, 221–47. Tokyo: United Nations University Press.

Jolly, Richard, Louis Emmerij, Dharam Ghai, and Fréderic Lapeyre. 2004. *United Nations Contributions to Development Thinking and Practice.* Bloomington: Indiana University Press.

Jones, Phillip W., and David Coleman. 2004. *The United Nations and Education: Multilateralism, Development and Globalization.* New York: Routledge Falmer.

Jubany, Floencia, and Judy Meltzer. 2004. *The Achilles' Heel of Latin America: The State of the Debate on Inequality.* Policy Paper, June. Ottawa: Canadian Foundation for the Americas.

Kay, Cristóbal. 2005. "Reflections on Rural Poverty in Latin America." *European Journal of Development Research* 17 (2): 317–46.

Keeling, David J. 2004. "Latin American Development and the Globalization Imperative: New Directions, Familiar Crises." *Journal of Latin American Geography* 3 (1): 1–21.

Kennedy, Paul. 2006. *The Parliament of Man: The Past, Present and Future of the United Nations.* New York: Random House.

Klasen, Stephan, and Felicitas Nowak-Lehmann. 2008. *Poverty, Inequality and Migration in Latin America.* Oxford: Peter Lang.

Klingebiel, Stephan. 1999. *Effectiveness and Reform of the United Nations Development Programme.* London: Frank Cass.

Korzeniewicz, Roberto Patricio, and William C. Smith. 1999. *Growth, Poverty and Inequality in Latin America: Searching for the High Road.* Working Paper, May 7. New York: Columbia University Institute for Latin America and Iberian Studies.

Krasno, Jean E., ed. 2004. *The United Nations: Confronting the Challenges of Global Society.* Boulder: Lynne Rienner.

Kumar Saha, Suranjit, and David Parker, eds. 2002. *Globalization and Sustainable Development in Latin America: Perspectives on the New Economic Order.* Cheltenham: Edward Elgar Publishers.

Landman, Todd. 1999. "Economic Development and Democracy: The View from Latin America." *Political Studies* 47 (4): 607–26.

Leipziger, David M., ed. 1980. *Basic Human Needs Approach to Development.* Westport, CT: Greenwood.

León, Franciso. 2000. *Mujer y Trabajo en las Reformas Estructurales Latinoamericanas Durante las Décadas de 1980 y 1990.* Santiago: United Nations Economic Commission for Latin America and the Caribbean.

Levine, Ruth, Amanda Glassman, and Miriam Schneidman. 2001. *The Health of Women in Latin America and the Caribbean.* Washington, DC: The World Bank.

Lewis, David, and Tina Wallace, eds. 2000. *New Roles and Relevance: Development NGOs and the Challenge of Change.* Williamsburg, MA: Kumarian.

Liverman, Diana M., and Silvina Vilas. 2006. "Neoliberalism and the Environment in Latin America." *Annual Review of Environment and Resources* 31: 327–65.

López, Ramón E. 2004. *Growth, Equity and the Environment: Elements for a Development Strategy for Latin America.* Washington, DC: Inter-American Development Bank.

———. 2006. "Structural Adjustment and Sustainable Development." In *Economic Development and Environmental Sustainability: New Policy Options,* edited by Ramón E. López and Michael A. Toman, 154–77. Oxford: Oxford University Press.

López, Ramón E., and Michael A. Toman, eds. 2006. *Economic Development and Environmental Sustainability: New Policy Options.* Oxford: Oxford University Press.

Lowenthal, Abraham F. 2000. "Latin America at the Century's Turn." *Journal of Democracy* 11 (2): 41–55.

Lustig, Nora, ed. 1995. *Coping with Austerity: Poverty and Inequality in Latin America.* Washington, DC: Brookings Institution Press.

Machinea, José Luis. 2007. "The Latin American Population Challenge." *ECLAC Notes* 53 (July): 2.

Machinea, José Luis, and Narcis Sierra, eds. 2007. *Visiones del Desarrollo en América Latina.* Santiago, United Nations Economic Commission for Latin America and the Caribbean.

Magariños, Carlos A. 2005. *Economic Development and UN Reform: Towards a Common Agenda for Action.* Vienna: United Nations Industrial Development Organization, January.

Mandeville, Eliz. 2009. *United Nations Development Programme.* New York: Routledge.

Massey, Douglas S., Magaly Sanchez, and Jere R. Behrman, eds. 2006. "Chronicle of a Myth Foretold: The Washington Consensus in Latin America." *The Annals of the American Academy of Political and Social Science* (Special Edition).

McHale, John, and Maqda Cordell McHale. 1979. *Basic Human Needs: A Framework for Action.* Houston: University of Houston Press.

Miller, Shawn William. 2007. *An Environmental History of Latin America.* Cambridge: Cambridge University Press.

Mingst, Karen A., and Margaret P. Karns. 2000. *The United Nations in the Post-Cold War Era.* Boulder: Westview.

Mische, Patricia M., and Mauricio Andres Ribeiro. 1998. "Ecological Security and the United Nations System." In *The Future of the United Nations System: Potential for the Twenty-first Century,* edited by Chadwick F. Alger, 315–56. Tokyo: United Nations University Press.

Mokate, Karen Marie. 2004. *Women's Participation in Social Development: Experiences from Asia, Latin America and the Caribbean.* Washington, DC: Inter-American Development Bank.

Montaño, Sonia. 2005. *Gender Indicators and Statistics in Latin America and the Caribbean.* Santiago: United Nations Economic Commission for Latin America and the Caribbean.

———. 2007. "Toward the Tenth Regional Conference on Women in Latin America and the Caribbean." *ECLAC Notes* 52 (May): 4–5.

Moon, Bruce Edward. 1991. *The Political Economy of Basic Human Needs*. Ithaca: Cornell University Press.

Moreno, Ana Rosa. 2006. "Climate Change and Human Health in Latin America." *Regional Environmental Change* 6 (3, September): 157–64.

Morrison, Judith. 2007. "Race and Poverty in Latin America: Addressing the Development Needs of African Descendants." *UN Chronicle* 44 (3, September): 44–47.

Moura Castro, Claudio de, Martin Carnoy, and Laurence Wolff. 2000. *Secondary Schools and the Transition to Work in Latin America and the Caribbean.* Washington, DC: Inter-American Development Bank, Sustainable Development Department.

Mousky, Stafford. 2002. "UNFPA's Role in the Population Field." In *An Agenda for People: The UNFPA Through Three Decades*, edited by Nafis Sadik, 211–47. New York: New York University Press.

Muravchik, Joshua. 2005. *The Future of the United Nations: Understanding the Past to Chart a Way Forward*. Washington, DC: AEI Press.

Murphy, Craig N. 2006. *The United Nations Development Programme: A Better Way?* Cambridge: Cambridge University Press.

Narayan, Deepa. 2002. *Empowerment and Poverty Reduction*. Washington, DC: World Bank.

Navarro, Marysa, and Virginia Sánchez Korrol. 1999. *Women in Latin America and the Caribbean*. Bloomington: Indiana University Press.

Ñopo, Hugo, Jaime Saavedra, and Maximo Torero. 2007. "Ethnicity and Earnings in a Mixed-Race Labor Market." *Economic Development and Cultural Change* 55 (4, July): 709–34.

Nussbaum, Martha C. 2001. *Women and Human Development: The Capabilities Approach*. Cambridge: Cambridge University Press.

Ocampo, José Antonio. 2004. "Latin America's Growth and Equity Frustrations During Structural Reforms." *Journal of Economic Perspectives* 18 (2, Summer): 67–88.

Olave, Patricia. 2001. *La Pobreza en América Latina*. Mexico D. F.: Instituto de Investigaciones Económicas, Universidad Nacional Autónoma de México.

Otto, Dianne. 1996. "Nongovernmental Organizations in the United Nations System: The Emerging Role of International Civil Society." *Human Rights Quarterly* 18 (1): 107–41.

Oxhorn, Philip. 2003. "Social Inequality, Civil Society, and the Limits of Citizenship in Latin America." In *What Justice? Whose Justice? Fighting for Fairness in Latin America*, edited by Susan Eckstein and Timothy P. Wickham-Crowley, 35–63. Berkeley: University of California Press.

Oxhorn, Philip, and Graciela Ducatenzeiler, eds. 1998. *What Kind of Democracy? What Kind of Market? Latin America in the Age of NeoLiberalism*. University Park: Pennsylvania State University.

Pan American Health Organization. 2004. *Exclusion in Health in Latin America and the Caribbean*. Washington, DC: Pan American Health Organization.

Parpart, Jane L., M. Patricia Connelly, and V. Eudine Barriteau. 2000. *Theoretical Perspectives on Gender and Development*. Ottawa: International Development Research Centre Books.

Pellegrino, Adela. 2003. *La Migración Internacional en América Latina y el Caribe: Tendencias y Perfiles de los Migrantes*. Santiago: United Nations Economic Commission for Latin America and the Caribbean.

Pietilä, Hilkka, and Jeanne Vickers. 1998. "The United Nations System in the Vanguard of Advancement of Women: Equality, Development and Peace." In *The Future of the United Nations System: Potential for the Twenty-first Century*, edited by Chadwick F. Alger, 248–81. Tokyo: United Nations University Press.

Piras, Claudia. 2004. *Women at Work: Challenges for Latin America*. Washington, DC: Inter-American Development Bank.

Poggio, Sara, and Montserrat Sagot. 2000. *Irrumpiendo en lo Público: Seis Facetas de las Mujeres en América Latina*. San José: Universidad de Costa Rica.

Portes, Alejandro. 1997. "Neoliberalism and the Sociology of Development: Emerging Trends and Unanticipated Facts." *Population and Development Review* 23 (2, June): 229–59.

Portes, Alejandro, and Kelly Hoffman. 2003. "Latin American Class Structures: Their Composition and Change during the Neoliberal Era." *Latin American Research Review* 38 (1): 41–82.

Postero, Nancy Grey, and Leon Zamosc. 2004. *The Struggle for Indigenous Rights in Latin America*. East Sussex: Sussex Academic Press.

Razavi, Shahrashoub, ed. 2009. *The Gendered Impacts of Liberalization*. New York, Routledge.

Roberts, J. Timmons, and Bradley C. Parks. 2004. *People and the Environment on the Edge: Environmental Vulnerability in Latin America and the Caribbean*. London: Catholic Institute for International Relations.

Roberts, J. Timmons, and Nikki Demetria Thanos. 2003. *Trouble in Paradise: Globalization and Environmental Crises in Latin America*. New York: Routledge.

Roberts, Kenneth. 2002. "Social Inequalities without Class Cleavages in Latin America's Neoliberal Era." *Studies in Comparative International Development* 36 (Winter): 3–33.

Robinson, William I. 1999. "Latin America in the Age of Inequality: Confronting the New 'Utopia.' " *International Studies Review* 1 (3, Fall): 41–68.

——. 2008. *Latin America and Global Capitalism: A Critical Globalization Perspective*. Baltimore: Johns Hopkins University Press.

Rodrik, Dani, ed. 2003. *In Search of Prosperity: Analytic Narratives on Economic Growth*. Princeton: Princeton University Press.

Romero, Aldemaro, and Sarah E. West, eds. 2005. *Environmental Issues in Latin America and the Caribbean*. New York: Springer.

Ros-Tonen, Mirjam A. F. 2006. *Partnerships in Sustainable Forest Resource Management: Learning From Latin America*. Leiden: Brill Academic Publishers.

Rugendyke, Barbara, ed. 2007. *NGO's as Advocates for Development in a Globalising World*. New York: Routledge.

Sachs, Jeffrey D. 2008. *Common Wealth: Economics for a Crowded Planet*. New York: Penguin.

Sadik, Nafis, ed. 2002. *An Agenda for People: The UNFPA Through Three Decades*. New York: New York University Press.

Sahn, David, and Stephen Younger. 2005. *Changes in Inequality and Poverty in Latin America: Looking Beyond Income to Health and Education*. Ithaca: Cornell Food and Nutrition Policy Program Working Paper No. 165, June.

Salzinger, Leslie. 2003. *Genders in Production: Making Workers in Mexico's Global Factories*. Berkeley: University of California.

Sánchez-Rodríguez, Roberto, and Adriana Bonilla. 2007. *Urbanization, Global*

Environmental Change, and Sustainable Development in Latin America. São José dos Campos: Inter-American Institute for Global Change Research.

Sanwal, Mukul. 2007. "Evolution of Global Environmental Governance and the United Nations." *Global Environmental Politics* 7 (3): 1–12.

Savedoff, William D. 2009. *A Moving Target: Universal Access to Healthcare Services in Latin America and the Caribbean.* Washington, DC: Inter-American Development Bank.

Schaefer, Brett D. 2006. "The Status of United Nations Reform." *Heritage Lectures* 966 (September 11).

Schatán, Claudia. 1999. *Contaminación Industrial en los Países Latinoamericanos Pre y Post Reformas Económicas.* Santiago: United Nations Economic Commission for Latin America and the Caribbean.

———. 2000. *Desarrollo Economico y Medio Ambiente.* Hamburg: IberoAmerican Institute.

Scott, Maurice Fitzgerald. 1991. *A New View of Economic Growth.* Oxford: Oxford University Press.

Segura-Ubiergo, Alex. 2007. *The Political Economy of the Welfare State in Latin America: Globalization, Democracy and Development.* Cambridge: Cambridge University Press.

Shaull, Richard, and Waldo Cesar. 2001. *Pentecostalism and the Future of the Christian Church: Promises, Limitations, Challenges.* Grand Rapids: Eerdmans.

Shaw, D. John. 2001. *The World Food Programme and the Development of Food Aid.* New York: Palgrave.

Shawn, Eric. 2006. *The United Nations Exposed.* New York: Sentinel H. C.

Shepard, Bonnie. 2006. *Running the Obstacle Course to Sexual and Reproductive Health: Lessons from Latin America.* Westport, CT: Praeger.

Sieder, Rachel, ed. 2002. *Multiculturalism in Latin America: Indigenous Rights, Diversity and Democracy.* New York: Palgrave Macmillan.

Siegle, Joseph T., and Stephen Gudeman. 2004. *The Demise of the Rural Economy: From Subsistence to Capitalism in a Latin American Village.* London: Routledge.

Sierra Castro, Enrique. 2000. *Desempleo y Pobreza: Globalidad y Latinoamérica Tránsito del Siglo 20 al 21.* Quito: Ediciones Cultural y Didáctica.

Simms, Andrew, and Hannah Reid. 2006. *Up in Smoke? Latin America and the Caribbean: The Threat of Climate Change to the Environment and Human Development.* London: New Economics Foundation.

Singer, H. W. 2001. *International Development Cooperation: Selected Essays on Aid and the United Nations System.* New York: Palgrave Macmillan.

Smallman, Shawn. 2007. *The AIDS Pandemic in Latin America.* Chapel Hill: University of North Carolina Press.

Smith, Peter H., Jennifer L. Troutner, and Christine Hunefeldt, eds. 2007. *Promises of Empowerment: Women in Asia and Latin America.* Lanham: Rowman and Littlefield.

Smith, William, and Roberto Patricio Korzeniewicz, eds. 1997. *Politics, Social Change and Economic Restructuring in Latin America.* Miami: North-South Center, University of Miami.

Socolow, Susan Migden. 2000. *The Women of Colonial Latin America.* Cambridge: Cambridge University Press.

———. 2005. "Colonial Gender History." *Latin American Research Review* 40 (3): 254–65.

Sojo, Ana, and Andras Uthoff. 2007. *Desempeño Económico y Política Social en América Latina y el Caribe*. Santiago: United Nations Economic Commission for Latin America and the Caribbean, March.

Solimano, Andrés. 2006. *The International Mobility of Talent and Its Impact on Global Development*. Santiago: United Nations Economic Commission for Latin America and the Caribbean.

Solimano, Andrés, and Claudia Allendes. 2008. *Migraciones Internacionales, Remesas y el Desarrollo Económico: La Experiencia Latinoamericana*. Santiago: United Nations Economic Commission for Latin America and the Caribbean.

Sollis, Peter. 1996. "Partners in Development? The State, NGOs and the United Nations in Central America." In *NGOS, the United Nations, and Global Governance*, edited by Thomas G. Weiss and Leon Gordenker, 189–206. Boulder: Lynne Rienner.

Soubbotina, Tatyana P. 2004. *Beyond Economic Growth: An Introduction to Sustainable Development*. Washington, DC: World Bank.

Sparr, Pamela, ed. 1994. *Mortgaging Women's Lives: Feminist Critiques of Structural Adjustment*. London: Zed Books.

Stahler-Sholk, Richard, Glen David Kuecker, and Harry E. Vanden. 2008. *Latin American Social Movements in the Twenty-first Century*. Lanham: Rowman and Littlefield.

Steigenga, Timothy J., and Edward L. Cleary. 2008. *Conversion of a Continent: Contemporary Religious Change in Latin America*. New Brunswick: Rutgers University Press.

Stern, Nicholas, Jean-Jacques Dethier, and F. Halsey Rogers. 2006. *Growth and Empowerment: Making Development Happen*. Cambridge: Massachusetts Institute of Technology Press.

Stirton Weaver, Frederick. 2000. *Latin America in the World Economy: Mercantile Colonialism to Global Capitalism*. Boulder: Westview.

Streeten, Paul. 1982. *First Things First: Meeting Basic Human Needs in Developing Countries*. Washington, DC: World Bank.

Stromquist, Nelly P. 2007. *Feminist Organizations and Social Transformation in Latin America*. Boulder: Paradigm Publishers.

Swinton, Scott M., Germán Escobar, and Thomas Anthony Reardon. 2003. "Poverty and Environment in Latin America: Concepts, Evidence and Policy Implications." *World Development* 31 (11, November): 1865–72.

Taylor, Paul. 2000. "Managing the Economic and Social Activities of the United Nations System: Developing the Role of the ECOSOC." In *The United Nations at the Millennium: The Principal Organs*, edited by Paul Taylor and A. J. R. Groom, 100–141. London: Continuum.

Taylor, Paul, and A. J. R. Groom, eds. 2000. *The United Nations at the Millennium: The Principal Organs*. London: Continuum.

Thirlwall, A. P. 2006. *Growth and Development*. New York: Palgrave Macmillan.

Thorin, Maria. 2001. *The Gender Dimension of Globalization: A Review of the Literature with a Focus on Latin America and the Caribbean*. Santiago: United Nations Economic Commission for Latin America and the Caribbean.

Thorp, Rosemary. 1998. *Progress, Poverty and Exclusion: An Economic History of Latin America in the Twentieth Century*. Washington, DC: Inter-American Development Bank.

Tiano, Susan. 2001. "From Victims to Agents: A New Generation of

Literature on Women in Latin America." *Latin American Research Review* 36 (3): 183–203.

Titi, Vangile, and Naresh Singh. 1997. *Empowerment for Sustainable Development: Toward Operational Strategies.* London: Zed Books.

Tokman, Victor E. 2007. "The Informal Economy, Insecurity and Social Cohesion in Latin America." *International Labour Review* 146 (1–2, March): 81–108.

Toye, John, and Richard Toye. 2004. *The United Nations and Global Political Economy.* Bloomington: Indiana University Press.

Tulchin, Joseph S., and Ralph H. Espach, eds. 2000. *Combatting Corruption in Latin America.* Washington, DC: Woodrow Wilson Center Press.

United Nations. 1945. *Charter of the United Nations.* New York: United Nations.

———. 1948a. *Technical Assistance for Economic Development.* General Assembly Resolution 200, December 4. New York: United Nations.

———. 1948b. *Universal Declaration of Human Rights.* General Assembly Resolution 217A. New York: United Nations.

———. 1952. *Convention on the Political Rights of Women.* General Assembly Resolution 640 (VII), December 20. New York: United Nations.

———. 1961. *United Nations Development Decade: A Programme for International Economic Cooperation.* General Assembly Resolution 1710 (XVI), December 19. New York: United Nations.

———. 1962. *Permanent Sovereignty Over Natural Resources.* General Assembly Resolution 1803 (XVII), December 14. New York: United Nations.

———. 1966a. *International Covenant on Civil and Political Rights.* General Assembly Resolution, A/RES/2200A (XXI), December 16. New York: United Nations.

———. 1966b. *International Covenant on Economic, Social and Cultural Rights.* General Assembly Resolution, A/RES/2200A (XXI), December 16. New York: United Nations.

———. 1967. *Declaration on the Elimination of Discrimination Against Women.* General Assembly Resolution 2263 (XXII), November 7. New York: United Nations.

———. 1968. *Problems of the Human Environment.* General Assembly Resolution 2398 (XVIII), December 3. New York: United Nations.

———. 1972a. *Declaration of the United Nations Conference on the Human Environment.* Adopted at the United Nations Conference on the Human Environment, Stockholm, Sweden, June 5–16, 1972. New York: United Nations.

———. 1972b. *Institutional and Financial Arrangements for International Environmental Cooperation.* General Assembly Resolution 2997 (XXVII), December 15. New York: United Nations.

———. 1973. *Report on the United Nations Conference on the Human Environment.* New York: United Nations.

———. 1974a. *Declaration for the Establishment of the New International Economic Order.* General Assembly Resolution 3201 (S–VI), May 1. New York: United Nations.

———. 1974b. *Programme of Action on the Establishment of the New International Economic Order.* General Assembly Resolution 3202 (S–VI), May 1. New York: United Nations.

———. 1974c. *Universal Declaration on the Eradication of Hunger and Malnutrition.*

Adopted by the World Food Conference, Rome, Italy, November 5–16, 1974. New York: United Nations.

———. 1975a. *A United Nations Structure for Global Economic Cooperation.* New York: United Nations.

———. 1975b. *Declaration on the Equality of Women and their Contribution to Development and Peace.* Adopted by the First World Conference on Women, Mexico City, Mexico, June 19–July 2, 1975, UN Doc. E/Conf.66/34. New York: United Nations.

———. 1975c. *Report of the Group of Experts on the Structure of the United Nations* (Gardner Report, May 20). New York: United Nations.

———. 1975d. *Report on the World Food Conference.* New York: United Nations.

———. 1978. *Final Declaration.* Adopted by the International Conference on Primary Health Care, Alma-Ata, Kazakhstan, September 6–12, 1978. New York: United Nations.

———. 1979. *Convention on the Elimination of All Forms of Discrimination against Women.* General Assembly Resolution A/RES/34/180, December 19. New York: United Nations.

———. 1985. *Nairobi Forward-Looking Strategies for the Advancement of Women.* Adopted at the Third World Conference on Women, Nairobi, Kenya. July 15–26, 1985, A/Conf.116/29/Rev. New York: United Nations.

———. 1986. *Declaration on the Right to Development.* General Assembly Resolution A/RES/41/128, December 4. New York: United Nations.

———. 1992. *Rio Declaration on the Environment and Development.* Adopted by the United Nations Conference on Environment and Development, Rio de Janeiro, Brazil, June 3–14, 1992, A/CONF.151/26/Vol. 1. New York: United Nations.

———. 1994. *Programme of Action of the International Conference on Population and Development.* Cairo, Egypt, September 5–13, 1994, A/CONF.171/13. New York: United Nations.

———. 1995a. *Beijing Declaration and Platform of Action.* Adopted at the Fourth World Conference on Women, Beijing, China. September 4–15, 1995, A/CONF.177/20. New York: United Nations.

———. 1995b. *Copenhagen Declaration on Social Development.* Adopted at the World Summit for Social Development, Copenhagen, Denmark, March 6–12, 1995, A/CONF.166/9. New York: United Nations.

———. 1997a. *Governance and Democratic Development in Latin America and the Caribbean.* New York: United Nations.

———. 1997b. *Reconceptualising Governance.* Management Development and Governance Division, Discussion Paper 2. New York: United Nations.

———. 2000. *United Nations Millennium Declaration.* General Assembly Resolution A/RES/55/2, 18 September. New York: United Nations.

———. 2001. *Road Map towards the Implementation of the United Nations Millennium Declaration.* Report of the Secretary General (A/56/326), September 6. New York: United Nations.

———. 2002a. *Johannesburg Declaration on Sustainable Development.* Adopted at the World Summit on Social Development, Johannesburg, South Africa, September 2–4, 2002. New York: United Nations Department of Economic and Social Affairs, Division of Sustainable Development.

———. 2002b. *Johannesburg Plan of Implementation.* Adopted at the World Summit on Social Development, Johannesburg, South Africa, September 2–4, 2002. New

York: United Nations Department of Economic and Social Affairs, Division of Sustainable Development.

——. 2002c. *Strengthening the United Nations: An Agenda for Further Change.* Report of the Secretary-General, September 9. New York: United Nations.

——. 2003. *Monterrey Consensus of the International Conference on Financing for Development.* Monterrey, Mexico, March 18–22, 2002. New York: United Nations.

——. 2004. *We the Peoples: Civil Society, the United Nations, and Global Governance.* Report of the Panel of Eminent Persons on United Nations-Civil Society Relations, A/58/817, June 11. New York: United Nations.

——. 2005a. *2005 World Summit Outcome.* Adopted at the 2005 World Summit, September 14–16, 2005, General Assembly Resolution A/RES/60/1. New York: United Nations.

——. 2005b. *Funding for United Nations Development Cooperation: Challenges and Options.* New York: United Nations.

——. 2006a. *Delivering as One: Report of the Secretary-General's High-Level Panel on UN System-Wide Coherence.* November 9. New York: United Nations.

——. 2006b. *Investing in the United Nations: For Stronger Organization Worldwide.* Report of the Secretary-General A/60/692, March 7. New York: United Nations.

——. 2006c. *Reflections on United Nations Development Ideas.* New York: United Nations.

——. 2006d. *Trends in Sustainable Development.* New York: United Nations.

——. 2007a. *The Millennium Development Goals Report.* New York: United Nations.

——. 2007b. *The United Nations Development Agenda: Development for All.* New York: United Nations.

United Nations Children's Fund. 2004. *Annual Report 2003.* New York: United Nations Children's Fund.

——. 2005. *Annual Report 2004.* New York: United Nations Children's Fund.

——. 2006a. *Annual Report 2005.* New York: United Nations Children's Fund.

——. 2006b. *The State of the World's Children 2007: Women and Children: the Double Dividend of Gender Equality.* New York: United Nations Children's Fund.

——. 2007a. *Annual Report 2006.* New York: United Nations Children's Fund.

——. 2007b. *The State of the World's Children 2008: Child Survival.* New York: United Nations Children's Fund.

——. 2008a. *Annual Report 2007.* New York: United Nations Children's Fund.

——. 2008b. *The State of Latin American and Caribbean Children 2008.* New York: United Nations Children's Fund.

United Nations Development Programme. 1997a. *Building Alliances for Development: UNDP and Civil Society Organizations.* New York: United Nations Development Programme, Bureau for Development Policy.

——. 1997b. *Governance for Sustainable Human Development.* New York: United Nations Development Programme.

——. 1997c. *Sustainable Human Development: From Concept to Operation.* New York: United Nations Development Programme.

——. 2000. *Mainstreaming the Policy and Programming Response to the HIV Epidemic.* Issues Paper 33. New York: United Nations Development Programme.

——. 2001a. *Second Country Cooperation Framework for Brazil 2002–2006.* New York: United Nations Development Programme.

——. 2001b. *Second Country Cooperation Framework for Chile 2001–2003.* New York: United Nations Development Programme.

——. 2001c. *Second Country Cooperation Framework for Guatemala 2001–2004.* New York: United Nations Development Programme.

——. 2001d. *Second Country Cooperation Framework for Haiti 2002–2006.* New York: United Nations Development Programme.

——. 2001e. *Second Country Cooperation Framework for Peru 2001–2003.* New York: United Nations Development Programme.

——. 2001f. *Second Country Cooperation Framework for Uruguay 2001–2003.* New York: United Nations Development Programme.

——. 2002a. *Cooperation Framework for Panama 2002–2006.* New York: United Nations Development Programme.

——. 2002b. *Country Programme Outline for Bolivia 2003–2007.* New York: United Nations Development Programme.

——. 2002c. *Country Programme Outline for Cuba 2003–2007.* New York: United Nations Development Programme.

——. 2002d. *Country Programme Outline for Venezuela 2003–2007.* New York: United Nations Development Programme.

——. 2002e. *HIV/AIDS and Poverty Reduction Strategies.* Policy Note, August. New York: United Nations Development Programme.

——. 2002f. *Second Country Cooperation Framework for Argentina 2002–2004.* New York: United Nations Development Programme.

——. 2002g. *Second Country Cooperation Framework for Colombia 2002–2006.* New York: United Nations Development Programme.

——. 2002h. *Second Country Cooperation Framework for Costa Rica 2002–2006.* New York: United Nations Development Programme.

——. 2002i. *Second Country Cooperation Framework for El Salvador 2002–2006.* New York: United Nations Development Programme.

——. 2002j. *Second Country Cooperation Framework for Honduras 2002–2006.* New York: United Nations Development Programme.

——. 2002k. *Second Country Cooperation Framework for Mexico 2002–2005.* New York: United Nations Development Programme.

——. 2002l. *Second Country Cooperation Framework for Nicaragua 2002–2006.* New York: United Nations Development Programme.

——. 2002m. *Second Country Cooperation Framework for Paraguay 2002–2004.* New York: United Nations Development Programme.

——. 2002n. *Second Country Cooperation Framework for Trinidad and Tobago 2002–2006.* New York: United Nations Development Programme.

——. 2002o. *The United Nations and the Millennium Development Goals. A Core Strategy.* New York: United Nations Development Programme.

——. 2003a. *Country Programme Outline for Ecuador 2004–2008.* New York: United Nations Development Programme.

——. 2003b. *UNDP and Gender Equality Challenges in Latin America and the Caribbean.* New York: United Nations Development Programme.

——. 2004a. *Annual Report 2004: Mobilizing Global Partnerships.* New York: United Nations Development Programme.

———. 2004b. *Country Programme Document for Guatemala 2005–2008*. New York: United Nations Development Programme.

———. 2004c. *Regional Report on the Achievement of the Millennium Development Goals in the Caribbean Community*. New York: United Nations Development Programme.

———. 2005a. *Annual Report 2005: A Time for Bold Ambition*. New York: United Nations Development Programme.

———. 2005b. *Country Programme Document for Guyana 2006–2010*. New York: United Nations Development Programme.

———. 2005c. *Investing in Development: A Practical Plan to Achieve the Millennium Development Goals*. New York: United Nations Development Programme.

———. 2006a. *Annual Report 2006: Global Partnerships for Development*. New York: United Nations Development Programme.

———. 2006b. *Country Programme Document for Brazil 2007–2011*. New York: United Nations Development Programme.

———. 2006c. *Country Programme Document for Jamaica 2007–2011*. New York: United Nations Development Programme.

———. 2007a. *Annual Report 2007: Making Globalization Work for All*. New York: United Nations Development Programme.

———. 2007b. *Human Development Report 2007–2008: Fighting Climate Change: Human Solidarity in a Divided World*. New York: United Nations Development Programme.

———. 2008. *Annual Report 2008: Capacity Development: Empowering People and Institutions*. New York: United Nations Development Programme.

United Nations Economic Commission for Latin America and the Caribbean. 2003a. *Handbook for Estimating the Socio-Economic and Environmental Effects of Disasters*. Santiago: United Nations Economic Commission for Latin America and the Caribbean.

———. 2003b. *Meeting the Millennium Poverty Reduction Targets in Latin America and the Caribbean*. Libros de la CEPAL 70.

———. 2004. "Poverty and Inequality from a Gender Perspective." *Social Panorama of Latin America 2002–2003*. Santiago: United Nations Economic Commission for Latin America and the Caribbean.

———. 2005a. *América Latina: Proyecciones de Poplación Urbana y Rural*. Santiago: United Nations Economic Commission for Latin America and the Caribbean.

———. 2005b. *Millennium Development Goals: A Latin American and the Caribbean Perspective*. LC/G. 2331-P, June. Santiago: United Nations Economic Commission for Latin America and the Caribbean.

———. 2006a. *Economic Survey of Latin America and the Caribbean 2005–2006*. Santiago: United Nations Economic Commission for Latin America and the Caribbean.

———. 2006b. *International Migration, Human Rights and Development in Latin America and the Caribbean*. Santiago: United Nations Economic Commission for Latin America and the Caribbean.

———. 2006c. *Shaping the Future of Social Protection*. Santiago: United Nations Economic Commission for Latin America and the Caribbean.

———. 2006d. *Water Governance for Development and Sustainability*. Santiago: United Nations Economic Commission for Latin America and the Caribbean.

———. 2007a. "Children and Adolescents Most Lack Access to Drinking Water and Sanitation." *ECLAC Notes* 54 (September): 7.

———. 2007b. *Economic Survey of Latin America and the Caribbean 2006–2007.* Santiago: United Nations Economic Commission for Latin America and the Caribbean.

———. 2007c. *El Costo del Hambre: Impacto Económico y Social de la Desnutrición Infantil.* Santiago: United Nations Economic Commission for Latin America and the Caribbean.

———. 2007d. *Foreign Investment in Latin America and the Caribbean.* Santiago: United Nations Economic Commission for Latin America and the Caribbean.

———. 2008a. *Economic Survey of Latin America and the Caribbean 2007–2008.* Santiago: United Nations Economic Commission for Latin America and the Caribbean.

———. 2008b. *Millennium Development Goals: Progression Towards the Right to Health in Latin America and the Caribbean.* Santiago: United Nations Economic Commission for Latin America and the Caribbean.

———. 2008c. *Social Panorama of Latin America 2007.* Santiago: United Nations Economic Commission for Latin America and the Caribbean.

———. 2008d. *Social Panorama of Latin America 2008.* Santiago: United Nations Economic Commission for Latin America and the Caribbean.

United Nations Economic and Social Council. 1997. *Report of the Economic and Social Council for 1997.* New York: United Nations Economic and Social Council.

———. 2005. *Mainstreaming a Gender Perspective into all Policies and Programmes in the United Nations System.* New York: United Nations Economic and Social Council.

United Nations Education, Scientific and Cultural Organization. 1990. *World Declaration on Education for All and Framework of Action for Meeting Basic Learning Needs.* Adopted by the World Conference on Education for All, March 5–9, 1990, Jomtien, Thailand. Paris: United Nations Education, Scientific and Cultural Organization.

———. 2000. *Dakar Framework for Action: Education for All: Meeting Our Collective Commitments.* Adopted by the World Education Forum, April 26–28, 2000, Dakar, Senegal. Paris: United Nations Education, Scientific and Cultural Organization.

———. 2004. *La Conclusión Universal de la Educación Primaria en América Latina: Estamos Realmente Cerca? Informe Regional Sobre los Objetivos de Desarrolo del Milenio Vinculados a la Educación.* Oficina Regional de Educacion de la UNESCO para América Latina y el Caribee.

United Nations Environmental Programme. 1992. *Agenda 21: Programme of Action for Sustainable Development.* Adopted at the United Nations Conference on Environment and Development, June 3–14, 1992, Rio de Janeiro. Nairobi: United Nations Environmental Programme.

———. 1997. *Nairobi Declaration on the Role and Mandate of UNEP.* GC.19/L.44/REV.1, February 7. Nairobi: United Nations Environmental Programme.

———. 2002. *Latin American and Caribbean Initiative for Sustainable Development.* LAC-SMIG.I/2, May. Nairobi: United Nations Environmental Programme.

——. 2003. *Annual Report 2002*. Nairobi: United Nations Environmental Programme.

——. 2005a. *Annual Report 2004*. Nairobi: United Nations Environmental Programme.

——. 2005b. *Bali Strategic Plan*. Nairobi: United Nations Environmental Programme.

——. 2006. *Annual Report 2005*. Nairobi: United Nations Environmental Programme.

——. 2007a. *Annual Report 2006*. Nairobi: United Nations Environmental Programme.

——. 2007b. *Elements for the Proposal of the Regional Action Plan 2008–2009*. UNEP/LAC-IGWG.XVI/6, November. Regional Office for Latin America and the Caribbean.

——. 2007c. *Final Report of the Meeting of High-Level Government Experts*. UNEP/LAC-IGWG.XVI/4, November. Regional Office for Latin America and the Caribbean. November.

——. 2007d. *Final Report of the UNEP Regional Forum for the Civil Society of Latin America and the Caribbean*. UNEP/LAC-IGWG.XVI/Ref.7, December. Regional Office for Latin America and the Caribbean.

——. 2007e. *International Environmental Governance and the Reform of the United Nations*. UNEP/LAC-IGWG.XVI/7, October. Regional Office for Latin America and the Caribbean.

——. 2007f. *Regional Application of the Work Programme of UNEP, including the Regional Implementation of the Bali Strategic Plan*. UNEP/LAC-IGWG.XVI/8, November. Regional Office for Latin America and the Caribbean.

——. 2007g. *Report on the Fulfillment of the Decisions of the Fifteenth Meeting of the Forum of Ministers of the Environment of Latin America and the Caribbean*. UNEP/LAC-IGWG.XVI/5, November. Regional Office for Latin America and the Caribbean.

——. 2008a. *Annual Report 2007*. Nairobi: United Nations Environmental Programme.

——. 2008b. *Report on the Latin American and Caribbean Initiative for Sustainable Development: Five Years After it was Adopted*. UNEP/LAC-IGWG.XVI/3/Rev. 2, January. Regional Office for Latin America and the Caribbean.

United Nations Population Fund. 1995. *Proposed Projects and Programmes for Costa Rica 1995–1997*. New York: United Nations Population Fund.

——. 1998. *Proposed Projects and Programmes for Colombia 1998–2001*. New York: United Nations Population Fund.

——. 2000a. *Proposed Projects and Programmes for Ecuador 2001–2003*. New York: United Nations Population Fund.

——. 2000b. *Proposed Projects and Programmes for Guatemala 2001–2004*. New York: United Nations Population Fund.

——. 2000c. *Proposed Projects and Programmes for Peru 2001–2005*. New York: United Nations Population Fund.

——. 2001a. *Proposed Projects and Programmes for the Dominican Republic 2002–2006*. New York: United Nations Population Fund.

——. 2001b. *Proposed Projects and Programmes for Guatemala 2002–2006*. New York: United Nations Population Fund.

——. 2001c. *Proposed Projects and Programmes for Haiti 2002–2006*. New York: United Nations Population Fund.

——. 2001d. *Proposed Projects and Programmes for Honduras 2002–2006*. New York: United Nations Population Fund.

——. 2001e. *Proposed Projects and Programmes for Mexico 2002–2006*. New York: United Nations Population Fund.

——. 2001f. *Proposed Projects and Programmes for Nicaragua 2002–2006*. New York: United Nations Population Fund.

——. 2001g. *Proposed Projects and Programmes for Paraguay 2002–2006*. New York: United Nations Population Fund.

——. 2002a. *Country Programme for Bolivia 2003–2007*. New York: United Nations Population Fund.

——. 2002b. *Country Programme for Colombia 2003–2007*. New York: United Nations Population Fund.

——. 2002c. *Country Programme for El Salvador 2003–2006*. New York: United Nations Population Fund.

——. 2002d. *Country Programme for Venezuela 2003–2007*. New York: United Nations Population Fund.

——. 2002e. *Proposed Projects and Programmes for the English and Dutch Speaking Caribbean Countries 2002–2006*. New York: United Nations Population Fund.

——. 2003a. *Country Programme Document for Cuba 2004–2007*. New York: United Nations Population Fund.

——. 2003b. *Country Programme for Ecuador 2004–2008*. New York: United Nations Population Fund.

——. 2004. *Country Programme Document for Guatemala 2005–2008*. New York: United Nations Population Fund.

——. 2005a. *Annual Report 2004*. New York: United Nations Population Fund.

——. 2005b. *Country Programme Document for Peru 2006–2010*. New York: United Nations Population Fund.

——. 2005c. *Reducing Poverty and Achieving the Millennium Development Goals: Arguments for Investing in Reproductive Health and Rights*. New York: United Nations Population Fund.

——. 2005d. *State of World Population 2005: The Promise of Equality*. New York: United Nations Population Fund.

——. 2006a. *Annual Report 2005*. New York: United Nations Population Fund.

——. 2006b. *Country Programme for Brazil 2007–2011*. New York: United Nations Population Fund.

——. 2006c. *Country Programme for the Dominican Republic 2007–2011*. New York: United Nations Population Fund.

——. 2006d. *Country Programme for El Salvador 2007–2011*. New York: United Nations Population Fund.

——. 2006e. *Country Programme for Honduras 2007–2011*. New York: United Nations Population Fund.

——. 2006f. *Country Programme for Panama 2007–2011*. New York: United Nations Population Fund.

——. 2006g. *Country Programme for Paraguay 2007–2011*. New York: United Nations Population Fund.

——. 2006h. *State of World Population 2006: A Passage to Hope*. New York: United Nations Population Fund.

———. 2007a. *Annual Report 2006*. New York: United Nations Population Fund.

———. 2007b. *Country Programme Document for Bolivia 2008–2012*. New York: United Nations Population Fund.

———. 2007c. *Country Programme Document for Colombia 2008–2012*. New York: United Nations Population Fund.

———. 2007d. *Country Programme Document for Costa Rica 2008–2012*. New York: United Nations Population Fund.

———. 2007e. *Country Programme Document for Cuba 2008–2012*. New York: United Nations Population Fund.

———. 2007f. *Country Programme Document for Mexico 2008–2012*. New York: United Nations Population Fund.

———. 2007g. *Country Programme Document for Nicaragua 2008–2012*. New York: United Nations Population Fund.

———. 2007h. *State of World Population 2007: Unleashing the Potential of Urban Growth*. New York: United Nations Population Fund.

———. 2008a. *Annual Report 2007*. New York: United Nations Population Fund.

———. 2008b. *State of World Population 2008: Reaching Common Ground: Culture, Gender and Human Rights*. New York: United Nations Population Fund.

United States Agency for International Development. 2003. *Economic Opportunities and Labor Conditions for Women: Perspectives from Latin America*. Office of Women in Development, Bureau of Global Programs. Washington, DC: United States Agency for International Development.

Van Den Berg, Hendrik. 2001. *Economic Growth and Development*. New York: McGraw Hill.

Vanden, Harry E., and Gary Prevost. 2008. *Politics of Latin America: The Power Game*. Oxford: Oxford University Press.

Villarroel, Ricardo Cifuentes. 2006. "Environmental Conflicts and the Plundering of Resources in Latin America." *Development* 49: 32–37.

Vuletin, Guillermo Javier. 2008. *Measuring the Informal Economy in Latin America and the Caribbean*. Washington, DC: International Monetary Fund.

Wade, Peter. 1997. *Race and Ethnicity in Latin America*. London: Pluto Press.

Webber, Jeffrey R. 2007. "Indigenous Struggle in Latin America: The Perilous Invisibility of Capital and Class." *Latin American Politics and Society* 49 (3): 191–205.

Weinstein, Barbara. 2006. " 'They Don't Even Look Like Women Workers': Femininity and Class in Twentieth-Century Latin America." *International Labor and Working-Class History* 69 (1, Spring): 161–76.

Weiss, Thomas G., and Leon Gordenker, eds. 1996. *NGOS, the United Nations, and Global Governance*. Boulder: Lynne Rienner.

Westmeier, Karl-Wilhelm. 2000. *Protestant Pentecostalism in Latin America: A Study in the Dynamics of Missions*. London: Associated University Presses.

White, Nigel D. 2000. "The United Nations and Democracy Assistance: Developing Practice within a Constitutional Framework." In *Democracy Assistance: International Cooperation for Democratization*, edited by Peter Burnell, 67–89. London: Frank Cass.

Wiarda, Howard, and Harvey F. Kline. 2006. *Latin American Politics and Development*. Boulder: Westview.

Wise, Carol, and Riordan Roett, eds. 2003. *Post-Stabilization Politics in Latin America: Competition, Transition, Collapse*. Washington, DC: Brookings Institution Press.

Wodon, Quentin T. 2000. *Poverty and Policy in Latin America and the Caribbean.* Technical Paper 467. Washington, DC: World Bank.

Wolff, Laurence. 2001. *Public and Private Education for Latin America.* Washington, DC: Inter-American Development Bank, Sustainable Development Department.

Wolff, Laurence, and Claudio de Moura Castro. 2000. *Secondary Education in Latin America and the Caribbean: the Challenge of Growth and Reform.* Washington, DC: Inter-American Development Bank, Sustainable Development Department.

Wolff, Laurence, Ernesto Schiefelbein, and Paulina Schiefelbein. 2002. *Primary Education in Latin America: An Unfinished Agenda.* Washington, DC: Inter-American Development Bank.

Wood, Charles H., and Bryan R. Roberts, eds. 2005. *Rethinking Development in Latin America.* University Park: Pennsylvania State University Press.

World Bank. 2001. *Engendering Development: Through Gender Equality in Rights, Resources and Voice.* Policy Research Report. Washington, DC: World Bank.

——— . 2004. *Inequality in Latin America and the Caribbean: Breaking with History?* Washington, DC: Latin American and Caribbean Studies Program, World Bank.

World Commission on Environment and Development. 1987. *Our Common Future: Report of the World Commission on Environment and Development* (Brundtland Commission Report). Oxford: Oxford University Press.

World Food Programme. 2000. *Development Project. Peru. Promotion of Sustainable Development of Andean Micro-Watersheds.* Rome: World Food Programme.

——— . 2001a. *Country Programme for Guatemala 2001–2004.* Rome: World Food Programme.

——— . 2001b. *Development Project. Cuba. Nutritional Support to Vulnerable Groups in the Five Eastern Provinces.* Rome: World Food Programme.

——— . 2005a. *Annual Report 2004.* Rome: World Food Programme.

——— . 2005b. *Development Project. Ecuador. Integrated Approach for the Protection of Vulnerable Populations Affected by the Colombian Conflict on Ecuador's Northern Border 2006–2008.* Rome: World Food Programme.

——— . 2006a. *Annual Report 2005.* Rome: World Food Programme.

——— . 2006b. *Development Project. Central America. Assistance to Strengthen Disaster Preparedness and Mitigation among Marginalized Populations in El Salvador, Guatemala, Honduras and Nicaragua 2007–2009.* Rome: World Food Programme.

——— . 2007a. *Annual Report 2006.* Rome: World Food Programme.

——— . 2007b. *Consolidated Framework of World Food Programme Policies.* Policy Issues, Agenda Item 4. Rome: World Food Programme, October.

——— . 2007c. *Country Programme for Bolivia 2008–2012.* Rome: World Food Programme.

——— . 2007d. *Country Programme for Honduras 2008–2011.* Rome: World Food Programme.

——— . 2007e. *Country Programme for Nicaragua 2008–2012.* Rome: World Food Programme.

——— . 2007f. *Protracted Relief and Recovery Operation for Haiti 2008–2009.* Rome: World Food Programme.

——— . 2008a. *Annual Report 2007.* Rome: World Food Programme.

——— . 2008b. *Protracted Relief and Recovery Operation for Colombia 2008–2011.* Rome: World Food Programme.

World Health Organization. 1981. *Global Strategy for Health for All.* General Assembly Resolution 36/43, November 19. New York: United Nations.

——. 2003. *Situación de Salud de las Américas: Indicadores Básicos de Salud.* Geneva: World Health Organization.

Yashar, Deborah J. 2005. *Contesting Citizenship in Latin America: The Rise of Indigenous Movements and the Postliberal Challenge.* Cambridge: Cambridge University Press.

Ziccardi, Alicia. 2001. *Pobreza, Desigualidad Social, y Ciudadanía: Los Limites de las Políticas Sociales en América Latina.* Buenos Aires: Consejo Latinoamericano de Ciencias Sociales.

Index